15 DAYS TO STUDY POWER

Philippe Roy Falkenberg

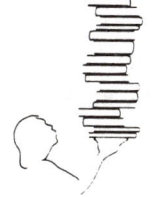

Greencrest Press Inc.

To My Students

Copyright © 1981, 1985, 1994
Philippe R. Falkenberg

Published by:

Greencrest Press Inc.
Box 7746
Winston-Salem, North Carolina 27109
(910) 722-6463

All rights reserved.
Printed in the United States of America

Library of Congress Catalogue Card No.: 81-81330
ISBN 0-939800-03-9 (cb)
ISBN 0-939800-04-7 (pb)

Photographs by Bill Ray III

PREFACE

This book was written from Dr. Falkenberg's extensive experience with student's learning problems. He has interviewed over 2,000 students about their study problems. He teaches psychology at Wake Forest University in Winston-Salem, North Carolina where he is also an academic advisor to freshmen and sophomores.

In 1971 he created the Learn-to-Learn course for the university to help students with their learning skills. He has taught this course to packed classes (they have added another teacher), ever since then. That summer he offered the course to local high school students, and since then over 1,500 of these students have taken the course.

In addition to his experiences as a teacher and counselor, he is a behavioral scientist. He has conducted and published research in the area of human memory and learning. His knowledge of the theory and facts of human learning and memory enables him to see to the core of a student's study problem. He can show that student how to improve his reading, or notetaking, or examination skills based upon sound scientific laws.

His own experiences as a student in high school and college give him a special empathy for students with problems. He dropped out of college the first time he tried it, lasting only two months at the University of Alberta. When he returned to school nine years later he set about becoming an efficient learner. He had to, because he had a wife and three children to support. He succeeded well enough in his search for learning efficiency that he was able to collect over a dozen scholarships, fellowships and prizes during his undergraduate and graduate years.

The Publisher

TABLE OF CONTENTS

Fifteen Days to Study Power

Table of Contents	4
Author's Preface	3
Introduction	6

- I. A Plan for Success — 12
  1. Fifteen Days to Study Power — 14
- II. Self Study — 26
  2. Readrite — 28
  3. Co-Teach — 44
  4. Reading Speed — 54
- III. Classroom Work — 69
  5. In Class — 71
  6. Notetaking — 84
  7. Examinations — 101
  8. Student-Teacher Relations — 120
- IV. The Study Habit — 130
  9. A Place and a Time — 131
  10. Using Time — 143
  11. Concentration — 153
  12. Record Keeping — 165
  13. Fight Boredome with Variety — 178
  14. Motivation — 186
- V. The Laws of Learning — 198
  15. Gradualness — 199
  16. Stimulus Control and Specific Practice — 211

	17.	Reinforcement, Repetition, and Active Learning.	219

VI. Appendixes   231

	A.	Test Record	232
	B.	Study Problems List.	233
	C.	Reading Tests	234
		1. Clouds-A Pilot's View.	234
		2. Raising a Family - Zebra Finch Style	248
		3. When Memory is Super Good or Super Bad.	261
		4. Tables - Reading Times, Scores and Indexes by Class Grades.	277
	D.	Reading Power Drill - Calculation Form, Words per Page	280
	E.	Reading Speed Record	281
	F.	Reading Speed Graph.	282
	G.	Reading Speed Table	283
	H.	Action Plan	287
	I.	Chapter Tests	297
	J.	Answers for Chapter Tests.	319
	K.	Learnometers	327
	L.	Time Sheets	363

References.   369

Index   371

Knowledge is power. **Francis Bacon**

Power-vigor, force, strength, influence, authority, sway, rate of work, might, potency, control, superiority, ability, energy, domination.
Roget's Thesaurus

Power-ability to do. **Webster's Dictionary**

STUDY POWER–all of this. **The Author**

INTRODUCTION

What can this book do for you?

Briefly, this book will show you how to:

>Become a more powerful learner.
>Study textbooks with high efficiency (more learning – less work).
>Read more in less time.
>Enlist other students to help you to learn.
>Use classroom time and classrooms themselves to greater advantage.
>Achieve better grades by writing better exams.
>Take notes to boost your learning.
>Make study easy through better study habits.
>Train yourself to concentrate.
>Use your time most effectively.
>Improve your self-motivation.
>Cope with the boredom of study.
>**And you can do all this in 15 days.**

If you don't think any of this will be helpful to you then this is not the book for you. If you don't feel that you have mastered your craft, being a student, then possibly this book will be useful to you. First of all lets consider what is meant by study power.

Study Power

What is meant by Study Power?

The word *power* has two quite different meanings. In one sense power means control over people and events. President Reagan can shape people's lives and move events to suit his desires. He is powerful. In another sense power means efficiency. The astronauts would think of power as the ability of a rocket to do so much work, in so much time, burning so much fuel. A one horsepower motor performs 33,000 foot-pounds of work in one minute. A ten horsepower motor can do far more work in the same time.

When a student develops his study power he does so in both of these senses of the word "power". He increases his control over people, his teachers, friends, relatives and most important of all, himself. At the same time he improves his work efficiency. He does more work in less time, and the quality of work is better. That is what is meant by study power.

Being a powerful student is not all brains and ability. Too many students have both, but still are far from achieving what they could because they do not know how to apply their talents. Even Michelangelo needed to be shown the proper way to cut rock with a chisel, before his great talents could create the beautiful statue of *David*, or the moving sculpture of Mary and Jesus, *Pieta*.

Dr. David Hills, former director of the Center for Psychological Services at Wake Forest University coined the phrase "the A-to-D student" to describe those people who did brilliantly in high school, but disastrously when they came to college. The center refers such students to the Learn-to-Learn course. Susan Rushing was such a student. *

Poor Susan

Susan had just made a D grade on a quiz in the beginner's psychology course, and she was upset.

"I studied hard for that test, Dr. Falkenberg, and I blew it!", she wept.

When she had calmed down a bit I asked her how she had studied.

"I read my lecture notes and the textbook, again and again," she said.

When I asked her if she had practiced her remembering she looked confused. I kept on with my probing trying to find out how much work she had done, and how she had done it. No, she did not make reading notes. No, she did not look at the material before reading it. No, she did not check to see if she could remember what she had read. Yes, she had studied four hours the night before the test (her roommate confirmed this). The payoff? A grade of D.

---

* Many of the students mentioned here are still in school. Since their faults as well as their virtues are paraded on these pages, their names have been changed to avoid embarrassing them.

Susan was a passive reader. She felt that if she was seeing the printed words, and felt their meanings in her mind she was learning. She was intelligent, her SAT and high school record showed an average college level ability. She was being swamped by her freshman year workload. Because she was bright, she never really had to develop any efficient learning skills. When I (and probably four or five other professors) assigned 200 pages from a textbook for a short quiz, her old methods could not handle it. It took but a few minutes to show her a better study method. She used it from that day on and started making B's.

Susan represents that large group of able students who have not yet mastered their craft. They have not learned and practiced the learning skills that are needed by efficient students.

Learning Skills

What is a learning skill?

It is a *tool* a student uses to help him learn. Sometimes this tool is called a method, a procedure or a technique. Sometimes a learning skill involves real physical objects like notebooks or pens, just as a carpenter's skills involve physical tools like hammers, chisels, or screwdrivers. A learning skill can be a tool of the mind, knowledge that will allow the student to learn efficiently. Knowing how to read a textbook to learn from it with the minimum effort and time spent is an example of a mental tool.

There are many skills that are secondarily learning skills, but are mainly devoted to another purpose. Reading and writing are two examples of such skills. A twentieth century student would find it very hard to learn without these two skills, and competence in both of these areas will benefit a student, but the main purpose of writing and reading is communication, not learning.

Students are *self taught learners*. Rarely has a student had a class or whole course devoted to learning skills. How often have courses with the titles "Study Habits," "Notetaking for Rapid Learning," or "Remembering Through Reading" been offered in your school's regular curriculum. Seldom, if at all, I'll bet. The result of this lack of training is that many students operate far below their peak efficiency as learners. They read pages many more times than necessary; they take rambling, disorganized notes, and their time budget for study is wasteful.

Self taught learners are like self taught swimmers. Every movement a swimmer makes must be exactly correct or his energy is uselessly dissipated as turbulence. Olympic gold medalists Shirley Babashoff and Mark Spitz cleave the water like otters, swift, seemingly effortless. Then watch your Aunt Maude or Uncle Herman, who taught themselves to swim twenty years ago and brag that they "never took a lesson." When they swim smoothly, they are slow. When they try to go fast, they splash and thrash about and don't go fast at all. But they do swim, they stay up and move forward.

In our school system most students stay up in their studies and move forward. Because they are not "drowning" in their studies, they have the illusion that they are OK. A student may feel a bit put out when a girl next door gets higher grades and seems to work a lot less than he does, but he usually shrugs that off.

"Guess she's got more brains than me," he thinks.

Ordinary students who feel that the only difference between the "gifted" student and themselves is natural endowment are copping out. Let's look at the swimmers again.

Olympic gold medalists must be gifted. They compete against the swiftest swimmers in the world. Without natural talent they would not be in the Olympics at all, but talent alone would not get them there either. Babashoff and Spitz spent years perfecting their swimming techniques. They sought the best coaches and spent hours every day perfecting their skills. Talent plus superb training got them to the Olympics, not just talent alone. The ordinary swimmer does not have the talent of an Olympic athlete, but he can learn the same techniques and skills.

That girl next door combines a talent for learning with the proper use of learning skills. She may even succeed at her studies despite a lack of talent. She may not be so bright, a brain so to speak, but she may have been well coached. In her early school years a teacher or parent may have coached her in study techniques. Her learning is "easy" because she knows *how to learn*, not just because she is gifted at it.

The student untrained in learning skills may believe that he is learning as well as his talents will let him, but he's wrong. Time taken to improve learning skills will pay off in future years. *The pay-off can come immediately!*

Who Needs Study Power?

All kinds of students have taken the Learn-to-Learn Course. (This is the study skills course given at Wake Forest University in Winston-Salem, N. C. for college and high school students, from which this book was developed). Some of these students are scholarship students, students who make straight A's in their classes. Many are students, like Susan, who have ability that they do not seem to be realizing. Some students who take the course have never been successful students and desperately want to improve their grades.

Some students study learning skills to polish up on a particular skill. Mike Sandman, who you will meet in the chapter on reading speed, specifically wanted to increase his reading rate. Shirley Hobbs wanted to improve her notetaking. Mary Anne Layton, who won a Morehead Scholarship to the University of North Carolina at Chapel Hill, wanted to polish up all her learning skills before she went away to college. Jeff Thetford had made up his mind that he wanted to be an electronics engineer. Jeff was 16 years old entering grade 11, and realized that he had a long period of study ahead of him before he could realize his goal. Each student's reason for increasing his study power is different, and all of them are good.

All good craftsmen constantly work at improving their craft. Your craft for the next few years is being a student. You have to keep on improving your craft, developing your study power.

Organization of the Book

The four major sections of the book deal with the three major problem areas that students have, plus a section on the laws of learning. The first section is the fifteen-day plan. Since most learning in our school systems comes from books the second section will show you better methods of book study, an easy way to improve your reading speed, and an improved method of working with your fellow students. The third section will help you with your classroom work: classroom strategy, notetaking, examinations, and student-teacher relations. The fourth section will help you strengthen your study habits.

The book's fifth section will provide you the reasons for doing the skills you learned in the first four sections. To develop your study power you must first know what to do; that's most important. To perform intelligently as an efficient student you will need to know why you are doing what the book says. That's the purpose of the last section on the laws of learning.

The first part of each chapter will show you what to do, and the second part will offer some explanation and examples. To improve your study power you have to learn the material in the first parts perfectly. The second part is cake icing, nice but not essential, but the second part of each chapter will deepen your understanding of the chapter.

If you have decided to take the plunge, to develop your study power by learning and using these skills as fast as you are able follow the fifteen day plan. This plan is used in the Learn-to-Learn Course and has been tremendously successful over the last ten years in training students to develop their study power.

The Laws of Learning

Finally, I want to introduce you to the Laws of Learning. These are natural laws discovered by researchers over the last 150 years that summarize our knowledge of the learning process. The six laws cited below are not all the laws of learning, but they are most important to you, the student. No one of these laws is more important than the others, so I have arranged them so that their first letters spell the word GRRASP. This word should help you remember the laws. The last three chapters of the book discuss these laws in detail, but you will need some familiarity with them for the earlier chapters, hence this brief introduction. The laws are:

Gradualness: Learning is most efficient if it is paced properly, not too fast and not too slowly. Since students tend to rush their learning (cram!), the emphasis is put on taking it easy, gradualness.

Repetition: This one is so widely known that it hardly bears repeating; the more often you use material the better it is learned and remembered. 'Nuff said.

Reinforcement: Learning must be rewarding. That's a good first approximation of this law, although you will find out later that it is a bit trickier than that, and very, very powerful.

Active learning: Be active in your learning, not passive. The more ways you can use material, the better it will be learned.

Stimulus Control: Take control of the things and people around you to aid your learning. The more closely the learning situation resembles the remembering situation the better you will remember.

Practice (specific): Use the material you are learning, exactly as you will use it later on when you have to remember it.

These laws will be referred to over and over again throughout this book. They will provide the thread that will weave together all the different skills you will learn.

Acknowledgements

First of all thank you to all my students who have taught me what it really means to be a student craftsman.

My thanks to my family for being very patient with my late night typing and preoccupation. My colleagues at work deserve thanks for tolerating my absent mindedness, and for all their encouragement.

I am grateful for all the advice and help I received from the many professionals in the printing and publishing trades.

2,440 Words

SECTION I.
A PLAN FOR SUCCESS

You must put study skills to work right away if you want to become a more efficient student. Reading this book will not make you a super student, but reading and practicing skills as you go will definitely improve your ability. The work plan in Chapter 1, *Fifteen Days to Study Power*, has evolved over the ten years of teaching the Learn-to-Learn Course at Wake Forest University to both college and high school students. Students who followed this plan in the fifteen-day-course increased their study power. You can also.

13

CHAPTER 1 - FIFTEEN DAYS TO STUDY POWER

You can master Study Power in 15 days. Over 2,000 students have done this in the Learn-to-Learn Course at Wake Forest University. This chapter details a step-by-step plan to help you make dramatic improvements in your learning efficiency.

Each day of the plan requires a couple of hours reading and practice. Divide this time so that you do not do it all at once. If you are already in the midst of a school semester you might find that completing this plan in 15 days is too much. In that case spread the assignments over several days each week; make it a 15 week plan.

The Study Group

Try to interest one or more fellow students to work with you on the 15 day plan. The exercises can be done by yourself (except co-teaching), but all of them will be much more fun if done with others. You need to meet only an hour a day. Having one other person you can discuss your work with, practice your co-teaching with, or to alternate as timer and prompter for reading speed drills will give you a big motivational lift.

DAY 1 BEGINNINGS

1. **Read** — Read the Introduction to this book (note how long it takes you to read the Introduction). (pages 6 to 11, 2440 Words)
   Chapter 12 — Record Keeping (page 234

2. **Test—** Take the first reading test in Appendix C-1 to establish your learning efficiency before you read this book or do any of the exercises. (page 11)

3. **Equipment—** You must have the following equipment. No substitutes will do:
   a. A hard-cover, 3 ring looseleaf notebook (8½ x 11 inch size)
   b. A set of index tabs (five will do)
   c. Lined notepaper with margins
   d. A pen (ballpoint preferred), black or dark blue ink.

4. **Do This—**
   a. Find a good *study place* (See Chapters 9 and 19 if you want to know why. If you can hold your curiosity until day 4 of the plan you will find out why. You will do many things in

this plan that will not be explained until later. It is important that you start to do them now, even before you know why, so be patient.)

b. Find *one particular time* each day that you can work on your study power. Any time will do.

c. Be at your study place, at your study time each day for the next 14 days of the plan, *without exception*. No other place will do. If you cannot work at the same time each day, choose a particular time for each day of the plan, in advance, and stick to it. For example, you might have to study at 6 p.m. Monday, Wednesday, and Friday, but at 7 p.m. on Tuesday and Thursday. Do not work at this plan more than five days a week. You need the breaks. Work at your study power for *at least 30 minutes* each day.

d. Complete the Study Problems Form in Appendix B. (page 233)

e. Fill out a Learnometer for the day. (page 327 following)

The first day is a "get-things-together-and-get-started day." You may feel that you have not accomplished much towards increasing your study power, but you have. All the steps above are necessary, and have been worked out over the years with many students. Today's work will set you firmly on the road to increased learning efficiency.

DAY 2 LOOK–IT–OVER

1. **Read–** Chapter 2

2. **Test–** Take the test on Chapter 2 (see page 302) and score using the key. Enter your score in your Test Record on page
IMPORTANT - For each question you answered wrong, go back to the chapter and study that section again. Do not leave any question until you know the correct answer. Follow this *Re-study procedure* for all of the chapter tests you will take. One hundred percent true learning of this book is your Study Power goal.

3. **Equipment–**
   a. Select a couple of textbooks you can practice READRITE upon. Paperbacks will do. Do not use a textbook from a course you are taking now, but a book from a previous course is all right. The rule in selecting these practice books -

is don't care about the contents, because they are study skills practice not actual learning.

b. A watch or clock that tells time in hours, minutes and seconds. You will need this for the next 13 days.

4. **Do This—**

a. Turn to the first chapter in a practice book and *Look-it-Over*. Complete your Look-Over in three minutes.

b. Label three of the index tabs in your 3-ring looseleaf notebook "Reading", "Practice", and "Tests." Place some notepaper in each of these three sections. Number the first page in each section "1."

c. Write the current date at the top left of page 1 in the Practice section. Beside the date write "Practice Day 2 - Look-it-Over." On the line below this write as much as you can remember from your Look-Over.

d. Look-over the next chapter in your practice book, within three minutes.

e. Write as much as you can remember of that Look-over. Head this second bit of writing, "Day 2 — Look-it-Over-2." From now on every time you write to practice some Study Power skill, do it in this Practice section of your notebook. Label each day's practice with the correct date, and an explanatory heading. Number all pages in sequence.

f. Fill out today's Learnometer.

That's enough for today.

DAY 3 CO-TEACH

1. **Read—** Chapter 3 and 9

2. **Test—** Take the chapter test on chapters 3 and 9 (see pages 298 and 307).

3. **Equipment—**Every day you will need your notebook, this textbook, and a pen, and also your practice book. The abreviation NTP will be used from now on to remind you of this set of materials. Although a person can hardly be classified as equipment, that

is the most important item you will need for today's work. Find a good listener.

4. **Do this—**

   a. Did you Look-Over chapter three before you read it. You didn't! When does reality take over? The sooner you start to apply your study skills in real learning situations the faster they will become part of your personality and be useful to you.

   b. Look-Over a chapter in your practice book. Do it in three minutes. Repeat this exercise, and this time jot a few notes as you Look-it-Over. Stay within the three minutes. Remember, you are not trying to learn the whole chapter in three minutes, you're only interested in familiarizing yourself with its contents, that's all.

   c. Today's new exercise is co-teaching, in three easy steps. Choose some material that you feel you will be comfortable with, material you can talk to someone about. Find that someone, and tell them what you know. Let's elaborate on those three steps.

   You could use Chapter 3 as the material. I'm going to use it here as an example. Look-it-Over and jot down notes. Take a bit more time on this Look-Over, say 5 minutes. After you have finished review your notes to see that they make sense to you. Find that person. This does not need to be a big deal, although it will be helpful for future practice if you can arrange to work with someone regularily. All you need to do today is grab a friend, or brother or sister, or whomever for ten minutes. You can do it in your room, or in a car, or in a cafeteria at lunch. The only explanation you need to make could sound like this:

   "Hey Charlie. I'm trying to learn some stuff here. Would you listen to me for a minute or so, so I can check myself out?"

   When you have captured your audience (your co-teaching student), tell him about chapter 3 as quickly and as well as you can. Keep your notes at hand, and refer to them IF YOU HAVE TO. Try to say your piece from memory. Don't be a bore, keep it short.

   d. There it's done! Your first co-teaching. How do you feel

about it? Happy? Exhilarated? Great! Do another one on another chapter. Pooped? Unsure of yourself? OK, you'll get better with practice, but knock it off for the day.

e. Fill out your Learnometer. As well as your study place and time, you can check Look-it-Over for each one you did, and the same for Co-teach.

DAY 4 READRITE

1. **Read—** Review Chapter 2. *Reminder*: Look-Over each of the chapters in this book before you read it.

2. **Tests—** Chapter 2, again. See if you can make 100 percent.

3. **Equipment—** NTP, and a co-teaching student

4. **Do This—**
   a. Do a three minute Look-Over in your practice book as a warm-up.

   b. Today you want to start to practice the *Notes* step in the Readrite technique. Select a chapter from your practice book, Look-it-Over (no notes for this step), then read the chapter using Notes. Use your usual style of notetaking. (If you have been reading ahead in the book and have read the chapter on Notetaking you might be trying to start a new style. Don't. Do one thing at a time.) Be mechanical about notetaking for the first few times you try it. Stop at the end of each paragraph and jot a note or two. This serves to check if you remember what you have read, and starts the habit of read-remember-write, read-remember-write that you want to develop. Do the whole chapter. This will take some time the first time you do it so it will be the only practice for today.

   c. Check Notes on your Learnometer as well as the other skills you did today.

DAY 5 SELF TESTING

1. **Read—** Chapter 17 - Reinforcement, Repetition, and Active Learning.

2. **Tests—** Take the Chapter test on Chapter 17. *Reminder:* after you have scored your chapter tests return to the chapter to re-read the paragraphs dealing with the questions that you go wrong.

Always leave a test knowing the correct answers to missed questions.

3. **Equipment**—NTP, a person, *or* a parakeet *or* a dog *or* a tape recorder.

4. **Do This**—

    a. Inspect your *study place* carefully. Does it meet all the criteria set for a good study place in chapter 9? Could you improve on it. Is your *study time* ideal or does it conflict with something else you want to do. Sometimes shifting the start of a study time a few minutes can improve it a lot. For example, if you are late arriving at your study time each day you are failing a bit in the performance of this skill. Set your time back ten minutes to eliminate that late start. Be strict with yourself about your study place and time. Make them as close to the ideal as possible.

    b. Look-Over, read and take notes, on a practice chapter for 15 minutes.

    c. Co-teach this chapter to a friend, no more than that. *Test yourself* on the material, using your notes, before you co-teach. You want to co-teach the material perfectly from memory. Keep your notes handy so you can refer to them if you really get stuck.

    d. Repeat b. and c. If you can't find a patient soul to listen to your co-teaching again, teach it to your parakeet, or dog or even better your tape recorder. Play it back and check what you hear against your notes. The recorder is not really a substitute for a co-teaching partner, but it is better than mumbling it into your waste basket. Test yourself on your learning before you try your co-teaching.

    e. Learnometer.

DAY 6 CONCENTRATION TRAINING

Take a couple of days off before you start this day's work. The five days of work you have completed would fit into a normal work week. You need a weekend off. As you will discover when you read chapter 15 the proper pacing of learning is important. By taking some rests you will increase the speed of learning, not slow it down. Take a break.

1. **Read**— Chapter 11 Concentration

2. **Tests—** Take chapter test on Chapter 11.

3. **Equipment—**NTP, person or tape recorder, and something to read that you enjoy a lot like a good novel, or playing your guitar.

4. **Do This—**
    a. You know what to do to practice Readrite and Co-teach. You have to practice these techniques until you can do them exceptionally well and automatically. From now on I'll just write the words in this section to tell you to practice them, like this.

    b. Readrite and co-teach a practice chapter.

    c. Be sure you understand the five steps of the *concentration training* drill. You need to choose something to read that will be boring. The telephone book or the legal notices in the in the morning's paper might work. Start to read this tedious material. As soon as you catch your mind wandering do a concentration drill. Keep your break to 2-3 minutes, return and repeat. (If you find the telephone book fascinating, try reading the dictionary. Don't miss any words now!) On your breaks leave your study place (even a few feet will do) and enjoy your novel, or guitar, or whatever as a positive reinforcer.

    d. Learnometer. Concentration drill is your latest skill.

DAY 7 THE CLASSROOM

1. **Read—** Chapter 5 - In Class, and Chapter 8 - Student-Teacher Relations

2. **Tests—** Take the chapter tests on chapters 5 and 8.
    Take the second Reading Test. You know how to read to learn, the Readrite technique. Here is your chance to see if it has improved your ability. Use it on the material of the Second Reading Test. Your reading speed will be effected by using Readrite, but don't worry about that. You are going to start to work on that tomorrow. (Reading Test on page 248)

3. **Equipment—**NTP, a classroom, a co-teaching partner, a telephone book

4. **Do This—**
    a. Readrite
    b. Co-teach

c. Concentration Drill

d. Change your seat in class. (I am assuming here that you are taking classes) Improve it according to the criteria in chapter 5. Even if you can't improve it, change it. That seat you have been sitting in wasn't chosen for the best reasons, was it? Get out of it. If your teacher wonders what you are doing, explain. If she wants you to stay where you are, argue – up to a point. Don't make a federal case out of it (see Chapter 8), but get the best seat you can in each of your classes.

e. Learnometer.

DAY 8 READING SPEED

1. **Read—** Chapter 4. This is a complex and technical chapter, but once you have mastered it you will be able to do each day's drill well and benefit from it.

2. **Tests—** Take the test on chapter 4.

3. **Equipment—** NTP, a book with lots of words and few pictures, for example a paperback novel. Use a book that you can write in, because you are going to mark it up a lot. Choose a good book, because you are going to work in it for the next seven days.

4. **Do This—**

   a. Today you are going to do one reading speed drill, correctly. If you don't do it correctly the first time, repeat it until you do. That's important. A few tips: once you have calculated the number of words on a full page of your book write this figure on the inside front cover so that you won't need to calculate it again.

   This drill goes much more smoothly and effectively if you work with other people. Set up your own speed reading group if you can, but you can work by yourself.

   Your reading speed on the First Reading Test is a "before" measure. That's probably your basic textbook reading speed now, before any speed training.

   The pattern of reading speeds you are looking for after each drill is completed is something like this: 0-1, 200 WPM; 0-4, 400 WPM; 4-5, 210 WPM. The 0-4 speed should be much larger than the 0-1 speed, because this is your maximum overload. The 4-5 speed should be slightly higher than the 0-1 speed, signifying that the drill has increased your AFAYCWGC speed. If at first there is no 4-5 improvement, or if it even shows a drop, don't worry, it will improve shortly.

    b. Learnometer.

DAY 9 NOTETAKING

1. **Read—** Chapter 6 Notetaking

2. **Tests—** Take the chapter test on chapter 6

3. **Equipment—**NTP, Reading Speed book

4. **Do This—**

    a. You need an actual classroom setting to practice your lecture notetaking. To begin choose a teacher who is pretty well organized when she lectures, then use one of her lectures to practice *numbered outline notetaking*. Your goal for that lecture is to take the best notes you can. Don't try to do this in all of your lectures at first, pick and choose until you begin to feel confident about your notetaking.

    b. Readrite a chapter from your practice book, but this time use numbered outline notetaking. (You may feel that these notetaking exercises can be done anytime, but if you are to complete the plan successfully they *must* be started today. My experience shows that you are ready for this step now).

    c. Do a reading speed drill. You will do one of these each day now for the next six days. They only take 10 minutes to do, and a few minutes to complete your calculations and records. Once you have started to build your speed you need daily practice.

    d. Learnometer

DAY 10 PRACTICE, PRACTICE

1. **Read—** Chapter 15 — Gradualness. This chapter will help you understand the why's of many of the techniques you have been learning.

2. **Tests–** Take the chapter test for chapter 15.

3. **Equipment–**NTP, Reading Speed book, practice book, co-teaching partner.

4. **Do This–**
    a. You won't start any new exercises today. Continue your work on the skills you have achieved.

    b. Readrite with numbered outline notetaking.

    c. Co-teach.

    d. Notetaking practice in a lecture.

    e. Concentration drill.

    f. Reading speed drill.

    g. Learnometer.

You have just completed the second week's work in the Fifteen-Day Plan. Although the exercises above will take some time, you will finish the week with a flourish, and achieve a lot of satisfaction at your progress. Take the weekend off. Dismiss Study Power from your mind for a couple of days.

DAY 11 EXAMINATIONS

1. **Read–** Chapter 7 Examinations.

2. **Tests–** Take the chapter 7 test.

3. **Equipment–**NTP, Reading Speed book, time sheets.

4. **Do This–**
    a. All of the chapter tests fall into the category of short answer, objective tests. Today, concentrate on using the proper techniques for taking this kind of test when you take the chapter test. In your classes, the first time an essay or objective test is given concentrate very hard on doing it the correct way. Memorize the steps for each test and perform them thoroughly.

    b. Reading Speed drill.

    c. Using the time sheets in Appendix K keep track of your

activities for the next 24 hours. You will need a watch or access to a clock to do this. You may want to read chapter 10 before you try this. Keep track of your activities in at least 15 minute chunks. It is better to jot down each new activity when you do it and note the time. Carry your time sheets with you all day. DO NOT try to remember your activities for an hour before you write. You can't do this accurately.

  d. Learnometer.

DAY 12 USING TIME

1. **Read–**   Chapter 10 Using Time.

2. **Tests–**   Take the chapter 10 test.

3. **Equipment**–NTP, Reading Speed book, time sheets, co-teaching partner.

4. **Do This–**

  a. Readrite a practice chapter with numbered outline notes.

  b. Co-teach the entire chapter to a partner, from memory.

  c. Reading speed drill. You can be adding a page at a time in the drill now.

  d. Prepare a schedule for tomorrow's activities. Base it upon your activity sheet from yesterday, and your knowledge of what your day is going to be like tomorrow. Work your schedule tomorrow.

  e. Learnometer.

DAY 13 THE ACTION PLAN

1. **Read–**   Chapter 16 Stimulus Control and Specific Practice.

2. **Tests–**   Take the chapter 16 test.

3. **Equipment**–NTP, reading speed book.

4. **Do This–**

  a. Reading speed drill.

  b. Complete your Action Plan in Appendix H. By preparing a

plan of action now you will ensure the smooth transition from the Fifteen Day Plan to your regular schoolwork. Think carefully about your plan. Make it practical.

   c. Learnometer.

DAY 14 THE FINAL READING TEST

1. **Read–** Chapter 13 Fight Boredom with Variety.

2. **Tests–** Take the chapter test on Chapter 13, and The Third Reading Test.

3. **Equipment–**NTP, practice book, reading speed book.

4. **Do This–**

   a. Reading Speed Drill, add a page and a half today.

   b. Readrite the first five pages of a practice chapter.

   c. Take the final reading test to measure your progress to date.

   d. Learnometer. By now your learnometers should have many check marks each day.

DAY 15 TRANSITION

1. **Read–** Chapter 14 Motivation.

2. **Tests–** Take the chapter 14 test.

3. **Equipment–**NTP, Reading Speed book.

4. **Do This–**

   a. Reading speed drill. Compare your 4-5 speed with that of the First Reading Test. If you are going to maintain and continue to improve your reading speed you should do periodic drills. A reading speed drill is a good way to begin a day's reading in a textbook. You get off to a flying start. Note the changes in your test scores from the first to the third test, and also the changes in the Efficiency Indexes.

   b. Learnometer. Keep track of your skills. A record like the Learnometer is handy. You are off to a good start at improving your craftmanship as a student. The more you practice your skills the better student you will become. Good Luck.

3,473 Words

SECTION II.

SELF STUDY

The major part of learning for high school and college students happens when the student is working by himself. Most of this self study consists of reading, and learning what is read. The following three chapters will show you skills needed to make your self-study efficient, so that you get the best payoff in learning for the time you spend. The Readrite system shows you what to do to learn as you read. Co-teaching discusses ways you can work with your fellow students to learn better. The chapter on reading speed gives a simple everyday drill you can use to boost your reading rate.

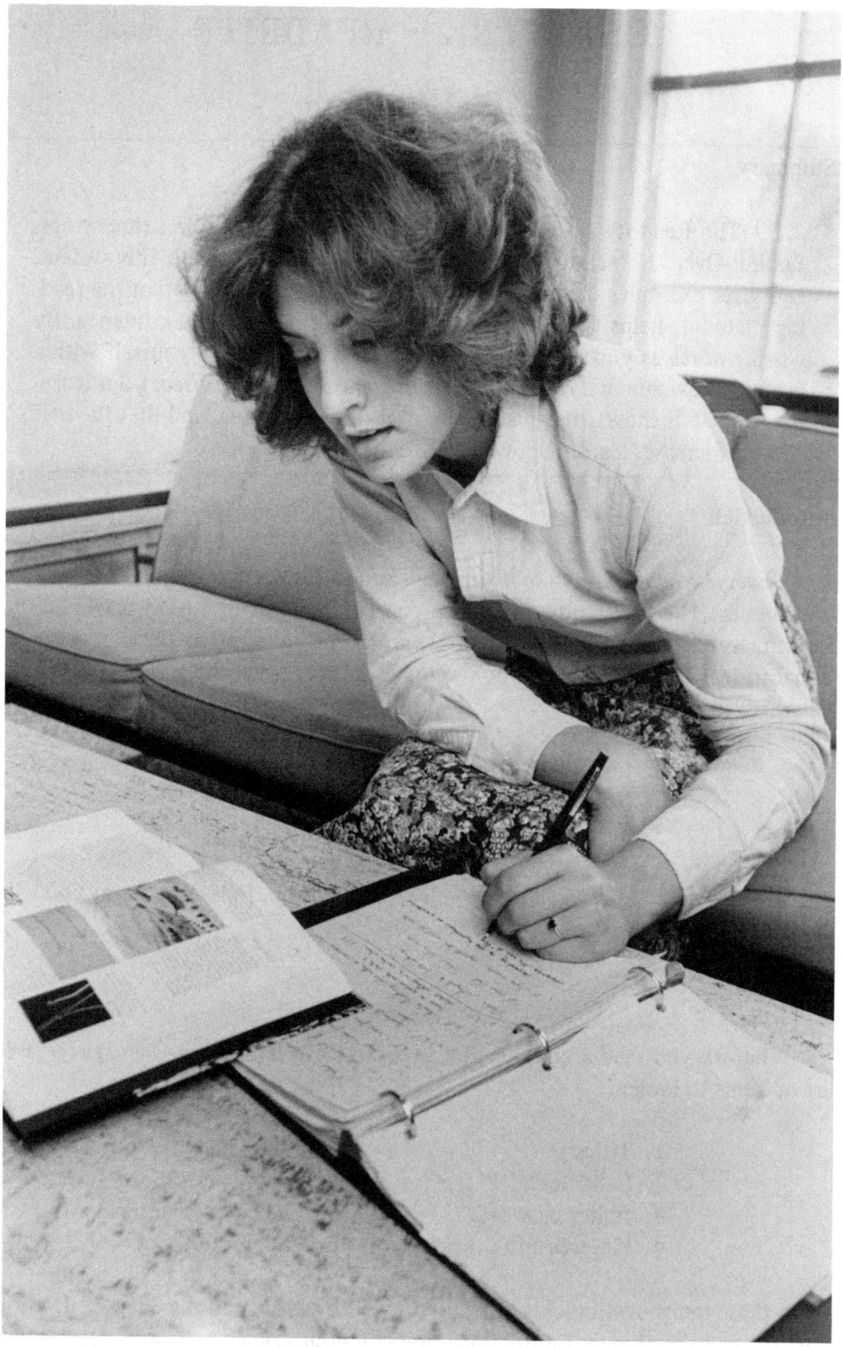

CHAPTER 2 - READRITE

> **Summary**
>
> The Readrite system of efficient book learning requires three steps, Look-it-Over, Notes, and Self Testing. This chapter explains this system, and gives examples of its use. The Look-Over gives you a map of the reading material, helps you evaluate it, and strengthens your confidence. By writing notes as you read you learn the facts and provide yourself with a useful review summary. The Self Testing checks and reinforces your learning. Research shows that reading by itself is not learning, and that the Self Testing increases learning power 200 to 300 percent.

Introduction

Every course you take from high school onwards depends on learning from books. The first study technique you will learn from this book will be the Readrite system (Read and write to Learn). This system has three easy steps. You can learn from any textbook using Readrite, since the system is general. The three steps are:

        1. Look-it-Over
        2. Notes
        3. Test yourself

The next three sections will show you how to Readrite. In later sections you will see why each of these three steps is necessary.

Look-it-Over

Before you read a chapter in a book to learn it, Look-it-Over. Here is a list of items to look at:

    1. Titles   5. Tables and graphs
    2. Subtitles   6. Boldface print
    3. Italicized words   7. The chapter summary
    4. Pictures and captions 8. Chapter outlines

Look these items over quickly and carefully before you read the chapter. Do not start to read the chapter before you complete your Look-over. Familiarize yourself with the chapter before you read it.

Notes

Once you have looked over the chapter you can begin learning. You will need a pen and a notebook.

Start reading. Read as much as you can remember. This may be a paragraph, a small section, or a few sentences. Then write a few words in your notebook to summarize your reading. Write your notes from memory. *Do not copy* from the textbook. If your memory fails, glance at the reading material again, then complete your notes. You *must* write your notes from memory. Be brief. (See Chapter 6 for notetaking techniques.)

You have completed your notes on the first paragraph. Read the next paragraph. Write notes on it, then the next one, and so on to the end of the chapter. This second step alternates reading and notetaking. Read as much as you can remember then write your notes from memory. Successful learning needs remembering and notes. You will find an example of the method in a couple of pages.

Learning your chapter cycles through the sequence, *read-remember-write, read-remember-write*, and so on to the end.

You have finished your reading and you have one more step to go.

Test Yourself

To be sure that you *have* learned that chapter, test yourself. Close the textbook, but keep your notes in front of you. See how much you can repeat to yourself without looking at your notes.

Start with the major sections of the chapter. Can you name all of the major section topics? How many are there? Recite the main points of the first major section. Again, how many are there? Do this for each major section in turn. When you get stuck, read your notes to refresh your memory. Quiz yourself again. Continue testing yourself this way until you are sure you know everything in your chapter.

Test yourself IMMEDIATELY after you have finished the Notes step. Don't delay this self testing until later, or even worse leave it until a quiz is upon you. *Immediate self testing* is the key to success in book learning.

That's all there is to READRITE. It's easy to do, and if you follow the method closely your learning will be guaranteed. Let's work through an example.

Example of READRITE

We will use the reading material from the first reading test to illustrate READRITE. Turn to *Clouds: A Pilot's View* and follow along (page 236).

The first step is to Look-it-Over. Examine the title, *Clouds: A Pilot's View*. You have your first hint of what the article is about. You find out more from subtitles: Horizontal Clouds, Weather Reports, Reading Clouds, Vertical Clouds, Storm Clouds, and Hybrid Clouds. A couple of these subtitles are a bit puzzling. You can read a book but how do you read a cloud? Are hybrid clouds something like hybrid corn? Don't look for answers to these puzzles now, leave that for the next step.

Glance through the chapter. Look at the pictures, tables, and underlined words. When you have completed looking it over, you will have a good idea what the article is about. You will also have a few puzzles you will want to solve. This Look-Over should not have taken more than two or three minutes. Keep all your Look-Overs SHORT.

The next step is Notes. Read the first three paragraphs that introduce the article, and jot down notes like this:

A. Introduction
 1. Cloud knowledge-lifesaver to pilot
 2. Two basic cloud types a. horiz b. vert.

These notes boil down 219 words in the paragraphs to 13 words. You can remember them because you read only a little bit. By jotting your notes from memory (instead of copying from the textbook) you checked on what you read, and started your learning.

On to the next section, Horizontal Clouds. You discover that the information here is a bit more complicated so take one paragraph at a time. First paragraph notes:

B. Horizontal clouds
 1. Clouds hide the ground

The second paragraph gleans these facts:

2. 1st layer - cumulo stratus - up to 6,000'

The third paragraph requires more detailed notes:

> 3. 2nd layer - <u>alto-stratus</u> – 6,-8,000' –
> smoother air = smoother clouds.
> a. lower air boils = rough clouds.
> b. middle air - smooth & horizontal

And the last two paragraphs can be summarized:

> 4. highest = 12,000' & up – thin <u>cirro stratus</u> (mares' tails) white ice crystals

Notice that the underlined words in the reading material are included in the notes and defined. The author is drawing attention to these words. Also notice that reading and note writing alternates in short spurts. Read only what you can remember.

Now you try it: Re-read some more of the article. Use Notes.

The third step is a test of what you've learned. Here are some questions you can try:

In one sentence, what is this article about? (title)

How many major sections in the article? (count them in your notes)

Name the topics in each section. (subtitles)

Start with the first section (the introduction). How many points? What were they?

Second section (Horizontal Clouds) — How many points? What were they?

And so on, all the way through the article. If you get stuck, check your notes. Repeat your questions and answer again. Be sure you get it all correct. Remember, you Self Test IMMEDIATELY upon completion of the Notes step. *Immediately!* That's important.

You know how to learn efficiently from books, both by description and example. Now you need to know why each of these three steps of READRITE is important.

Maps and Judgement

Any book you read to learn from is new. This means that the book's material is unfamiliar, even strange. Reading unfamiliar material is like taking a trip to a foreign land.

If you were going to drive to Mexico City, one of the first things you would buy is a road map. You would not dream of driving in a strange land without a map. If you did not use the map, you might end up in Canada, lost.

The Look-Over provides the map. The title describes the main route and the subtitles the major stops along the way. The pictures and graphs are your scenic attractions, while the italics and boldface print detail the spots of interest. The Look-Over shows you where you are going in your chapter, familiarizes you with the territory, and keeps you from losing your way.

You also need to *evaluate* what you are reading. You need to decide what is important, what must go into your notes, and what to ignore. How can you evaluate your reading if you know nothing about it? You can't. You need some

Figure 2-1 "Please Lord, let me pass this exam!"

familiarity with your subject to understand it. Here's a paradox: to learn you must evaluate, but to evaluate you need some background. Because the material is new you have no background. To break this vicious circle you look over the section before you read it. With the little bit of familiarity a Look-Over provides, you can better evaluate your reading.

If you know where your reading is going, and you can judge the value of what you read, your confidence in yourself improves. Having confidence will speed learning. A major difference between the experienced professional and the beginner in any field of work is self-confidence. For example, the rookie basketball player may know as much about the game as the veteran, but he does not have that edge of confidence the veteran's experience gives him. Veteran Duke University center Mike Giminski out-played Wake Forest University's freshman Jim Johnstone all season in 1978. In their last game, Johnstone decided, "enough," and out-scored and out-rebounded Giminski. Confidence.

Use it or Lose it

If you were learning to swim you would practice swimming.

If you were learning to speak Spanish you would speak Spanish.

If you were learning to carpenter you would saw and hammer wood.

If you were learning history you would . . .what?

Students believe that practical subjects like swimming, carpentry, and Spanish are easier to learn because they can *do* something with them. If a student is asked to do history or psychology or biology, he's at a loss. How can you practice an academic subject? Yet these academic subjects need to be practiced if you are to learn them. The sooner you start your practice, the faster will be your learning.

Let's use history and swimming as examples of learning an academic and practical subject. What if you had to learn to swim from a book? Never happen, you say. If you lived on an isolated ranch in Montana, with no swimming instructors for miles around, you might be forced to learn from a book. Would you only read the book, then believe that you knew how to swim a breast stroke? Of course not, you would go to the lake and practice until you could do each stroke.

Yet look at the history student. He reads his chapter, understands it, knows what he has read, and feels he has learned it. But he is wrong. He has not learned that chapter of history any more than the swimming student learned the crawl stroke by reading a chapter on it. The history student needs to practice just as much as the swimmer.

We're back at our original question; how do you practice an academic subject like history? The Law of Specific Practice (see Chapter 15) applies to all learning. Figure out how you will eventually use your learning, and practice right from the start. Let's analyze our two subjects.

In swimming you eventually will use the strokes you learn in the water, so you practice each stroke in the water. First you read the book to understand each stroke and know how they are done, then you get into the water and practice until you perfect each stroke.

In history you eventually will have to remember what you have read, and write it during tests. This will be the first use you will make of your history. So you must practice your r*emembering and writing*. After you have done your Look-Over, you start to read your history. Every so often you stop to see if you remember what you have read. Writing notes gives you the practice of writing you will eventually use in tests and papers. You are practicing your history.

The technique of pausing in your reading, remembering what you have read, and jotting notes on it, is a completely general method of practicing any subject. You can use it to learn Hindu poetry, advanced mathematics, or baking pies. If the subject you want to learn has a book, you can learn from the book by reading, remembering, then writing notes. This read-remember-write sequence is the Notes part of the Readrite system of learning. The sequence was named Notes to emphasize the note writing.

But, the average student is reluctant to take notes from a textbook.

"Why do I need to write it down if it is already written in the book?" one student asked me.

She misunderstood the purpose of the writing. You write notes as you read to practice what you will eventually *do* with the material, and to check on your memory. If your writing is a good summary of your reading, then you are sure you remember it correctly. If the swimmer tries a stroke and chokes, he could go back to the book to see what he did wrong. In history, if you can't write the event and date correctly, you know that you have to read again to find out what's correct. The rule is the same in both cases.

Another student asked, "Yvonne is a straight-A student, and she doesn't take notes from her reading. Why should I?

Don't confuse basics with advanced technique, as this student has done. You would not expect a beginning swimmer to use the techniques that Mark Spitz used to win seven Olympic gold medals. Yvonne has been a top student for years. She uses advanced techniques which she does in her head without pen

Figure 2-2 Underlining in textbooks is an adult version of finger reading.

and paper. She also has been using these techniques so long that she does them unconsciously and swiftly. The method taught here is basics, not "Olympics." You have to learn the basics first before you can progress.

Success

In Chapter 16 the importance of reinforcement to efficient learning is discussed. You have to see the results of your learning if you are to continue, otherwise you will soon quit. There are several ways of discovering the results of your study. Your teacher can reward with praise and good grades. That's one way. An even better way is for you to see what you can do . Success is the best reinforcement for learning.

When you write notes from memory, your success is laid before your eyes, in black ink on white paper. Every fact you learn is rewarded. "Hey, I did it!" This success, or reward, or feedback, or whatever you want to call it, is what the learning experts call reinforcement.

"Why can't I just practice my remembering?" asked a student during his interview. "Surely the notes are not necessary for me to see my success."

If students' memories were perfect, they would not make mistakes on tests. The notes provide a check on the accuracy of your remembering. If your notes are the same as the textbook, then you are sure you are correct.

Notes as an Aid to Review

The notes you take as you read will provide you a first-class study aid when you review for tests. A test can cover 50 to 100 pages of a textbook. Re-reading all of those pages again before the test is an inefficient method of study. Use your notes for review.

A recent Learn-to-Learn student complained that he was taking a lot of notes from his reading.

"I read a chapter of sociology last night, and I ended up with five pages of notes," he grumbled.

When I asked him how long the chapter was he told me, "40 pages." What's he complaining about? He has compressed 40 pages of text into 5 pages of notes. When he reviews for a test he has to study only 5 pages. That should take him less than one-eighth of the time it took him to read the original 40 pages. When I pointed that out to him, he appreciated the savings.

"One thing for sure," he commented as he walked away, "I learned that chapter one-hundred percent."

Underlining is a No - No

Sooner or later a grinning student will stick his hand up in a Learn-to-Learn class and say, "I've got a better system than notetaking from the textbook. I underline all the key points."

The grin disappears when I tell him that his system is one of the worst he could use. Underlining is a disaster. Three-quarters of every class I teach have used this study system and they are dismayed when I tell them how bad it is. They have been handicapping themselves for years by using it.

"My teacher says it's important to pick out those key points," the puzzled student says.

Agreed, but just because that student has found the important points does not mean that he has learned them. When the swimming student reads that he breaths "in" only when his face has rolled out of the water, he has discovered an important swimming skill. But, he needs to practice such breathing in the water while swimming before he can say he has learned it. Underlining words in books is not proper practice.

Ask yourself how often you are given a test in underlining. Can you imagine a teacher saying, "Underline the first three paragraphs in the textbook for your test today?" It's ridiculous. Underlining is adult finger reading. If you used your finger to follow the print when you were learning to read in elementary school, teacher would make you sit on your hands. She knew that finger reading was a bad habit that would slow you down. But clever adults have learned that they can finger read if they hold a yellow magic marker in their hand and mark "key words." They have even given it a name, highlighting. Highlighting, my foot! It's finger reading.

Figure 2-3 All the ingredients are here, but still no cake.

Underlining slows down your reading, and keeps you from properly practicing your work. In book learning correct practice is remembering and writing. Underlining keeps you from doing either of them. Don't use it.

Reading is not Learning

By now you see that I am making a distinction between reading and learning. Reading is not learning. I want to emphasize that. READING IS NOT LEARNING, READING IS NOT LEARNING, READING IS NOT LEARNING!

Reading is a necessary step towards learning, but by itself, it is not learning. So many students hold the idea that if they re-read a chapter often enough they will learn it better. That's true, but reading alone is a woefully inefficient method of learning. It's like trying to build a dam with a hand shovel. You have to do an enormous amount of work to show little progress. Table 2-A shows the results of an experiment where students used the re-reading method to study. Notice that the last group of students worked four times as hard as the first group, but only increased their grade by five percent. That's a poor payoff. Can you imagine getting a job that would pay you $10.00 for the first hour's work, but only 50 cents for the next three hour's work. You would not stay on that job long, yet students do use the re-read method, with its poor payoffs.

Table 2-A — Re-reading Experiment

	Test Results (%)
Read once	69
Read twice	74
Read three times	75
Read four times	74

Reading is necessary to learn from a book. You must collect that information before you can practice. The following analogy will show the difference between reading and learning. If you were baking a cake, the first step would be to collect your ingredients and tools. You would need flour, sugar, eggs, milk, flavouring, mixing bowls, spoons, pans, an oven, and so on. Once you had collected all that stuff together, you still would not have a cake. You need to *do* something with the ingredients before you have a cake. You measure, and mix, and put batter in pans, and put pans in a pre-heated oven, and then after the right amount of time in the oven, you would have your cake.

Reading is like collecting the ingredients. Once you have read the paragraph you have the ingredients, the information, for learning, but you must *do* something with this information to learn. In the Readrite system you practice your remembering and your writing. Only after you have completed the two "do" steps can you begin to say you are learning.

Test - Yourself Re-visited

Learning is no good if you cannot remember what you have learned. The purpose of the Test-Yourself step in the Readrite system is to ensure that you do remember. Your memory is like a huge filing system. Every time you learn a fact you store it in your filing system. The trouble with filing systems is that facts can get lost.

I'm sure that you have put something down and then not remembered where it was. You know it is around somewhere, but you can't remember where. Usually when that happens it occurs because you put the item down in an unusual place. I am always doing that with my car keys or sunglasses. As long as they are in my pocket or on my bureau in my bedroom, I have no trouble finding them. But if I casually leave them on the piano bench or beside the toaster I can hunt for them for hours. The bureau and my pants pockets provide automatic cues to help me locate my glasses or keys. I don't associate piano benches or toasters with my glasses so they are inadequate cues.

Filing systems work the same way. If you file a letter under the proper heading it is easy to find. It is even easier to find if it is filed under a number of headings. A letter from my father, Carl F. Falkenberg, would be found quickly if

Figure 2-4 The more activity while you learn, the better you will learn.

filed under his name, or under "Dad." If I got careless and filed the letter under "General Communications" or under "Edmonton" (where he lives), I might search for it a long time. The secret of a good filing system is using the best categories for filing.

Remember

The same is true of your memory. When you learn a fact you must tag it with a proper *retrieval cue*. If you do that well you will have no trouble using your memory, and finding what you need. How do you set up such cues?

A century of experimental research has given the answer to this question. You must make the learning situation resemble the remembering situation as closely as possible. When you do that, remembering is nearly faultless. This is the Law of Specific Practice.

For example: I learned that if I was to have my soccer team score goals, I had to have them practice shooting goals against opposition. Having them practice goal kicking without opponents was not good enough. They would forget to kick hard for the corners, and boot the ball directly at the goalie. But, if they practiced with two fullbacks trying to steal the ball and block their kicks, they remembered how to do it during games.

Another example: mathematics teachers know that having students memorize the rules in algebra is not enough if they want the students to solve problems. The students could know the rules perfectly, but would fail a problem-solving test miserably if they had not practiced problem solving. That's why algebra books are full of exercises. Students who work through these exercises do well on problem-solving tests.

Both of these examples tell us, *learn it as you plan to use it.* You must think ahead before you learn anything, and be sure you know how you are going to use it. Then you can practice your lesson that way and be sure that you will remember it later.

How to Practice

All students will use their knowledge to answer questions in tests, quizzes and examinations. The tests determine their grades, and show teachers how much their students have learned. All schools use tests.

Since you will be asked to remember what you have learned during tests, you must practice answering questions as you learn the material. That's why you have to Test-Yourself before you finish your Readrite. This last step provides you with the retrieval cues you will need to help remember later on.

You must Test-Yourself while you learn the material, not later on. IMMEDIATE self-testing is the secret to successful remembering. You would not wait until later to label a file before filing it, would you? If you said, "Oh, I'll just put this file away now, and label it later," you would never find it again. That's like dropping sunglasses behind toasters. If you carefully label the file when you first use it, you will always be able to find it when you need it.

The same with your learning. Label your facts with good questions so that when similar questions appear during a test they will automatically lead you to the fact. Here are a few questions you could have asked yourself after you had completed the *Clouds* article in the first reading test:

What two kinds of clouds are there? (answer – Vertical and Horizontal)

What is the most dangerous cloud? (answer – Cumulonimbus)

What is the symbol for an overcast sky? (answer – ⊕)

As long as you are quizzing yourself in some fashion you don't need to be as formal as this. Recalling all the points in a section of the book is an effective way of testing yourself. You really are answering the general question, "What's in this section?"

Is this last step really needed? After all, you have done your Look-it-Over, and Notes steps. You were able to make notes from memory. Is that not enough? No. This last step will double your remembering. Research has proved this.

Reciting Doubles Learning

Table 2-B summarizes the research of Professor Gates of Cornell

Table 2-B — Gates Experiment

Percent of Study Time Spent Reciting	Lists Immediate Test	Lists Retest Later	Biographies Immediate Test	Biographies Retest Later
0	35	15	35	16
20	50	26	37	19
40	54	28	41	25
60	57	27	42	26
80	74	48	42	26

University. He wanted to know if self-testing was worthwhile. To find out he asked New York school children to learn various materials, then immediately test themselves by reciting for different amounts of time. His results dramatically show the value of such work. Students who spent 80 percent of their study time reciting learned more than twice as much as students who did not do any reciting, and they remembered the facts three times better later on. Professor Gates's experiment has been repeated by other scientists who confirmed his results. *Immediate self-testing pays off.*

When you self test you are setting up those cues to remembering. For that reason you must do it as you learn, not later in the week, or just before a quiz. You have to label those facts in your memory as you file them. The more you can tie each fact to other facts (more labels) the easier it will be to find. The weather symbol for overcast skies (⊕) looks like someone has "crossed out the ground." That idea could help you remember the symbol later.

The Laws

The Readrite study system uses all the laws of learning. If you follow this system you take the easy road to knowledge, because you are working with these laws, not avoiding them or working against them. The laws are used as follows:

Gradualness — the system forces you to work with only as much material as you can remember at any moment. If you can't take notes from memory, then you are violating this law.

Repetition — you deal with each section of your book at least three times: once when you Look-it-Over, once when you take Notes, and once when you Test Yourself.

Reinforcement — Every time you jot down a note from memory, every time you answer a question during a self-test, you are succeeding. Success is the *best* reinforcement. Not a minute goes by in the Readrite system without reinforcement.

Active Learning — You look-it-over, you read, you remember, you write notes, you test yourself. You are busy.

Stimulus Control — A simple one, the pen and notebook. To learn you have to fill those pages with notes. No notes = no learning. Good notes = good learning.

Practice (Specific) — Eventually you will have to remember your reading material, and write answers to questions on tests. You start to practice your remembering, writing, and question answering right from the start.

Exercises

1. Look-over chapters in a practice textbook, not one from a regular course you are taking now. Do your look-overs in 2 to 3 minutes. Keep them short. Repeat this exercise often.

2. After you get the hang of exercise 1, start to jot a few notes from memory as you look over chapters.

3. Look-over then read-remember-write a chapter. Repeat this exercise several times over the next few days.

4. Add Self Testing to your Readrite. Repeat several times.

5. Use Readrite as you study all the remaining chapters of this book.

6. When you are confident about Readrite use it on a chapter from *one* of your regular course books.

7. If exercise 6 goes well continue Readrite for that course; if not return to your practice book.

8. *Slowly*, add exercises 6 and 7 for each of your courses. If it becomes too much, back off.

4,578 Words

CHAPTER 3 - CO-TEACH

To teach is to learn twice.
Joseph Joubert

Summary

Teachers know that the best way to learn is to teach. Extensive trials have shown that students can improve their preparation, motivation, and organization as well as their learning by co-teaching. In co-teaching students take turns at teaching their lessons to each other. Also, students who discuss their work, quiz each other on it, or recite their lessons to each other, help beat the problem of isolation and loneliness.

Re-discovery

Sometimes an old idea is reborn and becomes useful again. This is the case with co-teaching, the technique of *learning through teaching*. In this chapter, you will trace the method and discovery of co-teaching, learn how to use it, and discover its value as a learning skill.

When I began college teaching I discovered for myself that teaching is a superb learning technique. For example, I learned more about the mathematics of statistics the first time I taught that subject than I had in the five courses that I had taken as a student.

"It's an axiom among teachers that there is no better way to learn a subject than to teach it to somebody else," say Clifford Morgan and James Deese, two psychologists who are experts in study methods.

Could students who were not trained as teachers benefit by teaching their lessons to each other? I decided to find out. I required one of my classes to do this as a regular assignment. They thought this teaching was a strange assignment and they grumbled about the work, but they did it. After the final exam was over and graded the students were asked to turn in course critiques. Here are a few of the comments they made on their teaching assignments:

"I worked harder preparing those teaching sessions than I did in any other course."

"... the preparation for teaching taught me a lot."

"After I had taught a chapter I was surprised to find out that listening to another student teach the same chapter didn't bore me. I was alert and interested to see what sort of a job he would do."

"If I wasn't organized it really showed when I tried to teach."

"Knowing that I was going to have to face someone with my knowledge instead of just keeping it to myself really motivated me to work at it."

The method worked. I thought so, the students thought so. Since students worked in pairs teaching each other the materials of the course, I decided then to call this technique *co-teaching.*

The Method

The steps in co-teaching technique are:

1. Arrange to meet with a fellow student to *teach* him a section of your textbook. Set a definite time and place.

2. Study your section ahead of time, keeping in mind that you will have to teach the material *without the use of the textbook.*

3. Make *a brief outline* of your lesson on a small (3 by 5 inches) card, or piece of paper.

4. Teach the lesson to your friend. Keep the session short, no more than half-an-hour.

That's the skeleton of the method, now let's flesh it out. Students have asked many questions about this technique in the eight years that I have been teaching it in the Learn-to Learn Course and you probably have some yourself. Here's a typical class's session in which I answer their questions:

"Wouldn't I be better off to prepare first, then set up a teaching session with a friend?" a student asks.

"No. Definitely not," I replied. "You need the motivation provided by that future co-teaching appointment. If you know who you are going to teach it will help you organize your material better. Having a definite time set for your co-teaching forces you to prepare quickly and efficiently, instead of putting it off or letting your preparation drag out. Also, knowing that the studying you are doing is preparation for a co-teaching session with a particular friend is a tremendous boost to your motivation."

"Should I find an empty classroom to co-teach in?" said another student.

"Sure, if you can, but it's not necessary. You can co-teach anywhere that you and your friend can work undistracted; your home, your friend's home, even outside on a nice day. Exactly where you teach is not as important as having a set place. If you are going to co-teach regularly with your friend arrange *one* particular place for your co-teaching session; that's good stimulus control. In any event, arrange the place, as well as the time ahead of time so that you are both sure where you are going to be."

Figure 3-1 Teaching someone else is one of the best ways to learn the material yourself.

Finding a Student

Then a student asked a key question. "How can I convince somebody to be my student?"

The whole method depends upon *you* being able to get someone to be that student. "Why do you think I named the method co-teaching?" I asked.

"Uh, I don't know--wait a minute! It's because we teach each other," the student replied.

"Right! You alternate the teaching with your friend," I said. "That way you both get a chance to teach. You both get a chance to benefit from the technique. My experience has been that once a person sees how well the teacher in the co-teaching session has learned the material, they want to try co-teaching themselves. Convince your friend it's to his advantage."

"Is it okay to switch back and forth from being the teacher to being the student in one session?" I was asked.

"Be careful about that," I said. "The method works best when you prepare a particular section to teach. Both of you trying to teach the same section at the same session to each other will not work well. Let one person be a teacher for one session, then the other person can be teacher for the next session. This works best."

I then asked, "Can anyone think of a way to use co-teaching where you are the teacher exclusively?"

"Sure," said a student with a grin. "Be a tutor."

"Exactly. Find someone in your class who needs help. Your teacher usually knows who these people are. Set up a tutoring schedule. In that way you do your teaching and have the satisfaction of helping a friend who really needs it."

While in the Canadian Air Force I tutored some Turkish student pilots. Lieutenant Mehmet Senturk told me how important this tutoring was to them.

"If we fail a course here we are automatically sent home and busted back to ordinary soldiers. The difference between a soldier and an officer in Turkey is about as great as the difference between a starving peasant and an aristocratic landowner."

We worked very hard at our lessons; they as students and I as their tutor. We all passed our courses. I ended up at the top of my class, and I am sure now, as I look back, that my tutoring had much to do with my success.

Golden Preparation

"I've seen teachers' lesson plans. Sometimes they go on for pages, so why do you restrict our outlines to that small card?" asked a student.

"Your goal is to *learn* the material well. Forcing yourself to use the minimum amount of notes in your teaching will make you commit more of the material to memory. A teacher's lesson plan contains a lot of teaching technique which you can't use, so it has to be longer. Also, the teacher is already an expert in the area she is teaching, so she does not need to learn the material. You do." I replied.

"Does co-teaching really help me organize the material?"

"To teach anything you have to think about organization. To give an exaggerated example, a teacher must teach arithmetic before he teaches algebra, and algebra before he teaches calculus. They must be taught in this order if the student is to follow the lessons. When you organize a lesson properly you have to make judgments on what to teach first, second, third, and so on. This forces you to *evaluate, compare* one part with another part, and *think* about the material. This is superior learning, far better than rote memorization of facts. When you first start co-teaching you will probably try to teach the facts without organization, but you will soon find out how bad this is. Your student will tell you. Soon you will be organizing, and you will benefit a lot."

"I am a shy person. I think I would be too embarrassed to try to teach. What can I do?" asked one girl.

"That is a problem. Remember that you will be teaching your fellow students, your friends, the people that you like best. Also, you won't be standing up in front of a class to do this teaching. You and your friend will be working in private. One positive factor about co-teaching is that it might help you overcome some of your shyness," I told her.

"Turning on" to Co-teaching

Students work on this technique very hard in the Learn-to-Learn Course. By now we have accumulated thousands of classroom hours experience with the method. Watching students "turn on" to co-teaching is one of the exciting highlights of each class.

At first students are doubtful and hesitant about trying to teach each other. This teaching is made even harder because I make them teach strangers. They teach material they are not familiar with, and they must read and learn the material quickly. They also have to co-teach in public in the classroom with all the other students around them. I try to set up the worst possible situation that I can contrive in the classroom. If they can co-teach under these circumstances they *know* they can do it with anyone, on any subject, anywhere, anytime.

During these co-teaching practice sessions students are allowed five minutes to learn a short section of a book to teach. They work in new material, a subject that they are not familiar with, each time. Then they pair off and try to teach another student that material.

Figure 3-2 Discussion groups foster creative thinking, and enthusiasm.

For the first couple of days they are tongue-tied, and clumsy, spitting out a few disjointed facts and then they quit. During the first couple of practices they rarely speak for more than a minute. Once they see that nothing really bad is going to happen to them they begin to warm to the task. By the end of the course most of them can teach easily for five to ten minutes from a five minute preparation.

The Co-teaching Teacher

The student doing the teaching in a co-teaching session has the classic job of all teachers; present the facts clearly and see that the student undersstands them and learns them.

The Co-teaching Student

The co-teaching student can do a lot to make the session useful and enjoyable. He can do this by asking questions, and seeking explanations when the teacher is not clear. If the material being taught is unclear it usually means that the teacher is not clear in his mind. Discovering such vagueness is one of the major advantages of the co-teaching method. When studying by yourself you can slide over such difficult parts, believing that you know them well, when you don't. When a co-teaching student starts asking questions these weakly learned areas will show up and you can work on them later.

The best teaching happens when teacher and student talk to each other. Good teaching is a dialogue, not a monologue.

WORKING WITH FRIENDS

Discussion

Kicking around a few ideas with some friends is still one of the best ways of sharpening your knowledge of any subject. Good discussion is fun, fascinating, even exciting. Discussion often leads to argument where you try to convince another person of the rightness of your viewpoint. In marshalling your facts to argue you learn how to use them to your advantage.

In discussion you discover that there are many different ways of looking at one set of facts. For example, in a discussion on history you might argue that it was right for the American colonists to fight for their freedom from the British. You discover that your argument is used against you by a Southerner who contends that for the same reasons the South had a right to fight for its freedom from the North in the Civil War. You would have to counter his argument, and so the discussion would go.

Two people facing each other form the core discussion group, but any number can play. A discussion is best when it's spontaneous, but you don't have to idly wait around for one to ignite. Look for opportunities to start one. Start your discussions casually, anywhere. Asking a question or a person's opinion is a good way to ease into a discussion of a topic. People are pleased if you seek their advice. Make sure your question blends in with what was already being talked about. "I think we should discuss this," is a sure-fire way to turn off any chance for a good talk. The trick is to have a discussion topic in mind, then when a natural opportunity arises you can start your discussion. If you get really good at it nobody will ever know that you are leading discussion groups.

Quizzing

There's no point in studying what you already know. You need to concentrate your efforts on what you don't know. Teachers can't give quizzes often enough for you to find out where you need more work. Get together with a friend and quiz each other.

One of you sits with the textbook or class notes in his lap and fires questions at the other. Every question you can't answer shows you some area of the subject that you need to study some more. The question you answer correctly is a reinforcement, a repetition, and good practice for teacher's quizzes and exams. After awhile, you can switch jobs and ask your friend questions.

If you leave a quizzing session until just before an exam you may not have enough time to study those "don't know" areas. Give yourself a few days lead time.

Of course you could quiz yourself, but it's much more fun to do it with a friend.

Reciting

Sometimes you need a knowledgeable ear to find out if you really know your work as well as you hoped.

"Hey Peter, listen to this, will you?"

Then recite your part in the class play, or your geometry theorems, or your French, or whatever. If Peter is taking the same class with you he can correct your mistakes. Maybe he can't, but you get the benefit of hearing yourself recite, and being with your friend.

The Lonely Student

"The really hard part of studying is the loneliness," Charlie Kennedy complained. "I hate being by myself. I no sooner sit down with my books than my mind drifts off to my friends."

Charlie's complaint is a common one.

"Oh, I've got to have a radio on when I study for company," said Edith Norman.

"I like to be where I can see lots of people when I study, so I work in the library reference room," Robin Whitaker told me.

Whenever you sit down with your books to study, you briefly isolate yourself from your fellows. That is necessary and unavoidable. We all need to be alone occasionally, but too much solitude is punishing. In prisons they call it solitary confinement, and they use it as punishment. If you punish yourself for studying you will do it less and less, and develop a disliking for the whole study process.

Learning is an often repeated cycle. You listen in class, you read and study your textbooks. Every once in awhile your teacher gives you a test. Before you take that test you want to be sure you know your lessons. Co-teaching provides this assurance. Now the cycle becomes listen, study, co-teach, take the tests.

Don't leave your co-teaching until just before exams. Work it in often, every week if you can. You need time to correct your learning for those errors you discovered in your co-teaching sessions.

Work with your friends. Learning can be a warm friendly task if you do it well. The joy of a teacher is working with his students. The joy of a co-teacher is working with his friends.

The Laws

The laws of learning are followed in co-teaching:

Gradualness — The four steps in the co-teaching method lead you in easy steps to your final performance, the teaching.

Reinforcement — A successful teaching is a tremendous reinforcement. Now you know you have learned your lesson well. Being with friends is a powerful social reinforcer; it tops the list.

Active — when you study a lesson to co-teach, you are not just studying, you are studying with a purpose. The teaching itself is active.

Stimulus Control — by setting a time and place to co-teach in advance you schedule the work for yourself.

Practice (specific) — the organization and evaluation that you must do in preparing a co-teaching lesson make you think, which is the ultimate goal of all learning. The co-teaching itself gets you to remember the material and use the facts in clear manner. Thinking, remembering, using — all well practiced.

Co-teaching, discussion, quizzing and reciting are four ways to beat this loneliness of study. You can work with friends and learn your lessons. All of your study does not need to be done in isolation, and some of your best learning can be done happily working with others.

Why Does It Work?

Why do people learn better when they are teaching a subject than when they are not? Notice some of the key words that those students used in their course critiques: "preparation," "alert and interested," "organized," and "motivated." If you were alert and interested as you studied, as you prepared and organized your lesson to teach to a friend, you would learn better than if you were not. The secret in the effectiveness of co-teaching as a learning method lies in this *preparation*. That's the first benefit the method gives you.

Another benefit you gain by co-teaching is being with a fellow student, a friend. You enjoy being with your friends so that is *reinforcing*. The method also allows you to beat the loneliness of studying. Even while you are by yourself preparing for your co-teaching session you have the warm expectation of meeting with your friend in a short while. We all study with our friends occasionally, question and answer sessions before a quiz, discussion of course material, or work out problems together. Keep on doing this, it's excellent learning technique. Co-teaching goes a step further.

Exercises

1. Teach a short section from one of your practice books to a friend; keep the session very short about five minutes. You can handle that and your friend will tolerate it.

2. Make a list of people in the courses you are taking who might be willing to co-teach with you.

3. Ask these people, one at a time to be a student in a co-teaching session. You will get some rejections. Persevere. Make it a trade; offer to do something for them if they will do this for you.

4. Tell your school teachers that you would be willing to tutor if they have someone who needs it.

5. Have you got a hobby, a sport, something that really excites you. Teach some of your hobby to someone who knows little about it. Watch your own enthusiasm be reflected back from that person. That's the best kind of teaching!

6. The best co-teaching students are those who are taking the same course that you are. They are knowledgeable students. Working with them will increase your own learning in gigantic strides. They are worth cul

REMINDER: Co-teaching is sharing. One person helps

-18 Words

CHAPTER 4 - READING SPEED

> **Summary**
>
> If you can read fast you can complete your assignments more easily, and understand what you read better. The speed you read is a habit, and like any habit it can be changed. By using the athlete's technique of overload in a daily 10 minute drill, you can easily increase your comfortable fast reading rate. The records you keep of your daily reading rate will show you your progress and reinforce the faster reading. You achieve this faster speed by decreasing the number of fixations per line of print, and by eliminating regressions. Students using this drill show at least a 50 percent increasing in reading speed after only two weeks of practice.

Introduction

Mike Sandman was unhappy about his reading. During the interview with me he stared at the table before him, his tall, angular body shifting restlessly as he talked.

"I read only ninety words a minute in the first reading test," he said. His dark brows pulled together in a worried frown.

Ninety words a minute — what a handicap! He would spend over twice as long reading school assignments as the average student. I asked him if he drew books out of the library.

"No."

"Do you subscribe to any magazines," I asked?

"Nope."

"Do you read the daily newspaper?"

"Just the sports scores," he said after some hesitation.

Mike was a slow reader. Slowness was not his only reading problem, far but if he could read faster he might develop some confidence and be more.

The Reading Habit

Reading speed is only partly tied to the mental side of reading. Vocabulary size, using grammar well, and your reading experience do determine your reading speed. You develop these skills daily in school. If a student is weak in these mental skills he can take more English classes to improve, but this is a long-term project.

There is also a physical side to reading. Your eyes have to move to read the lines on this page, and muscles control your eye motions. Any behavior using the muscles of your body quickly becomes habitual, because that is efficient. You have developed a physical reading habit as well as a mental one. Mike's slow eye movements hampered his reading.

You can change bad habits easily, even slow eye movements. Think of all the bad physical habits that you have broken in your life, for example, chewing your nails, a faulty golf swing, or even smoking. Students in the Learn-to-Learn Course eliminate the slow eye movements that were handicapping their reading power by using the methods presented later in this chapter. Very slow readers (107, 146, 154 words per minute) improved their reading rates by 100, 200, or even 300 percent. Students who were fast readers to start with (244, 290, 266 words per minute) also showed dramatic speed improvements (see Tables 4-A and 4-B, at the chapter's end).

READING POWER

Reading power – to be able to read more, and understand it better in less time.

The average college freshman reads about 200-225 words a minute in textbook material. The average reading speeds for high school students have been measured from 150-200 words per minute.

The student who can read 50% more material in the same time as the average student is doubly blessed. He can read in two hours the material it takes the average reader three hours, or in the same amount of time he can read half again as much material. All of this can be done easily with no loss in comprehension. The secret of developing your reading power lies in the technique of overload.

Overload

If a weight lifter wants to increase his muscle power he overloads.

If a distance runner wants to run farther, he overloads.

If a typist needs to type faster to keep her job, she overloads.

Overload is a standard training technique for increasing speed, strength and power. The weight lifter heaves more weight each day. The runner increases training run lengths each week. The typist forces her fingers to fly. If a reader wants to increase reading speed, he must overload. Every day the reader conducts a training session during which he forces his eyes to flash over the page at high speed. This is the technique that will increase your *comfortable*, normal reading speed.

Reading Power Drill

The success of this drill lies in two simple facts:

1. Everyone can read at high speed for brief spurts.
2. You can read more quickly the second time through the material.

By clever use of these facts, students can dramatically improve their reading power and maintain it. A major advantage of this drill is that the student practices high speed reading on ordinary material. He uses books, not expensive machines. He uses his eyes in a normal fashion, although at a much higher movement rate. There are no distracting tricks, just powerful reading practice.

In this drill the student reads and re-reads a passage from a book while timing himself. Each time he re-reads he extends the amount read. The drill takes only ten minutes. At first, the student reads at his usual rate, then he starts to accelerate. At the end of the drill, the student measures his improvement, to get his immediate reinforcement. Here are the steps of the drill.

POWER READING

The Basic Drill

1. Read for *two minutes* as fast as you can with good comprehension.
2. Go back to where you started to read in 1. and re-read this passage, plus half a page more, IN TWO MINUTES!
3. Go back to the beginning, now read what you did in 2., plus half a page more, IN TWO MINUTES.
4. One more time, start at the beginning, read all you did in 3., plus a half page, again IN TWO MINUTES.
5. Now test your improvement. Start reading where you left off in 4. and read as fast as you can with good comprehension for two minutes.

Isn't that simple? Yes it is, but you have to pay careful attention to detail to make it work. You have to keep careful track of how much you read. Your timing has to be perfect, your concentration total. Do not worry about comprehension in steps 2, 3, and 4.

Comprehension

"Hey, wait a minute," you say. "Am I really reading *as fast as I can with good comprehension* in 1.?" Yes, you should be.

"If that's so, then I won't be able to comprehend as well in steps 2, 3, and 4, will I?"

"No you won't, and that's OK."

In any overload training something has to be sacrificed to gain the overload's benefits. The typist makes mistakes, the runner gets out of breath, the weight lifter exhausts himself, and the reader loses some comprehension. But, in every case that's OK, because in the long run it will correct itself.

You will never do your study reading at the breakneck speed you use in the Power Reading Drill. As you practice, your ordinary reading speed will increase. Your comprehension will be just as good, even better, if you started as a very slow reader. You only practice a few minutes every day, and during practice you sacrifice comprehension a bit. The effects of this practice carry over into your ordinary reading, and you read faster, quite comfortably and you understand what you read.

The weight lifter does get stronger, and the typist faster. Your everyday reading power will improve, so don't fret over the loss of comprehension during the drill.

Step-by-Step

Now we are going to lead you through a Reading Power Drill step-by-step.

Choice of practice book: — pick an easy one, a novel for instance, that you will enjoy. Choose one with pages filled with print, no diagrams or photos. You want words, lots of them.

Location: — sit at a desk or table. Avoid sofas and easy chairs. Use a good light.

Tools: — Get a pencil or ball point pen. You are going to write in this book (that means don't use a library book, use your own. A paperback is fine).

Clock: — You can't read fast and watch a clock at the same time. You need an alarm-timer. Borrow the one from the kitchen, or if you don't have one, buy one (They're only 5-7 dollars, and a good investment).

One of the best timers for these drills is a cassette tape recorder. Here's how to use it. Record your own stop and start signals. Turn the recorder on, wait a second or two then say "Start." Let the machine run for two minutes exactly then say "stop." Let the machine run for a few seconds for spacing then stop it. If you repeat the above sequence five times on the one cassette, you have a complete timing sequence for one Reading Power Drill, portable and convenient.

Some students have used the clicking sounds made by digital clocks to time their drills, while others have used the timers on their kitchen ovens.

Figure 4-1 Reading speed books are marked to show stops and starts

Have you got everything? OK, let's go.

1. Figure 4-1 illustrates the procedure we will describe here. Choose a starting place in your book and write zero (0) alongside the starting line of print, in the margin. Set two minutes on your timer and, GO! Read AS FAST AS YOU

CAN WITH GOOD COMPREHENSION for those two minutes (we're going to abbreviate that capitalized phrase, AFAYCWGC, pronounced A-FAY'-KWUG). Don't loaf, move right along, but *do understand* what you are reading. When the timer tells you that two minutes are up, mark a number one (1) in the margin alongside the line of print that you were reading at the end of the two minutes.

Now, estimate where a half-page beyond the number one is, and mark one-plus (1+) in the margin.

2. Go back to the beginning (zero), set two minutes on the timer, and try to read to one-plus (1+) WITHIN THAT TWO MINUTES! You have read most of this material once already, so you *will* be able to go through it faster. Reading to one-plus (1+) will not be that difficult. Do it, and when time is up, mark two (2) in the margin next to the line you were reading. You may not have reached 1+ or you may have gone beyond it. Wherever you are when the bell goes, mark 2.

Estimate a half page beyond 2, mark two-plus (2+) in the margin.

3. Go back to zero, set 2 minutes on the timer, and now try to read to 2+. Mark three (3) in the margin next to the line you were reading at the end of the 2 minutes.

4. One last time. Estimate a half page beyond 3, and mark three-plus (3+). Set your timer for two minutes, and starting at zero again drive yourself to reach 3+! Make it! When time finishes, mark four (4) in the margin.

Whew! Pant, pant, pant!

I'll bet you never dreamed that you could move your eyes that fast. Are you a bit confused? That's all right. Remember that this is the first time you have tried this. Practice will lessen the confusion.

You're not quite finished. You need a reinforcement.

5. Set the timer for two minutes. Start reading at four (4) this time, and read AFAYCWGC. When time finishes mark five (5) in the margin next to the line you were reading.

That's all there is to the Reading Power Drill. Daily practice for two weeks should show a fine improvement. More on that later. You probably want to know, "Why all those numbers?"

For this drill to be effective you must be able to see your day to day progress. You will use those numbers to calculate your reading speed each time you do the drill. You will compute three separate reading speeds for each drill; one for the first two minutes reading (from 0 to 1), one for the fourth two minutes of reading (0 to 4), and one for the last two minutes of reading (4 to 5). These calculations are very simple, and require that you count a few words and lines, do one straightforward division, then look up your reading speed in a table we have provided. Once you get the hang of it you will be able to do these calculations within a couple of minutes.

Keep a detailed record of these reading speeds from day to day using the Reading Speed Record in *Appendix E*, so that you can follow your progress and be reinforced for your efforts.

Summary – Reading Power Drill

Mark 0 next to the line you will begin reading.

1. PRE-TEST – Read for exactly two minutes AFAYCWGC, then mark 1 next to the line you were reading when the two minutes finished.

   Mark 1+ half a page beyond the 1 (or one page beyond, or two, or whatever you choose as you improve your speed).

2. FIRST OVERLOAD – Starting at 0 read for two minutes trying to reach 1+. Mark 2 when finished.

   Mark 2+ half a page beyond 2.

3. INCREASE OVERLOAD – Starting at 0 read for two minutes trying to reach 2+. Mark 3 when finished.

   Mark 3+ half a page beyond 3.

4. MAXIMUM OVERLOAD – Starting at 0 read for trying to reach 3+. Mark 4 when finished.

5. POST TEST – Starting at 4 read for two minutes AFAYCWGC: mark 5 when finished.

   REINFORCEMENT – Calculate your reading rate in WPM for the first two minutes (0-1), for the maximum overload reading (0-4), and for the last two minutes (4-5). Enter these figures in your reading speed record.

Reading Speed

RECORDS

The record keeping for the drill is straightforward and *absolutely necessary*. Without it you will get no reinforcement, nor will you see your day-to-day progress. This step cannot be skipped.

You need to know your reading rate (words per minute – WPM) at the start of each drill, at the end, and how hard you were pushing yourself. Since you already know how long you read (two minutes for each numbered passage), all you need to find out now is how much you read.

Words Read

You need to calculate the average number of words on a page in your book. Turn to a full page, one with print from top to bottom, and follow these steps.

1. Count the number of words in five *full* lines, then divide that number by five to give you the average number of words per line (WPL).

    EXAMPLE – Using this book, there are **75** words in the first five full lines on the previous page: **75** ÷ 5 = **15** WPL.
    Round any decimal to the nearest full number.

2. Now, count the number of lines on a full page. This will give you the lines per page (LPP).

    EXAMPLE – There are **37** lines on the next page of this book.

3. You now have the two figures you need to calculate the words per page (WPP). Multiply the words per line by the lines per page.

    EXAMPLE – WPL x LPP = WPP

    15 X **37** = **555** WPP in this book.

Obviously, the number of words on a page will vary, but this figure will serve as a useful and reliable estimate. As long as you continue to read in the same book you may use this WPP figure in your arithmetic. Write the WPP number inside the front cover of your book to serve as a handy reference.

It will save you time if you practice your Reading Power Drill in one book, rather than skipping around. After a short time, you will be able to calculate the WPP figure quickly and easily. Now, let's use it.

Reading Speeds

The numbers you wrote in the margins mark three different parts of the Reading Power Drill. In the first two minutes you read from zero to one (0-1), AFAYCWGC, and these lines are what you read before you overload. The 0-1 lines are a standard you will use to make a before-and-after comparison of your reading rate.

The lines between zero and four (0-4) are the words you read under maximum overload. You read this big chunk of material in two minutes at high speed. Your reading rate from 0-4 will show you how hard you pushed yourself to read fast.

The lines from four to five (4-5) were new material read AFAYCWGC, to show yourself how much benefit you got from the drill. The 4-5 block serves as a test and a reinforcement of your work to improve your reading power.

To summarize, you need to know your reading speed for:
1. 0-1, the before test,
2. 0-4, the maximum overload, and
3. 4-5, the after test.

Speed Calculations

The standard measure of reading speed is the number of words per minute (WPM) that a person reads. To work this out you need to estimate the number of pages you read for each of the three blocks, 0-1, 0-4, and 4-5. Count fractional pages, such as 1 1/2, or 1 3/4, or 1 1/3. Do *not* round to whole numbers.

> EXAMPLE — If you had been using this book and had read from the top of page 63 to the middle of page 64, you would estimate that you had read 1 1/2 pages.

If you turn to *Appendix D* in the back of the book, you will find a form that will make these computations easy.

Estimate the number of pages you read for each of the 0-1, 0-4, and 4-5 blocks. Do it now. Once you have these three page estimations you can find out your reading speed for each block by looking it up in the table in *Appendix G*. To use this table, you find the number of words per page (WPP) in the left column, then move your finger along that row of numbers until you reach the column that has the number of pages you read at the top. The number you have your finger on is your reading speed in words per minute. An example is shown on the first page of the table using 240 words per page and 2/3 of a page read. The reading speed is 80 WPM.

As soon as you have found your reading speeds for each of the three blocks enter it in your Reading Power Drill Recording Form *(Appendix E)*. Every time you do a speed drill enter these three reading speed figures on this form. Only by keeping an accurate and up-to-date record such as this can you show yourself that your reading speed is improving, thereby getting an immediate reinforcement.

If you have done all your calculations correctly they should show a characteristic pattern. The 4-5 speed should be higher than the 0-1 speed, and the 0-4 speed should be much larger than either of these other two blocks. Why? Remember, the 0-4 block was your maximum overload; you were pushing yourself very hard to read faster and faster. You were letting comprehension slide. In the 0-1 and 4-5 blocks you were reading AFAYCWGC, and since you were concerned with understanding what you read, you read slower than in the 0-4 block, as you should.

If your drill was successful, the 4-5 rate should be slightly faster than your 0-1 rate. Don't be upset if the first few times you do the drill you show no improvement or even a loss when you compare the 4-5 rate with the 0-1 rate. This is common, and merely indicates that you still have to overcome the newness of the drill.

Cumulative Records

Keep track of your improvements. The Reading Speed Record and graph in *Appendix E* will allow you to follow your progress for the first fifteen days. Fill them out daily, as well as showing your 4-5 rate on your Learnometer. This will give you the immediate and continuous reinforcement needed for speedy improvement. Don't let record keeping overshadow the importance of doing the drills. They come first.

Eye Movements

Your work to improve your reading speed will be more meaningful if you understand how you use your eyes when you read. The following sections explain the research behind reading speed improvement, and give you some demonstrations to try.

In 1879 a French scientist by the name of Javal made a startling discovery about the way eyes move when you read. You do not look at each letter as you read a line of print. Javal fashioned a plaster of Paris contact lens for a reader to wear. A slender stick stuck out from this lens and traced a path on a smoked drumhead as the reader read. From this very simple, and very uncomfortable apparatus came the foundation discovery of modern speed reading: The fast reader does not look at every letter on a line of print, he does not even look at every letter on a line of print, he does not even look at every word. The fast reader "looks" only three or four times a line as he is reading.

Javal's discovery has been confirmed over and over again, and today the same experiment is repeated using modern electronic machinery that does not require the reader to wear any equipment at all. Figure 4-3 shows the eye movement of a slow, a moderately fast, and a fast reader. Each vertical bar shows the place where a reader's eyes stopped as he looked at part of the line of print. Each stop and the movement preceeding it is called a saccad, and this form of stop and go movement is called *saccadic movement*. If you wish to see this saccadic movement by a reader for yourself, perform the demonstration in the box.

Demonstration: Saccadic movements, regression

To see saccadic eye movements you will need a partner, and a book with printing at the top of the page (this page will do). Ask your partner to read the ten lines at the top of the page at his normal reading speed. Also, ask him to hold the book so that the top edge of the book just hides the tip of your nose from his view: that way you can watch his eyes as he reads. Watch the jerky passage of his eyes from left-to-right, and their typewriter-carriage return at the end of each line. Once in a while you will see a pause in the eye movements across the page; that's a regression.

Figure 4-2 Watching Saccadic movements and regressions

This demonstration should also show you regressions, backwards saccads. As you can see in the numbering of the saccads in Figure 4-3, occasionally readers back up and look again at a part of the line they had already seen. These regressions slow down the forward pace of reading and interrupt the rhythm. Partly they are caused by a lack of confidence by the reader, partly they are habitual. If the reader is unsure of his ability to read material, he goes back often to check on what he has read. Once such a regression pattern has been established it takes on a life of its own and becomes habitual so that the reader continues to do it even in material he has some confidence in reading.

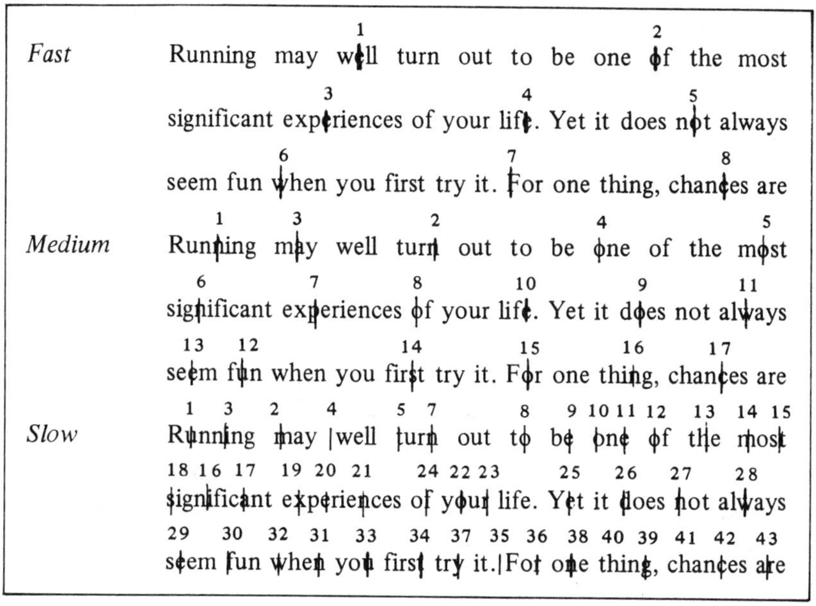

Fast

          1   2
Running may well turn out to be one of the most
         3   4   5
significant experiences of your life. Yet it does not always
    6   7   8
seem fun when you first try it. For one thing, chances are

Medium

  1   3   2   4   5
Running may well turn out to be one of the most
6   7   8   10   9   11
significant experiences of your life. Yet it does not always
13 12   14   15   16   17
seem fun when you first try it. For one thing, chances are

Slow

1   3   2   4   5 7   8   9 10 11 12   13 14 15
Running may |well turn out to be one of the most
18 16 17 19 20 21   24 22 23   25   26   27   28
significant experiences of your life. Yet it does not always
29   30 32 31 33   34 37 35 36 38 40 39 41 42 43
seem fun when you first try it.|For one thing, chances are

Figure 4-3 Eye fixations of three readers (saccads numbered in sequence) Adapted from Smith, 1958.

Movement "Blindness"

This stop-and-go reading looks inefficient, and you might wonder why it is necessary. Why not pass the eyes smoothly along each line of print? The answer, to see a word or phrase clearly the eyes must be fixed upon it. By analogy if you want to take a sharp picture with a camera, you must hold it still or the picture will be blurred. Your visual system acts the same way, only instead of blurred film as in the camera, the brain does not process information until the eyes have fixed upon an object.

Your brain will not handle information sent to it while your eyes are in motion from one fixation to the next. The object itself can be in motion, a car, a flittering barnswallow, or a falling leaf, but the gaze must be firmly fixed on the object for that object to be seen.

The brain behaves this way to achieve stability in a constantly shifting world. The wind keeps the trees, grass and clouds in nearly continuous motion. Even when you are sitting still, your head and eyes move many times each minute. To keep you from becoming dizzy and disoriented the brain "looks" at the world only when your gaze is fixed on an object. At all other times the brain just tunes out. If the eyes cannot fix on a stable object dizziness and occasionally nausea will occur — seasickness is an example of this. You can demonstrate this refusal to process information while your eyes are in motion to yourself.

Demonstration: Movement "Blindness"

Look at your face in a mirror. Fix your attention on the pupil of your left eye. Look at it steadily, now quickly shift your gaze to the pupil of your right eye. Did you see your eyes move?

Oh, you're not sure, eh? Well, try it again. Shift your gaze rapidly back and forth from left to right eye. Do it several times. NOW, did you see your eyes move? Still no!

Try it once again, only this time have a friend stand behind you to see if your eyes really are moving as you switch your gaze from eye to eye. Did your friend see your eyes move? Yes. Terrific! Did you see the motion? You didn't! Terrific! Yes, I said terrific. You are perfectly normal. You have not lost your vision. It is impossible for you to see your eyes move in the mirror.

Your day is a mixture of sharp visual pictures with a lot of blanks spaced in between the pictures. You probably object to this idea because you have not noticed the blanks. They really are there, but you have adapted to them and don't pay any attention to them. The hard fact that you cannot see when your eyes are in motion is important knowledge as far as improving your reading speed is concerned.

From the two facts of saccadic movement of the eyes needed to read and movement "blindness," you can see that you cannot improve your reading speed by trying to speed up the movements themselves. Your eyes move from one fixation to the next at almost top speed for all readers. Figure 4-3 gives a clue to what must be done. The fast reader has fewer saccads and regressions per line than the slow reader. To increase reading speed one needs only to decrease the number of saccads per line, and stop regressions.

The best way to improve reading speed is to force fast reading. Direct methods of decreasing saccads and regressions do not work well, so they have to be changed indirectly. Every successful speed reading method uses the indirect method of forced fast reading, sometimes called overload.

The Fast Reader

Tables 4–A and 4–B show the improvements made by high school and college students after only *seven days* of Reading Power Drills. Every Learn-to-Learn class shows this kind of improvement. Students started Reading Power Drills on day 8.

The ability to read fast with good comprehension requires periodic practice. It's like any complex physical skill in this respect. Stop playing tennis for ten days and the edge goes off your game. Stop reading fast for a few days and your reading rate will drop.

Your reading rate can be maintained if you do one, ten-minute Reading Power Drill each work day. This will maintain your speed and keep you aware of how fast you do read. The simplest way to do this is by incorporating the Reading Power Drill into your regular studies. When you sit down to read a textbook, start out each day's reading with the drill. In that way you get down to your regular work without delay, do your Reading Power Drill for the day, and get a real boost into your reading. When you slow down to a comfortable rate after the drill, your regular reading speed will be much higher for this boost. It's a triple plus.

Table 4-A Speed Reading of College Students
Words Per Minute

Student	Day 1	Day 7	Day 14 Pre-test	Day 14 Maxiumum Overload	Day 14 Post-test
1	146	285	600	1500	650
2	107	353	320	1960	360
3	244	186	660	7210	990
4	178	218	670	1360	705
5	207	238	555	1202	592
6	154	219	340	1302	365
7	292	333	525	1400	560
8	183	284	822	1716	1072
9	266	175	616	1288	772
10	201	220	402	1160	625

(continued on next page)

			Day 14		
Student	Day 1	Day 7	Pre-test	Maximum Overload	Post-test
11	237	164	1665	2775	1727
12	170	235	350	585	350
13	146	217	360	820	425
14	146	211	570	1300	580
15	225	259	561	1700	783

Table 4–B Speed Reading of High School Students

Student	Day 1	Day 7	Pre-test	Maximum Overload	Post-test
1	244	240	405	604	473
2	256	159	595	887	700
3	179	184	805	1668	920
4	146	251	320	520	480
5	122	300	960	660	
6	152	218	340	1360	453
7	155	161	210	467	280
8	150	151	525	750	638
9	213	227	340	680	556
10	47	81	133	200	150
11	183	170	320	720	400
12	146	197	200	260	213
13	125	191	390	990	450
14	122	110	175	350	210
15	244	143	300	900	375

4,356 Words

SECTION III.

CLASSROOM WORK

Although the brute force work of learning is done by you in your self study, the work you do in the classroom can accelerate your learning. A teacher helps speed learning. Use that help as best as you can. This means making the most of those classroom hours, and learning the best way to get extra help from teachers. Good management of routine matters such as class seating and your notetaking can improve your classroom efficiency. The next four chapters will show you some basic classroom skills to master.

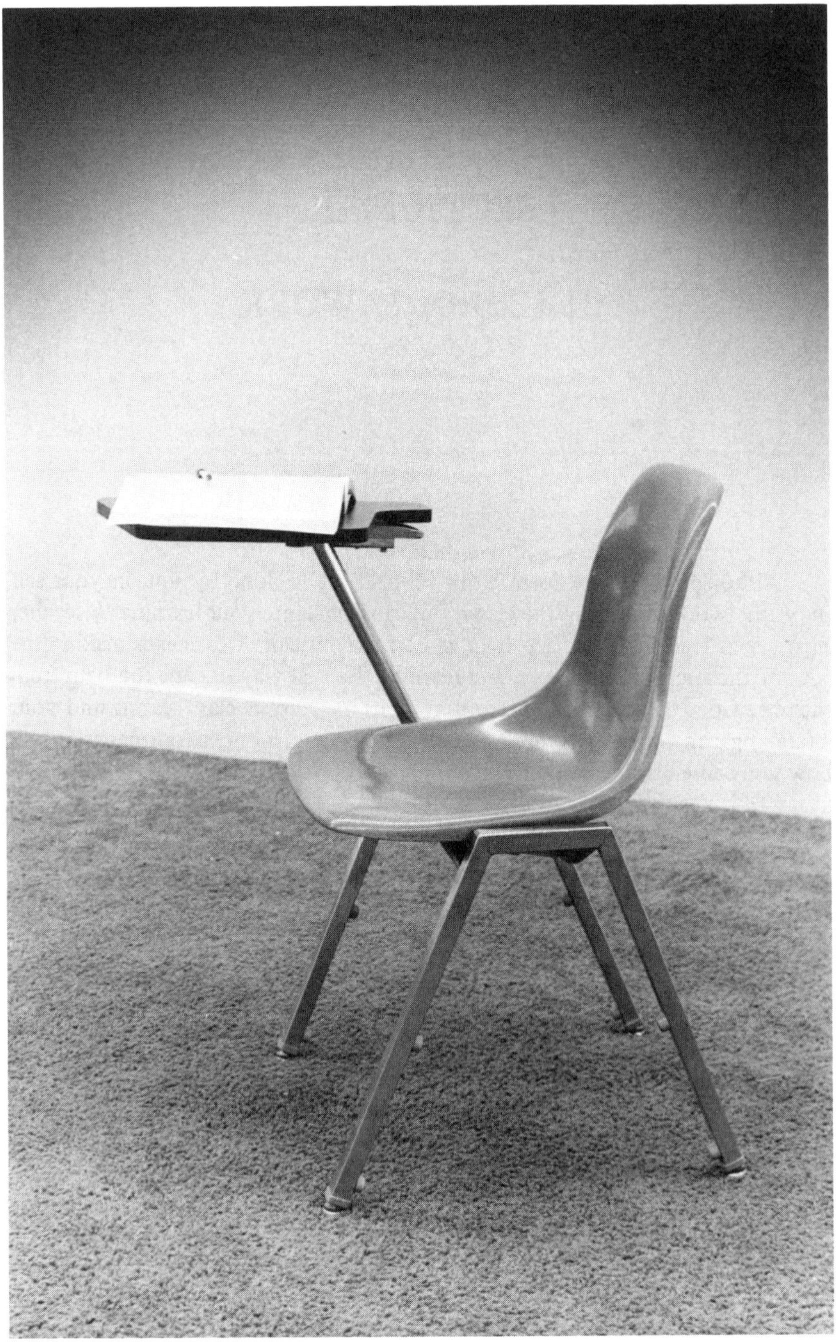

CHAPTER 5 - IN CLASS

> Summary
>
> Did you know you would spend about 5,500 hours in class during your high school and college career? You will, and for that it is most important to think about the seat you will sit in during all that time, and how you will make use of those hours.
>
> Students choose seats to sit near friends, out of habit, to avoid the teacher, or for fun. To increase your study power, choose your seat to maximize your learning. Choose one that avoids physical distractions and annoying people. A front and center seat is better than one at the back, or off to the side by the windows. Remember this formula: Seat Choice x 5,500 hours = *a very important decision.*
>
> Once you are sitting in the seat of your choice you have to make the best use of the class. Be prepared for each class. Have assignments completed, and be on time. Preview your notes or textbook before the class starts to warm up your mind for that class, and possibly discover some cloudy point from a previous class you would like cleared up. Take brief, numbered, outline notes of lectures. Ask questions during class, or if you can't, write them in your notes to be answered after class. Join discussions, and in general be as active as you can. Finally, the class is not completed until you test yourself on the material.

Introduction

You will spend over 3,600 hours in classrooms during your high school career. If you go to college you will spend another 1900 hours in classrooms. Use that classroom time well and you will get a good education; use it badly and your education will suffer. This chapter will show you how to use that classroom time to best advantage. First, we will discuss your use of classroom space, your seat, and then we will discuss how you can best use your time in class.

Your Class Seat

Look at the picture on the left, a typical classroom desk chair. Over a full year of waking hours will be spent in such a seat during your school years. Choose wisely.

If you are taking a class now, try to remember where you sit. Answer this question — Why am I sitting in that seat? Do you have a reason for sitting there? Did you plop yourself down in the first seat available? Students choose their seat for lots of reasons.

> Reason 1. "My friend Irene was there, so I sat next to her."
> Reason 2. "I don't know. I just sit over by the windows out of habit, I guess."
> Reason 3. "I don't like to sit up front where teacher can bug me."
> Reason 4. "My eyes aren't too good. I sit up front where I can see the blackboard easily."
> Reason 5. "If I sit in the back by the windows, I can sneak a smoke."

Figure 5-1 The farther back you sit the more distractions you see

Friends, habit, teacher, eyesight, and recreation are a few of the reasons students choose their seats. I'm going to add one more, learning. The student who wants Study Power chooses his seat so he can learn best. Here's how.

Physical Distractions

Avoid physical distractions.

Sitting next to a ventilating fan may be cool in summer heat, but the fan may be noisy. Sit far away from noisy machinery. Sitting by doors and windows can also be bad news. If the door is open you can be disturbed by the people walking by and noise from other classrooms. A seat by a window is an invitation to daydream. The world outside represents freedom and fun. Inside the classroom you work.

Be sure your seat is in good repair. A wiggling desk makes writing difficult. A loose chair leg can worry you enough to make you uncomfortable.

Physical distractions are pretty obvious. Do what you can to eliminate them. A wise person knows when to complain about a flaw in his world — do something about flaws that repeat day after day, and ignore the small ones that occur once or twice.

People Distractions

The number one, first class, top of the list distraction is people. We need to have people near us, but at times they can be irritating.

A mother phoned to ask if her daughter should be playing the stereo while she studied. I asked if her daughter was getting her work done.

"Yes, But, I don't see how she can concentrate with all that noise."

I asked the student about the "stereo-mother" problem next day.

"I need that stereo on to *help* me concentrate. Mom makes an awful racket in the kitchen. My baby brother yells all the time. The music helps drown out all that clatter so I can work," she said.

One person's noise is another person's music. People noises distract.

Your classmates constantly compete for your attention with the teacher. Two girls in the corner are having a giggling contest. A couple of the jocks are arm wrestling. And then there's that "friend" of yours in the next seat.

Teacher is saying, "A very important point to note is . . ."

While your friend whispers to you, "Boy! What a party we had over at Phyllis's house last night. Tony got smashed on his Dad's beer. They had some great records. We danced until nearly two, then her parent's kicked us out." And on and on.

What was that important point teacher was making? With a friend like this you don't need enemies. Sitting next to friends is an invitation to talk.

Choose who you sit with carefully.

Just seeing people can be distracting. The view from the back of the class includes all your classmates. There's 20 or more distractions before you in every class. The view from the front seat excludes most of them. Try it.

Habit

One of the strongest causes of seat choice is habit. Without really thinking about it, students will choose the same seat in a new class that they have sat in before in other classes. Chuck Hunter did that. He would shamble to the back of the room and squeeze himself into a corner seat. During a class discussion on seating, I asked why the people in the back row sat there.

Chuck said, "I was put back here by my teachers."

I asked why.

"I've always been big, all of my life. Some of my teachers were afraid of me, so they stuck me back here. Now I just head for the back when I enter a new classroom."

Figure 5-2 A front seat excludes distracting sights.

I was dumbfounded by this answer, although I could understand it. Chuck was a tackle on the varsity football team. He stood six-feet-two-inches and weighed two-hundred and eighty pounds. I have watched Chuck bench press a 450 pound bar-bell, so I can vouch for his strength. He was big, but there wasn't a threat about him anywhere. His curly blond hair and gap-toothed smile gave him a boy's face. During the last semester in college, he was followed around campus by a furry ball of a puppy, which he treated gently and affectionately. Those teachers did not look any deeper than Chuck's skin when they sent him to the back of the room.

Chuck moved to the front of the class that day, but he did not stay there. He was uneasy in front so he moved back the next day, but only half way back. Habits are hard to break.

This persistence of habits can work for you, as well as against you. Once a good habit is learned it gathers a momentum of its own that will keep it going when times are tough. Once you develop the habit of choosing a classroom seat to maximize your learning, it will become easier to do each time.

The Perfect Seat

In every class there is a perfect seat for you. There are positive reasons for capturing that seat, as well as the negative reasons mentioned above.

Choosing a seat for a sports contest is simple. You pick one on the fifty-yard line, the center line, or in midcourt down close to where the action is. You don't choose a seat up in the rafters of the stadium. You can see more of the action up close. Ditto in the classroom.

One of the laws of learning not mentioned at the end of the book is called the law of Stimulus Intensity Dynamism. That mouthful just means that the more intense a stimulus is the easier you can learn with it. The bigger, brighter, more colorful, louder, prettier a stimulus is the easier it is to remember it. Dullness is hard to learn.

In the classroom you can make your lessons bigger and brighter by moving up close to them. Sit at the front. The printing on the blackboard will appear larger, teacher's voice will be stronger, and demonstrations will have more impact. In the long run your learning will be better, even easier.

There is another good reason for sitting down front. It is easier to pay attention when you are closer to the teacher. Teachers are trained to hold students' attention with eye contact. As they talk to a class, they try to look the students in the eyes. It is difficult to ignore someone who is looking straight at you as they talk, unless that person is a long way off. If you are talking to a person in a crowded room, you automatically move closer so that you can hear and see them better. Teacher spends much of her time at the front of the room using the blackboard and the tools she has there. Move up close to her so you can get that eye contact, and have your attention locked onto what she says.

If you don't get that eye contact, you feel that you are being ignored. You know a person is not really attending to you if they look off into space as they talk to you. Who needs that?

Which Side of the Room?

If your teacher is right handed, sit on the right side of the room (your right side). For a left-handed teacher, sit on the left side of the room. This is especially important in classes where there is a lot of blackboard work. As a teacher writes on the blackboard she turns to talk to the class occasionally. If she intends to write some more she will make a half turn (see the picture), not a full turn. This means that the left side of the class gets to see her in profile, while the right side of the class gets full eye contact.

For all of the reasons mentioned above, the front seats in the center of the classroom are the best seats, FOR LEARNING. That's a general truth. But, a front row seat may not be your perfect seat.

Figure 5-3 A left side seat will give you a fine view of the back of a right-handed teacher's head.

Many students are intimidated by teachers. Teachers are older, more experienced in the world, and have more authority than the student. This makes them a little frightening. Many students are uneasy in close face-to-face encounters with teachers. Some students are shy. If you find that sitting in the front row is a bit uncomfortable, move back a row or two. Put a few students between yourself and the teacher. Don't move all the way to the back, just a couple of rows.

Time — The Great Multiplier

Does this seem to be a lot of fuss to make about where you sit in class? Does it really matter? Think about the amount of time you are going to spend in that classroom seat.

Time is the great multiplier, in both the physical world and the human world. A single raindrop or one thunderstorm erodes very little rock. But, multiply those storms by a million years and the Rockies will flatten, or your neighborhood creek can gouge a new Grand Canyon.

Think of all the people interactions of little consequence that blow up to great importance if repeated. Someone bumps you in the hall at school. You apologize to each other, and dismiss it from your mind. That happens all the time. The next day that person bumps you again. You give an embarrassed smile and a quick, "Sorry." The third time it happens you begin to wonder. On the tenth bump you are certain that person is trying to get your attention. Do they want to fight or be a friend? One bump means nothing, ten bumps is important.

How many TV or radio commercials do you know? A bunch, I'll bet. Do you really want to know all those cute words about Ex-lax, Alka-Seltzer, and Ban? I doubt it, but you hear them over and over again. The advertisers know about repetition and the multiplication effect of time.

3,600 hours + 1,900 hours = 5,500 hours - that's a lot of time to spend in a rotten seat, a lot of repetitions. Make that seat a good one.

USING CLASSROOM TIME

So much for the use of space in a classrooom, now let's see what you can do about time. All those hours mentioned above come in 50-minute chunks, since the typical class lasts about that long. This varies a bit from one school system to another, but it is pretty standard. The work you do during each class period depends on the class, of course. An art class will use 50 minutes quite differently than a social studies class, yet there are some general rules for all classes.

Before Class Starts

The Scouts have a phrase for it, *Be prepared.* Before the class starts have your mind in gear for that class. Sometimes this is not easy during a busy school day. You may have just left an algebra class and your brain is still full of "factors, polynomials, and radicals," but somehow you have to now get your mind on the next class. Sometimes you chat with a friend about parties and football games and such as you walk from one class to the next, and that's what is on your mind. Despite all these distractions you still have to get your mind on the present class. If you follow the steps below you will be in pretty good shape:

1. Have *assignments* done and with you. 'Nuff said.

2. *Be on time.* If you are late you can arrive flustered and breathless. Also, you could miss the most important part of the class, the introduction. A teacher will often start each day's class with some introductory remarks. He can go over last day's work and this is valuable to you since it will provide linkage between the two days' classes, and will give you a warmup. Teachers will start by outlining the material they are going to cover that day. This preview of the days work will give you the same kind of road map that a Look-Over gives you with your reading, and just as valuable. All of this can happen in the first couple of minutes of class. If you arrive late, you can handicap yourself by missing these items.

3. *Preview* – Do a brief preview of the work before the class starts instead of chatting with friends or staring out the window; use the minutes before the class gets under way to warm yourself up. Look over your notes from the last lecture of that class. See if you understand all of it, or if you have some questions. How often have you heard a teacher start a class, "Have you got any questions on what we have covered so far?" Don't miss that opportunity to start the class on a topic you want to hear. If you have done your preview you will have your question.

   This preview need not take more than a minute or two. If you find that you are always rushed getting to a particular class, and never have time to preview, then you might have to borrow some time earlier in the day, before school, at lunch, or during a study period. The preview is another "drop of water" item. By itself it does not seem important or necessary. But students with real study power do it, and over the years it pays large dividends.

During Class

Just at the phrase "Be Prepared" summarizes what you do before class starts, the phrase BE ACTIVE summarizes how you should behave during class.

Since you sit in most of your classes, it is not easy to see just how you can be active while you learn, but it can be done. You must be mentally active, and being physically active helps.

Classes where the teacher guides the action are no problem. A gym class, or a drawing class, or a language class where you are speaking are all active classes, and they don't present much of a problem for the student. When the teacher lectures a problem arises. Students feel that the appropriate behavior for them during a lecture is to sit and listen. Right and wrong. They must listen, but that is not all they can do.

Lectures are a trap. Students who treat the teacher's lecture as if it was a movie or a TV program, and just sit and listen won't learn as much as they would if they were more active. There are several ways that students can be active during a lecture.

1. *Take notes.* This is such an important form of lecture activity, as well as necessary for self study, that the entire next chapter deals with this. To summarize that chapter here, TAKE BRIEF, NUMBERED, OUTLINE NOTES.

2. *Ask questions.* You will have to judge your teacher on this. Some teachers do not want to be interrupted at all while they are lecturing. Others, myself for one, encourage students to ask questions at any time. My own view is that there is no point in continuing a lecture if I have lost the class. A question from a student can quickly tell me if the class is lost.

   There is no such thing as a dumb question from a student. If a student has a question, it usually needs an answer, and needs an answer right away. There are dumb students. I mean dumb in the sense that they don't speak up when they should, not in the sense of being stupid. Too many students sit on their questions, class after class, until they are hopelessly lost. Don't be a "dumb" student. Ask questions.

3. If it is impossible to ask questions during class, *write your questions into your notes.* If teacher refuses to allow questions during class, or the class is huge, or the class is a movie showing, you can't ask questions. Don't lose the question that occurs to you during class. Write it down. Later you can look up the answer, or ask the teacher after class. If you don't write the question down when it occurs to you, you might forget it, and the next time you will see your unanswered question will be on a test.

4. *Join discussions.* If teacher has started a discussion, or one has started spontaneously, jump in. Don't sit on the sidelines and be a hitchhiker to other people's ideas; contribute your own. You will learn more.

Figure 5 – 4 Eye contact with a teacher helps focus your attention

Sometimes you will make mistakes, but so what? We all can learn from our mistakes.

5. *Ask questions at the end of class.* Be sure you get all of your questions answered. Get answers from teacher or a classmate.

If you find yourself sitting in a class day after day without moving your hands or occasionally, your mouth, examine that class closely. You are not being active enough.

At the End of Class

The end of a class is like the end of a chapter in your textbook. You cannot be sure that you have learned what you heard in the class until you TEST YOURSELF. To be most effective this self testing has to be done *immediately*. The sooner the better. The very best would be before you leave the classroom.

Now there's a difficulty! You have to dash off to your next class, so how can you take the time to test yourself? You have to use your common sense and good judgment. If you can find two or three minutes at the end of a class,

Use them for self testing. You will gain more from those few minutes at the end of the class than you would if you wait to self-test that evening. Don't assume that you cannot do your self-testing if teacher is still talking. Sometimes teachers have really finished their class early and are merely filling in time until the bell rings. Sometimes the end of a class is used to answer other students' questions Tune out on all of that and quietly recite what you have just heard. Your notes will be your guide.

Do not let a day go by without testing yourself on what you have learned in each class that day. Although this last section is short, don't think it is unimportant. The most important learning skill you can use in the classroom is immediate self-testing. British educational researcher Philippe Duchastel discovered that students tested immediately after learning remembered *twice as much* two weeks later as those students not tested.

The Laws

Stimulus Control — Carefully selecting your class seat makes use of this law. Also, by realizing that each class has three parts, a beginning, a middle and an end, you use the proper technique for each part (beginning — preview, middle — activity, the end — self-test).

Gradualness — A preview allows you to ease into each class. When you self-test after each class you ensure that you learn that day's work on that day. If you learn each day's work as you go along you will not have to cram for exams.

Repetition — A preview is the first, the class itself is the second and your self testing is the third repetition for the day. When you review the material before an exam that's the fourth repetition.

Reinforcement — Every time teacher pays attention to you that's a reinforcement. Nobody likes to be ignored. Seating yourself where you can get eye-contact with teacher, and receiving answers to your questions is reinforcing. Finally, the self-testing shows you how successfully you have learned that lesson, and such success is reinforcing.

Active Learning — Taking notes, asking questions, and participating in discussion are all active learning.

Practice (Specific) — The more questions you ask and have answered, the more your learning resembles the tests you will take. Self-testing forces you to remember what you have heard. Writing and remembering as you learn are specific practices.

Exercises

1. Choose one of your classes and analyze your class seat in that class by the criteria set in this chapter. If your seat is not perfect, change it right away.

2. During one of your classes count the number of times you make eye contact with the teacher. Are you getting the individual attention you need?

3. Find out how many of your teachers are right or left handed. Note which ones commit the "half-turn" error while working at the blackboard. Which side of the room is your seat on for each of these teachers?

4. Calculate the exact number of hours you will be seated in your classrooms for this semester.

5. Ask at least two questions a day in one of your classes next week.

6. Test yourself on one of your classes each day for a week. Do this self-test before you leave the class; no exceptions. Keep the self-testing short. Don't be late for your next class.

3,716 Words

83

CHAPTER 6 – NOTETAKING

Now go, write it before them in a table, and note it in a book, that it may be for the time to come for ever and ever.

Isaiah 30:7-8

He listens well who takes notes.

Dante Alighieri, The Divine Comedy

Summary

Six major purposes of notetaking are introduced here: recording information, developing understanding, focusing attention, organization, review and learning. To take useful notes you need first class tools. The tools of the notetaker are notebooks, paper, and pens, and the ideal choice of each is presented here. The most powerful style of notetaking is the numbered outline style, because it forces you to be organized and to evaluate the material. This style of notetaking can be fitted into many different page formats, so the student has a great deal of flexibility in its use. The chapter concludes with a list of tips on good notetaking and a list of common errors that students make while taking notes.

Introduction

Notetaking is learning. Notetaking is learning. Notetaking is learning.

In a previous chapter the fact that "Reading is not Learning," was stressed. The stress is the opposite here. Notetaking is an active process. You have to write on paper to take notes, so there is nothing passive about it. Some students try to be passive about their notetaking, by either writing down all they hear like little tape recorders, or by taking few notes at all. Even these shoddy techniques will produce more learning than vacantly listening to the lecture, or passively reading the book.

Many students believe the only purpose for notetaking is to record what the teacher is saying in a lecture, or to copy some quotes for a term paper. They are only partly right. There are many reasons for taking notes. Six important ones will be considered here.

1. To *record information* that may not be available from any other

source. Teachers can present their lectures in such a unique way that you will not find the information anywhere else in that exact form. Sometimes the teacher is an expert in an area, like a college professor who does original research, and the information he lectures on has not reached the textbooks yet.

2. By struggling to make a clear set of notes your *understanding* of the material will improve. If you cannot write the material in a few clear words then you don't understand it and had better ask some questions.

3. Notetaking *focuses your attention* on the lecture or the printed page. When the lecture gets dull, start to take notes by the yard. When the lecture is clear you can take short notes. Forcing yourself to write like mad when the teacher is boring will help you keep your mind on the lecture, instead of on your daydream.

4. The amount of *organization* of your notes shows how well organized that topic is in your mind. Messy notes equal messy thoughts. A notetaking style, like the numbered outline style, forces you to organize the material. More on that later in this chapter.

5. Notes are essential for *exam review.*

6. The best reason of all to take notes is to *LEARN*. The act of listening, remembering, then writing is a natural learning process. You attend to the material, you specifically practice the acts of remembering and writing that you will use in later exams. If your writing is satisfying and makes sense, you are reinforced for your work. Notetaking *uses* the material immediately.

You can think of more good reasons for taking notes, I'm sure. Let's get on with the techniques of notetaking, and we will start with equipment.

NOTETAKING MATERIALS

The basic materials a student needs to take good notes are:

1. A hard-cover three-ringed notebook to hold 8½ x 11 paper.
2. Indexes with tabs to separate sections in the notebook.
3. Lined paper
4. A pen or pens (different colors)

The Notebook

The hard-cover three-ringed notebook is the *best* kind of notebook that you can use. It is not the only kind. Students use all kinds of books to take notes. The spiral notebook is very popular. Some students take notes on loose paper held on a clipboard, and later file their notes in file folders. Some students use the staple bound notebook. All of these notebooks are OK, but the advantages of the three-ringed notebook are so large that it is definitely the best.

Figure 6-1 The three-ring looseleaf notebook has more potential uses than any other type of notebook.

The really big advantage of the looseleaf notebook is its flexibility in use. You can move pages and sections around in the notebook simply by opening the rings. You can add new material or take out useless material just as easily. If you decide that you need to keep your notes in two books instead of one, you can take out half of your notes and transfer them to another looseleaf notebook in less time than it takes to type this sentence. Half way through a laboratory psychology course in college I realized that I would need a separate lab book. I was able to pull out all my lab reports from my regular notebook (a three-ringer), and start my new lab book easily.

If you decide that you don't like the organization of your notes, for a particular course you can reshuffle their order easily in a looseleaf, but it could be impossible in a spiral notebook without destroying the notebook itself.

The hard cover of the looseleaf provides you with a sturdy writing platform when you don't have a desk. Teachers sometimes say, "it's a beautiful day, let's have our class outside." Trying to take notes on a toadstool can be awkward; or on your knee in the gym, or on the floor. The three-ringer gives you a portable desk.

The vinyl pastic cover of a looseleaf notebook is waterproof and sturdy. Your book can get pretty beat up in a semester. You will sit on it, spill coke on it, use it to hit frisbees or friends. You need something rugged. Also, the plastic covered looseleaf notebooks sometimes have pockets inside the covers that can be used to carry pens, geometry sets, or salami sandwiches.

You can buy very large looseleaf notebooks, large enough to hold all of the notes you will take for all of your courses in a semester. Having all of your notes in one place is handy, but by the end of the semester that notebook will weigh a few pounds. You might like to try this trick. Carry a thin looseleaf notebook in which you can keep the notes for a couple of days and some blank paper. Once a week transfer each course's notes to its own notebook kept at home. In that way you never have to carry much, and you give yourself the insurance that if you lose your "carry-around" notebook, you would not lose all of your notes. Most of them would be safely at home.

Ten days before an exam Wake Forest University student David Humphry had a knapsack stolen from his car. He never got it back. Inside the knapsack were *all* of his notes for *all* of his courses for the semester. When I saw him just after the theft he looked like a steamroller had just flattened his pet dog.

By the way, never, never, lend your notebook to anyone, even your best and dearest friend. People are terribly casual about pieces of paper that don't belong to them. The klutz will lose your notes, and you'll lose your friend. If you want to be generous lend a couple of pages so your friend can copy the notes of the lecture he missed (skipped?). If you have a looseleaf, it's easy to take out a couple of pages. Be sure to ask for them back. In this day of Xerox machines your friend should be willing to pay 20 cents to copy your notes so that you do not have to give them to him. Another trick, if your friend asks you to take notes for him in a class, put a piece of carbon paper under your own notes and give him the carbons.

Index Tabs

Save yourself a lot of "thumbing through." Buy a set of index tabs for your notebook. You will need one tab for each course, maybe more if you have labs. They will keep your notes from getting too dog-eared from use, and will keep your blood pressure lower.

Paper

Anything smaller than the standard 8½" x 11" paper will give you problems. Dozens of special papers are available for three-ring looseleaf notebooks. This is a clear bonus for users of these books. Science and mathematics courses use graph papers of many kinds which can be bought and inserted into your notes in the appropriate place. A few examples of such paper would be:

1. Linear graph paper in both inch and metric sizes
2. Linear-logarithmic graph paper
3. Logarithmic-logarithmic graph paper
4. Polar projection graph paper
5. Graph papers with diagonal lines ruled upon them

In addition to specially ruled papers you can buy plain paper for diagrams, in white or any color you want. You can also buy ruled paper in different colors. Changing page colors is a dramatic way to mark off special sections, or add a little variety to the appearance of your notebook. Be careful of the colors you choose. A few hours study on pink paper could leave you tense and irritable.

None of these special papers can be used in spiral notebooks or any of the other permanently bound notebooks, unless they are included in the binding. Some notebooks for mathematics courses do have graph paper included, but you are limited to the type of paper included, and you have to use it where it is bound in the book. Your three-ring notebook allows you to insert any special paper you want exactly where you want it.

You can buy such paper with or without margins. The spacing between the lines can vary, so you must choose the one that suits you best. If you have a small to medium size handwriting you can use college ruled paper and write a lot of notes on a page. If your writing is large you will need to select wider line spacing.

Pens

One of the finest inventions to come out of World War II was the ballpoint pen. They are cheap, reliable, they don't leak ink as badly as a fountain pen does, and they will write through several carbon copies. If you buy the kind with the clip on the removable top you can minimize the chances of putting the ball-point in your pocket and leaving an unwashable splotch on the breast of your shirt.

Choose a dark colored ink for day-to-day writing, and for papers your teacher wants you to hand in. No matter how fair I try to be, I find my fury mounting as I struggle to read an essay written in violet ink on yellow paper by a girl who thinks this combination sweet and feminine.

Do buy colored pens. You can use them to jazz up your notes, emphasize points, or draw pictures or graphs. Students in my classes without colored pens go crazy. I use a full rainbow of colored chalk on my blackboard. Students trying to copy my blackboard work into their notebooks without using color themselves can produce some pretty obscure notes, losing the emphasis I was making.

Pencils are not so hot. If a pencil is soft enough to leave a good black mark, the mark is soft enough to smear easily. The rubbing together of pages can smear those precious words so that they cannot be read for final exams. If you use a pencil that is hard enough not to smear, it produces a thin light grey mark which can be hard to read.

STYLES OF NOTETAKING

Take your notes in the *numbered outline style*. This is the best style of notetaking. Every student is exposed to this form, but many do not use it fully. The form uses a system of lettering and numbering to show main ideas and subtopics. If a proper indenting system is also used your notes become a value picture. The form is illustrated in Figure 6-2.

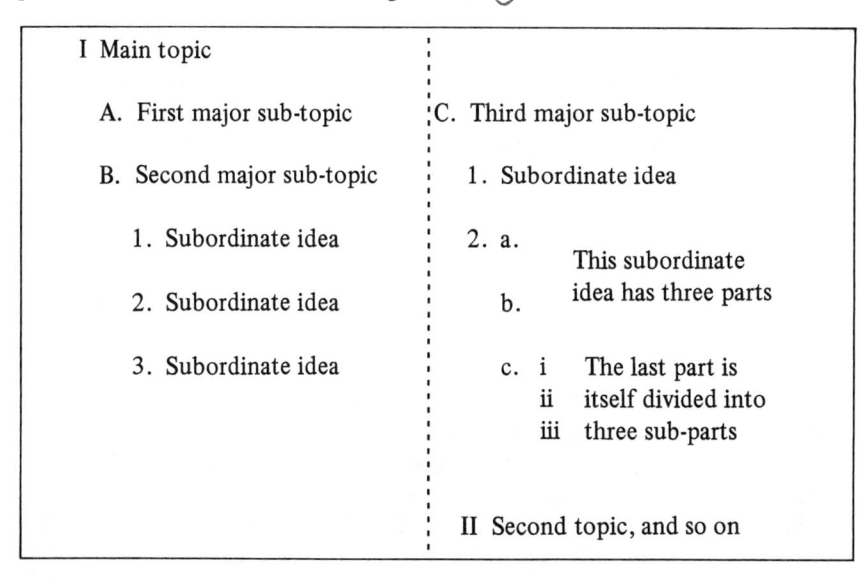

I Main topic	
A. First major sub-topic	C. Third major sub-topic
B. Second major sub-topic	1. Subordinate idea
1. Subordinate idea	2. a.
2. Subordinate idea	b. This subordinate idea has three parts
3. Subordinate idea	c. i The last part is ii itself divided into iii three sub-parts
	II Second topic, and so on

Figure 6-2 Numbered Outline Notes

Once you have the skeleton of the numbered outline style firmly in your mind any lecture or textbook material can be fitted to it. This form gives you a ready made system of organization. You are alerted to look for main topics, sub-topics, subordinate ideas and so on. It is much easier to find something when you know what you are looking for. For example, if I show a football crowd picture to a class and say, "There's an important man in this crowd see if you can find him," they will search for several minutes and not find that man. If I say, "Former President Kennedy is in this picture, see if you can find him," someone usually discovers him in a few seconds.

Use the numbered outline form of notes and you will be ready when the teacher changes the topic, or adds another idea to a topic he is developing. You are ready, you expect it because your notes naturally lead into that next change.

The indenting and numbering let you know at a glance the complexity of the subject matter. In Figure 6-2 the first major sub-topic, A, is very simple, B is pretty straightforward even though it has three ideas, but C is complex with two subordinate ideas, the last of which has three parts and the third part is also subdivided. All this can be seen at a glance.

This style of notetaking is infinitely flexible. It can be used for any subject matter. Because the framework of the style is logical and orderly it forces you to take logical and orderly notes. If teacher's lecture is a jumbled mess it will show up that way on your paper. Later you can repair the mess. Sometimes the disorganization on your page indicates the lack of organization in your head, and you need straightening out.

Figure 6-3 shows some actual uses of the numbered outline style by students. As you can see they took notes in several different courses, but they all used the numbered outline style. Each student's style is unique, but the same rules are used by all of them.

Examination Review

The numbered outline style offers a bonus when you come to study for exams.

It makes good sense when you are studying for exams to study what you don't know well, and by-pass what you do know well. If you are a bit insecure about your knowledge you usually spend time re-studying material that you already know "just to be sure." This is harmless if you have all the time in the world to prepare for the exam, but you do not. You have other exams to take, other tasks to perform. If you could discover what you did know, and did not know easily then you could work hardest where it would pay off the most, on the material you did not know.

Chapter 13

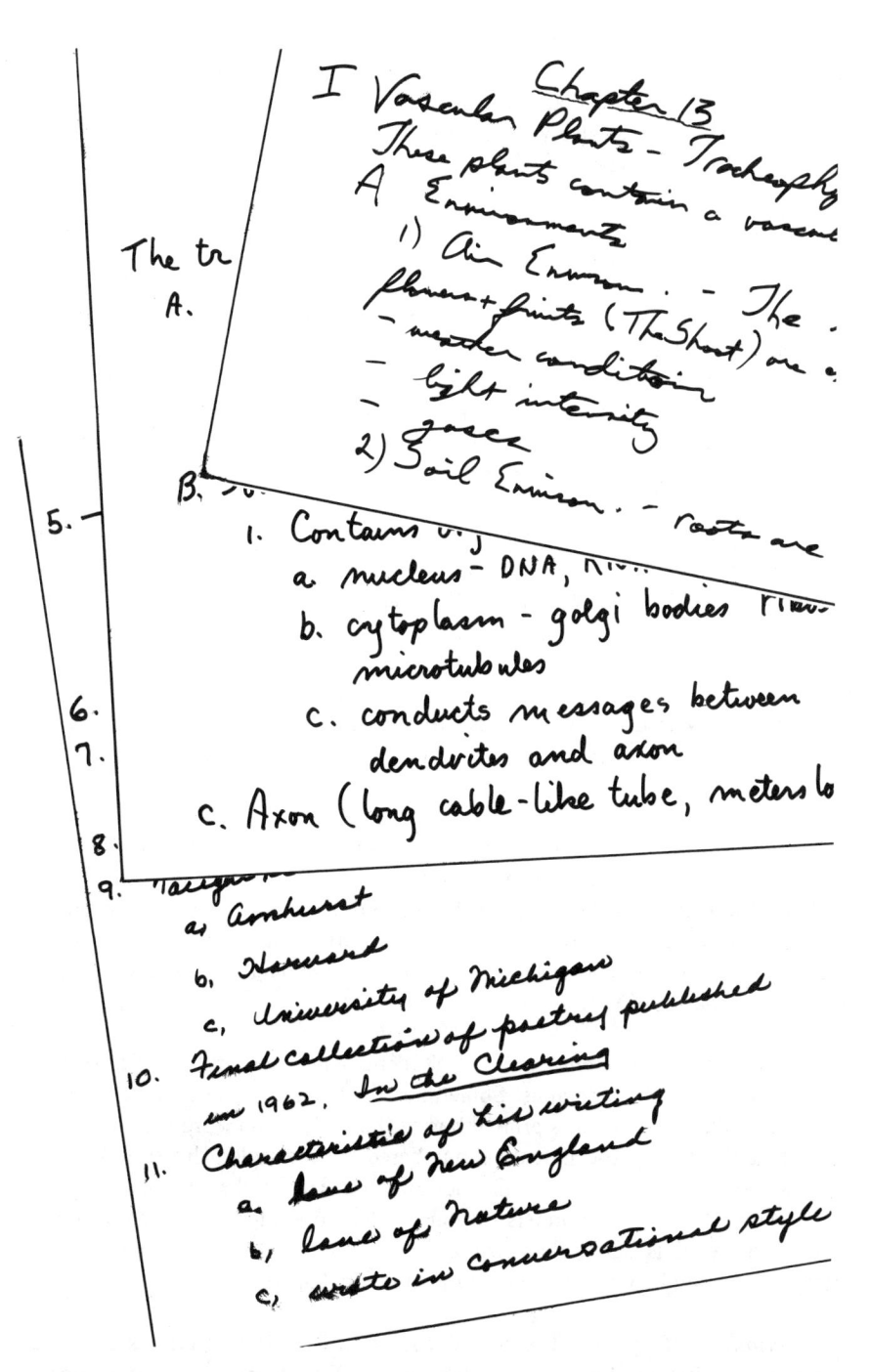

I Vascular Plants - Tracheophy
  These plants contain a vascu[lar]
  A. Environments
    1) Air Environ... - The
       flowers + fruits (The Shoot) are
       - weather conditions
       - light intensity
       - gases
    2) Soil Environ. - roots are

The tr[ee]
A.

B.
  1. Contains v..
     a. nucleus - DNA, R...
     b. cytoplasm - golgi bodies r...
        microtubules
     c. conducts messages between
        dendrites and axon
  C. Axon (long cable-like tube, meters lo[ng]

5.
6.
7.
8.
9.   ...
       a. Amherst
       b. Harvard
       c. University of Michigan
10. Final collection of poetry published
    in 1962. In the Clearing
11. Characteristics of his writing
       a. love of New England
       b. love of Nature
       c. wrote in conversational style

Figure 6-3 Students Outline Notes

The numbered outline system gives you a simple check on that knowledge. All you need to do is count and test yourself. For example in Figure 6-1 you can see at a glance that there are three major sub-topics under the main topic (A., B., and C.). Once you know how many sub-topics there are you can test yourself to see if you know them.

"Let's see, one of them is. . ., and the second one is. . ., but I can't think of the third one," you could say.

Right away you can see that you need to study the missing third one; you know the other two. After refreshing your memory on that third topic, you can proceed to the next level of detail in your study. Under B in Figure 6-1 there are three subordinate ideas, and a glance will show you that. You can then check to see how many of these ideas you remember, and how many you need to study. You can proceed this way for every level of your notes.

This exam study system allows you to focus your study on what you don't know. By testing yourself as you go, you practice the questions and answers you will have to deal with on the exam.

Other Styles

The numbered outline style is not the only style of notetaking used by students. Some other styles will be mentioned in descending order of usefulness.

Indent style — Students write main topics up against the margin, and indent when they come to subordinate topics. The numbered outline style includes the system of the indent style, and adds to it the numbering and lettering that makes the relationships among the parts clearer. If you are already using an indent style start using the letters and numbers as well, and you will increase the clarity of your notes.

Sentence or Paragraph Style — Students write their notes in full sentences or even in full paragraphs. Sometimes they number the sentences. Their notes look like the page of a printed book. This style is too wordy and lacks the clear organization of the indent or numbered outline style. This style is probably a carry-over from basic English lessons that stress full sentences and paragraph form. Notes are reminders to yourself, not fine literary writing. In notetaking one word is better than two, a phrase is better than a paragraph, and a paragraph should be written when ever it snows in August.

Primitive Messy — The title describes it. This is the style used by the student who has no idea how to take notes. Words, phrases and sentences trail down the page with all the order of a traffic jam. If this is where you are, you really need to work on your notetaking.

a. 2 Columns

b. uses only ½ page

c. Small right column useful for inserts

d. Key words in left margin

Figure 6-4 Notepage formats

Formats

The pages of notepaper you buy at the store usually have pale blue lines ruled horizontally for you to write upon, and a red margin about one inch from the left edge of the paper. Students usually use such paper by starting at the margin and writing across the page as far as they need to go, and continue to do so from top to bottom until the page is full. This is so widely accepted a system of using a page of notepaper, that students wonder why I comment upon it at all.

This is not the only way a sheet of notepaper can be used. There are other ways and one of them may be better for you than the one just mentioned.

If you take too many notes, and feel that this is a fault you would like to correct there is a simple trick that will force you to be briefer. Divide your page in half from top to bottom. When you write notes use the left column first, then the right column. Most people can only write from three to six words in a column. Because the space for writing is smaller, you will write fewer words. (See Figure 6-4, a.)

The *two-column format* is also good for students who are already brief notetakers. If you are using an outline style you start each seperate point on a new line. If you have summarized the points in less than half a line your notes will fill only the left half of the page (see Figure 6-4, b.). This really wastes half of the paper, and gives you double the number of pages of notes. By using the two column format you can put twice as many notes on a page. The more compressed your notes are the easier it is to review. The closer together the facts are placed the more likely you are to see relationships among them.

Sometimes a teacher will not be perfectly organized in lecture. He returns to topics to change what he originally said, or to add to the topic. Your notes can get pretty messy if you try to force these changes into the main body of the page. If you leave a *small column* - 1½ inches on the right of a page, you can insert the changes right alongside the place in the main body of notes where they belong. (See Figure 6-4, c.).

Some students draw a *wider left margin* than usual and use this space to place key words from their notes. This way they can build a glossary of terms from their notes, with the advantages of a running index. This system makes it much easier to find facts, and the list of key words is a boon when it comes to studying for exams. (Figure 6-4, d.).

You can think of many other ways to divide up a page for notetaking. How about a space at the bottom for footnotes? How about using one column for lecture notes and one column for notes from your reading? The only limit to using a page is your imagination, and how useful the format is to you.

ORGANIZATION

Notetaking helps you organize what you see and hear. Organized material is always easier to remember than unorganized material. Within the science of psychology there is an entire sub-science that explores how we organize words before we store them in our memory. These scientists even have their own journals, for example, the *Journal of Verbal Learning and Verbal Behavior*. The one broad conclusion these scientists have reached is that organized material is always learned and remembered better than unorganized materials. The organization that you give to your notes is going to be very personal, and that is just what you want. The organization has to be meaningful to *you*, not necessarily to anyone else.

Any organization that helps you learn the material is good. Very often you will use the organization that the teacher gives in class, or that the author of your textbook uses. Teachers and authors help students by providing organization in their lectures and books. If the material you are trying to learn is badly organized, or has no organization at all, organizing the material in your own way will help you learn it. The organization you make needs to make sense only to you, but it is also useful if the organization has some general meaning as well. Consider the following example.

Hippos 'n Snakes

Imagine that for some strange reason you had to remember the following list of animals:

sparrow, dove, lamprey, hippopotamus, possum, ostrich, iguana, sea snake, man, penguin, flying fish, shark, and bat.

There are several ways that you could organize this list to help you remember it. You could list the animals alphabetically (see Figure 6-5, b.). That's not much of an organization, but if that was the best you could do that might help. You could help your learning of the list by clumping the first letters of each name to help you memorize (bdfh--ilmo--ppsss). Again that's a pretty meaningless organization, and might not prove very useful. Let's try another.

If you could visualize the list in your mind easily it might be helpful to list the names in order of the size of the name (Figure 6-5, a.). Hippopotamus is the longest word and man and bat are the shortest. Not too good, I agree. I wouldn't use this kind of organization, unless I was desperate. Yet it could be better than a list of random words. The next two organizations are much more meaningful.

You could organize the list of animals according to the size of the animals starting with the hippo and ending with the bat. You might even subdivide this grouping into large, medium or small animals (Figure 6-5, c.). You might decide to organize the list according to how the animals move about, walkers, swimmers or fliers. Both of these organizations have the advantage of meaning, they make sense. If you have studied some biology you could organize the animals by their biological classification. This last organization would have the advantage of making sense to a lot of people, not just yourself. You could talk about the animals with others using this organization.

a. *By Name Size*

Hippopotamus
flying fish
sea snake
lamprey
ostrich
penguin
sparrow
possum
iguana
shark
dove
man
bat

b. *Alphabetically*

bat
dove
flying fish
hippopotamus
iguana
lamprey
man
ostrich
penguin
possum
sea snake
shark
sparrow

c. *By Animal Size*

Large - hippopotamus
ostrich
man
shark
Medium - sea snake
penguin
iguana
possum
flying fish
lamprey
Small - dove
sparrow
bat

d. *By Locomotion*

Walk - hippopotamus
possum
iguana
ostrich
man
Swim - sea snake
penguin
shark
lamprey
Fly - flying fish
bat
sparrow
dove

e. *By Biological Category*

A. Cold Blooded
  I Reptiles
     1. sea snake
     2. iguana
  II Fish
     1. flying fish
     2. shark
     3. lamprey

B. Warm Blooded
  I Birds
     1. sparrow
     2. dove
     3. penguin
     4. ostrich
  II Mammals
     1. hippopotamus
     2. possum
     3. bat
     4. man

Figure 6-5 Ways of Organizing a List of Animals

Related vs Unrelated

If you look closely at the different organizations in Figure 6-5 you will see that they can be classified in two ways. The organizations that use word size or the alphabet are forced and unnatural. There is no real relationship between the animals and their names, so this type of organization is *unrelated* to the material itself. This kind of organization is used as a last resort for learning nonsense material.

We do use unrelated organizations with lots of success, so don't ignore this type. "Every Good Boy Deserves Fudge," helps us remember the lines of the music score, EGBDF. "Thirty days hath September, April, June, and November. . .," and so on, does help us remember the number of days of each month. Consider this jawbreaker used by centuries of medical students to help them remember the names of the 12 cranial nerves: "On Old Olympus's Towering Top, A Finn And German Viewed Some Hops." The first letter of each word in the jingle matches the first letter of a particular cranial nerve. All of these little tricks, called *mnemonics* (memory aids), do help us remember, when a better system is not available.

Yet a far better aid to learning is to use an organization that is related to the material to be learned. The last three organizations in Figure 6-5 use this *related organization*. These related organizatons make use of some property of the material itself to help organize it, in these cases the animals size, or the way it moves, or its biological classification. This type of organization is best.

Finally, notice that the first two organizations in Figure 6-5 do not allow any grouping of the animals. The third and fourth organizations do allow some grouping so an indent note style is possible, and the last organization allows for the full use of the numbered outline style. In this last organization the animals are really organized three ways, first according to their body heat mechanism (warm blooded or cold blooded), and lastly according to the numbered outline form. This is a deep organization. The first two are pretty shallow. The more ways a subject can be organized when you learn it the easier it will be to remember later on.

NOTETAKING TIPS

Diagrams — Make liberal use of diagrams, tables and graphs. If teacher draws on the blackboard be sure to copy the drawing into your notes. "One picture is worth more than 10,000 words, " the old Chinese proverb says, and it's true. Pictures can save a lot of writing, and sometimes there is no substitution for a picture (describe Cheryl Tieg in a bikini). Draw good sized pictures so that all of your labels will make sense, and have room.

Key Phrases — Underlining key words or phrases in your notes, or writing them in the left margin is a useful study aid. You make your own glossary this way, and the emphasis of underlining makes each section stand out.

Questions — If you think of a question write it in your notes, and label it with a cipher (?), or a "Q", or a "Ques." in the margin so it will stand out. If you don't write questions when they occur to you they will get lost, and show up again as a surprise on an exam.

Cross Reference — The more you can relate one part of a subject to another part the better your knowledge becomes. For example, you can study the anatomy of the circulatory system, the nervous system, the skeletal system, and so on, but you have to understand how they all work together to make a living person. If a section on page 5 of your notes relates to one on page 33 cross reference them. Beside the page 5 item write, "See p. 33," and beside the page 33 item write, "See p.5." Of course this assumes that you know how to paginate.

Paginate — This is a fancy word for numbering pages. Every page of your notes should be numbered in sequence. If you keep separate notes for class, reading, and laboratory work, number the pages in each section separately. That way you will be able to cross reference. You will also be able to put your notes back together after you drop your notebook and scatter notes all over the steam table in the cafeteria. When you lend a friend some notes you will discover they are missing by the missing page numbers--the night before the exam.

Dates — Teachers often keep track of lectures by date. Date lecture notes so that you can ask teacher, "Did you really say last Monday that the world was flat and supported on the backs of four elephants?"

Opinions — Write your opinions in your notes. They add spice. Be careful to separate your opinions from those of the teacher or textbook author. The traditional way to indicate an editorial comment, like your opinion, is to separate it from the rest of the writing with brackets, [like this]. That way you can comment on the teacher's appearance that day [dyed her hair a ghastly blond], the dullness of the lecture [George Washington's a bore], or the new girl in class [Sheila—cute], without any fear that you might repeat them in an exam.

Emphasis — *Underline titles for emphasis. Nothing is duller than a solid page of writing without any attempt to stress points. If you have a whole section you wish to emphasize draw a box around it. The two letters "NB" mean "note well" in Latin (nota bene), and can be jotted for such emphasis like, "It's especially important to note..."*
You will soon develop your own system of stressing points.

Immediate Review — Review your notes immediately after they are made. That way you can catch any errors before the lecture or book chapter blurs in your mind. If you test yourself from your notes immediately you increase the learning, and the later remembering.

Common Errors

Here's a short list of common notetaking errors.

1. Copying directly from the textbook, or in lecture
2. Taking dictation
3. Illegible handwriting
4. No organization
5. Using a whole bunch of words where one word will do (wordy)
6. No pagination
7. Using shorthand (encourages non-thinking)
8. Doodling (the footprints of a wandering mind)
9. Using pencil
10. No notes at all

Avoid them.

The Laws

As a learning skill notetaking is one of the best. All of the laws are used.

Gradualness — Taking notes is a step by step process. You cannot force yourself to go any faster than you write. This gives your brain time to process information from short-term to long-term memory.

Repetition — You hear or read the information. You write your notes. You review, and then test yourself. Four repetitions, all built right into the notetaking.

Reinforcement — As you succeed in capturing the lecture on your pages you are reinforced. Writing from the textbook in your own brief form is another form of success. Both are instant reinforcements.

Active Learning — Writing *is* active. You listen, you evaluate, you summarize, then you use your pen and notebook.

Stimulus Control — When you finish a lecture or chapter you know you must have notes. The equipment and material demand that you convert ideas, spoken words into words on paper.

Specific Practice — Writing what you hear and read from memory is specific practice. Right away you practice your remembering. Even better, you remember by writing it down, which is exactly what you will have to do during exams.

Exercises

1. Select a numbering and lettering system for your notes. Use your own or the one from this chapter.

2. Take notes from 10 pages in your practice book. Use the numbered outline style. Be brief.

3. Use these notes (2.) to help you co-teach.

4. Take outline notes of a chapter from one of your textbooks.

5. Use these notes (4.) to review before you co-teach that chapter.

6. Choose the teacher who is the most organized lecturer you have and start outline notetaking in his/her class.

7. When your attention wanders in class, take notes furiously.

8. Spend one day observing the notetaking materials used by your fellow students. Compare them to yours.

9. Try a new page format for your notes. Better? Worse?

10. REMEMBER: Notes are *reminders,* not the whole story. Edit unnecessary words from your notes. After awhile you will stop writing those words.

5,207 Words

CHAPTER 7 - EXAMINATIONS

> **Summary**
>
> You will be shown how to best handle the two basic examinations that you will face in most courses, essay and objective exams. The five steps to consider in writing an essay exam are: 1. Use your subconscious memory as well as your conscious memory, 2. Answer the most difficult questions last, 3. Read the questions carefully and answer the questions asked, 4. Rough outline your answer, 5. Write your answer in the standard three part format, then review your answer.
>
> Objective exams require a different approach: 1. Start answering questions quickly and proceed as fast as you can to the end, 2. Skip over tough questions and leave them until the last, 3. Guess at answers you are not sure of, 4. Look over your paper before you leave it.
>
> Exam pacing often determines your grade. Learn how to properly time your exams by using the marks set for each question and the difficulty of the questions. The best way to study for an exam is to conduct an exam rehearsal, much as an actor rehearses a play. Your attitude toward the exam will determine your results, so be aware of this factor.

Payday

You have studied hard all week and now you are going to take the weekly quiz--payday; or, the end of the course is at hand, and the final examination is on the desk in front of you--payday. In both of these instances you and your teacher are going to find out how much you have learned--payday.

If you want to make a good grade on examinations you have to have learned the course material (so what else is new?). You also need to know how to take exams; you need examination skills (that's what's new!). You might expect by the time students reached high school and college they would know all about taking exams, but they don't. Believe me, they don't! Maybe you are the exception, eh? Let's find out. Do every one of the following statements apply to you?

1. You use techniques to tap your subconscious knowledge during exams.

2. You always use your examination time according to the marks a

question is worth, and your ability to answer it.

3. You rehearse for your examinations.

4. Every exam is an invigorating challenge, not a fearful ordeal.

If you can answer "Yes, all those statements apply to me," then skip this chapter, you have these skills already. If not, read on.

Examination Types

Although there are many kinds of examinations, most can be classed into two types, the essay examination and the objective examination. (In this chapter the word "examination" is used to include any form of test, quizzes, weekly tests, final examinations, and its short form "exam," will be used.)

The *essay exam* usually has few questions, and requires the student to do a lot of writing. The student writes answers as paragraphs or full essays. *The objective exam* has many more questions than the typical essay exam, and requires very short answers. True-false quizzes, multiple choice tests, fill-in-the-blank tests, and matching tests are all examples of objective exams. In the objective exam the student has to do more reading than writing.

The objective exam requires that the student recognize the correct answer when he sees it, or recall a fact. The essay exam goes further than this: the student must be able to recall facts, but he must also be able to evaluate the material, select those facts that are pertinent to the question asked, organize the material and then write his answer in good English. The essay exam is far more demanding upon the student than is the objective exam, although both measure a student's knowledge of facts equally well.

Students often mistakenly believe that they can study differently for these two kinds of exams. You can memorize facts for an objective exam if you are satisfied with a mediocre grade. Teachers can ask questions in an objective examination that require the student to evaluate, select, and organize just as much as on an essay exam. One of the toughest exams the author ever had to take was a multiple choice exam to obtain his license to practice psychology in North Carolina. The questions described experimental, counselling, or clinical events, asked a question, then provided four answers *any one of which could be right!* The examinee had to make careful judgments to select the *best* answer to obtain full marks.

Teachers use questions like the one just described to find out who has been thinking about what they have learned. Memorizing facts is straightforward and can get the student middling grades. If he studies for every quiz *as if it was going to be an essay exam,* he will get higher grades as a by-product of a deeper and broader understanding of the material learned.

During student interviews in the Learn-to-Learn Course I have questioned students about studying for exams. A strong distinguishing characteristic of the student who makes better grades is that he studies for every quiz as if it was going to be an essay exam.

Essay Exams

Since essay exams require the student to write long answers, they usually have few questions. Such an exam may have from one to 10 questions to be answered in a class period, compared to twenty-five to one hundred questions for an objective exam. Because there are so few questions it is possible for the student to read all of the exam's questions before he answers any one of them, and he should do just that.

The first important technique a student can use in taking an essay exam is *read all the questions before answering any of them.* Doing this will help you remember more, and allow you to write better answers, especially on those questions that are difficult for you. By using this technique the student taps into a vast storehouse of knowledge that would not be available to him otherwise, his subconscious memory.

We all know far more about any particular topic than we can recall at any one time. Most of our memories are stored deep in our subconscious. They exert subtle influences upon our behavior without ever coming into consciousness. Sometimes, though, we become aware of the workings of our subconscious. Here are a couple of examples.

Bob Lane stood outside the classroom where he had just written an examination with a puzzled frown on his high forehead. When another student left the exam he stopped her.

"Betsy, what was the answer to question eight," he asked.

When she told him he screwed up his face as if in pain and exclaimed, "I knew that! Why couldn't I remember that during the exam?"

Has that ever happened to you? Bob's knowledge was there in his subconscious memory banks, but he was not able to tap into it.

Another example. A week ago, I was picking my son up at his high school when I met a teacher in the hallway. She recognized me and greeted me, and I felt that her face was familiar, but I could not remember where I had met her or her name. I mumbled something about it "being a long time," and hurried away, embarrassed that I could not remember her name. In the school office, I asked the secretary who the lady was that I had just been talking to, and was told that she was Mrs. Higgins, the assistant principal.

A flood of memories hit me! Her first name is Dawn, her husband's name is Ed and he is a lawyer, and she had worked for me six years earlier as a teacher in the Learn-to-Learn Course! I also remembered that she was a much bigger woman when I knew her, and she confirmed this when I spoke to her the second time; she had lost seventy-five pounds since I knew her.

Notice in both of these examples that the memories were held in storage, but were unavailable until cued. Bob recognized the correct answer when he heard it, and I recalled many facts about Mrs. Higgins as soon as I heard her name.

Such stories hardly make good scientific evidence. Is there any good research data to support the idea that we have a subconscious memory?

Tip-of-the-Tongue

Everyone at some time or other has had a fact, a person's name, or a date on the tip of his tongue. Psychologists Roger Brown and David McNeill investigated this interesting state in an ingenious experiment. They read definitions of rarely used words to groups of students. If a student knew what the word was, or was sure he did not know what the word was, he was not required to do anything. If a student felt that he did know the word but could not remember it (tip-of-the-tongue) he was asked to write down as much as he could about that word.

Here's an example of the definitions: "An instrument used in measuring the angular distance between objects, used chiefly by navigators in determining position by measurement of the angle between a heavenly body and the horizon." A student in the tip-of-the-tongue state on this definition might write as follows:

"The first letter is "s," the word has two syllables, and it sounds something like 'secant.' It looks like a telescope mounted on a triangle attached to a semi-circle. The word is not 'transit' because that instrument is used by surveyors, and I think the last letter is 't.'"

These researchers obtained over 100 tip-of-the-tongue reports like the one above, and found that people were astoundingly accurate in their recalls of related facts about the word, even though they could not say the word. Brown and McNeill call this type of memory generic memory. This memory tells us when we have a fact buried in our subconscious even though we cannot recall it at that moment. Oh yes, the word is "sextant."

Joseph Hart, a psychologist from California, demonstrated experimentally that people use their generic memory to predict whether they have information in their subconscious that they cannot retrieve (see the demonstration). People can recognize correct answers even when they cannot recall them. Hart proved that when people cannot recall an answer they can still predict with 90 percent accuracy whether they could recognize the correct answer in a later test.

We must know what we have in our memory storage to use it efficiently. This ability keeps us doggedly searching our minds for an answer we know is there, and tells us that a search is useless if the information is not there. Without this ability, this generic memory, we might spend our lives in useless search for facts that we never learned, or even worse, give up our searches for known facts.

Demonstration-Subconscious memory: Part I

Written below are five important dates in English history. At one time or another we have all studied these dates and the events associated with them. If you can, write down the events associated with these dates. If you cannot, check one of the last three squares beside each date.

Date	Historical Event	I know it for sure.	I might know it.	I never knew it.
55 B. C.		___	___	___
1066 A. D.		___	___	___
1215 A. D.		___	___	___
1588 A. D.		___	___	___
1939 A. D.		___	___	___

Now turn over to the next page and answer the multiple choice questions about these dates.

Subconscious Memory

As well as such scientific experiments as those just mentioned, there is a large body of evidence from clinical studies demonstrating subconscious memory. Psychoanalysis has given us numerous instances where patients recall events of their former lives that they had not thought of in decades, but had lain deep in their subconscious all of these years.

To demonstrate subconscious memory in class I ask students if anyone had returned to a city or town that they had not lived in for many years. A couple of students in each class put their hands up.

"When you returned to that city, did you find yourself remembering names, places, and events that you had not thought of at all in the intervening years," I ask.

They always agree, and usually volunteer an example or two. Such subconscious memory storage is in all of us, not just those people who take part in experiments, or who are psychiatric patients.

During an exam the information you have previously learned can be thought of as being held in two bins, one of which is readily available for immediate recall, the other is the huge bin containing subconscious memories. These latter memories need time and an accumulation of retrieval cues to become available.

When you read *all* the questions at the beginning of the exam, you enable your brain to start sorting its way through that subconscious bin. Here's the sequence of events in tapping that bin:

Step 1: You read each question in turn, and right away you begin to recall facts and ideas which you jot down as rough notes, briefly and without developing them. (These facts and ideas come from the easily-available bin.) Once you have finished jotting ideas for that question you read the next one, jot notes, and so on for all the questions. You have not answered any questions, or even made an outline for any one question. Your brain is now using those questions to pull further facts from the less available subconscious memory bin and make them available to you.

Step 2: Read each question carefully, and analyze its parts. Exactly what is it that the teacher wants you to write about? Count how many parts there would be to a complete answer. Look for those key words in the question that tell you exactly how the teacher wants you to answer it.

There are dozens of such key words; here's a short list — illustrate, evaluate, describe, draw, explain, criticize, outline, define, relate, solve, review, summarize, measure, organize, match, label, identify, prove, calculate, and compute. Be sure you write the answer that is asked for and not some other answer, or you'll lose marks.

Step 3: The third step in essay exam technique is to answer the questions from easy to hard. You probably do this anyways, most people do. By leaving the hard questions until last you benefit first, by generating ideas for the more difficult questions, and second, by giving yourself more time for your brain to dredge up deeply stored facts from your subconscious memory.

Demonstration – Subconscious Memory: Part II

Check the correct answer in the following multiple choice test.

1. In 55 B. C.
    a. the English channel formed between Britain and France.
    b. the Romans invaded Britain.
    c. the Emperor Hadrian built his famous wall.
    d. the feudal system was established in Britain.

2. In the year 1066 A. D.
    a. Britain beat France in the battle of Agincourt.
    b. British yeomen first obtained the vote.
    c. the Normans conquered Britain in the Battle of Hastings.
    d. the British navy beat Napoleon's fleet.

3. The year 1215 A. D. is famous for
    a. British entry into the Crusades in Palestine.
    b. the hanging of Robin Hood.
    c. the signing of the Magna Charta.
    d. the invention of the steam engine by James Watt.

4. The year 1588 A. D. was crucial in British history because
    a. the Spanish Armada was driven from British shores.
    b. Henry the VIII beheaded his queen, Anne Bolyn.
    c. Britian broke with the church of Rome.
    d. Britain lost her empire in India.

5. The year 1939 A. D. was a crisis year for the British because
    a. they declared war on Nazi Germany.
    b. they entered the Great Depression.
    c. their armies were beaten in the Boer War.
    d. the invention of the airplane lost them the protection of the English Channel.

Answers. 1. b, 2. c, 3. c, 4. a, 5. a.

Some examples:

a. The word "discuss" is an open invitation to write about the question as you see fit. b. If the question asks you to "diagram" something, but you write a description instead, you will not get full marks. c. Is there any difference between a question that asks you to "compare" and one that asks you to "contrast?" You bet there is, because the "contrast" asks you to show differences, while the "compare" asks you to show both differences and similarities.

Demonstration: Question analysis

How many parts will there be to a full answer to the following questions? You don't need to know any sensory psychology to answer this, only the ability to read carefully and analyze an English sentence.

"Discuss the two major theories of human color vision, and give anatomical, physiological, and psychological evidence to support each theory."

Answer:

There are eight parts in all: parts one and two are the discussions of the two theories, while the other six parts are the three separate pieces of evidence for *each* theory. If your answer had less than eight parts it would be incomplete, and would not receive full marks.

Step 4: Scribble a rough outline of your answer before you write it. This will help you to put first things first, and write your answer in the fewest words. Every essay, no matter how short or how long, has three parts — an introduction, the body, and a conclusion. A test grader is more willing to give higher marks if the essay is well organized, than if it is a dangling string of facts. Think, outline, then write.

Step 5: Write your answer. Be precise and concise. Don't pad your answer, because teachers can spot this easily and it will sour them on your work.

Step 6: After you have answered all the questions, look over your answers to see if you have made any silly mistakes, or left out something obvious. Who needs to lose marks because he overlooked something in the rush of finishing? Not me. Not you.

Objective Examinations

Your approach to an objective examination has to be very different from the one you take in an essay exam. Objective exams have a lot of questions. If you read all of the questions in an objective exam before answering the first one, you won't have time to finish the exam.

Step 1: Glance quickly over the exam to see how the marks are allotted, how many questions there are, how the questions are distributed. For example, a mid-semester biology quiz in high school had 50 multiple choice questions worth 50 marks, two label-the-diagram questions worth 25 marks, and a set of matching questions worth another 25 marks, giving a total of 100 answers to be given worth 100 marks. The teacher has set a long exam, long so that only the best prepared students *who work quickly and efficently* through the test will finish all of the answers.

Figure 7-1 A watch on the desk ensures accurate exam timekeeping.

This kind of objective exam is called a speeded test, and is used by teachers to test a student's knowledge of facts. Not all objective exams are speeded, of course, but the pattern of questions above is typical, namely, a lot of questions to be answered briefly.

Step 2: Evaluate your time and the way the marks are given; (see following section on pacing) allot your time accordingly. Time allotment in an objective exam is usually easier than in the essay exam, because there are so many questions. Each question is only worth a few of the total marks, so that no really difficult decisions must be made about time rationing. In the example on the previous page, the student would have to watch out that he did not spend too much time on any one block of questions. Multiple choice questions are the quickest to answer, so getting through them first would be a good idea. The example requires 100 answers for 100 marks, so the marks are evenly distributed. The student answering this test should move as quickly as he can at an even pace through all of the questions.

Step 3: This step is the key to achieving the highest grades in objective tests. When you read a question that you cannot immediately give the correct answer, *mark a cipher (?) in the margin beside it and move on to the next question.* Leave all of your uncertain questions until the end, and then go back to try to answer them as best as you can.

Doubtful questions are time traps. While you ponder your answer to them, the second hand on the clock spins around draining off the valuable minutes you need to answer other questions.

"I did not finish the test," one student told me. "I took too much time on a couple of questions that I found tough, so I did not get to the end of the paper."

Don't lose easy marks by fumbling around with tough questions. By skipping over such questions you gain the use of your subconscious memory once again. You have read the question, so your brain can now operate on it as you answer other questions. When you come back to that skipped question at the end of the exam, your brain may have dredged up an answer out of your subconscious memory bin. Also, questions further along in the test may suggest the answer to that skipped question.

Step 4: *Guess.* On multiple choice exams, when in doubt, guess. Don't be tricked into leaving blank answers by instructions that threaten, "A correction for guessing will be made." Always guess.

Once again, your subconscious memory can come to your aid. As we have already shown, you have much more information stored in that memory than you can readily tap. Even though your memory may not allow you to recognize the correct answer for sure, it can help you get rid of some of the obviously wrong answers, and increase your chances of guessing correctly. The odds will be in your favor.

The formula used to correct for guessing is:

$$\text{Score} = \text{Right} - \frac{\text{Wrong}}{(N-1)}$$

where N is the number of choices in each question. For example, in a true-false exam, the score would be calculated by subtracting the number wrong from the number right (N is 2 in this case), or in a five-choice exam, the score would be the number of answers right minus the number of answers wrong divided by four.

This formula is based on the simple idea that in any test where a student can get some right answers by guessing he will. Since the mathematics of chance results is well known, the above formula subtracts enought points from the exam to give a score in which "pure" guessing will not be a factor. Theoretically, such a correction does work over large groups of students. Practically, **the formula is unfair to every individual student.**

The student who does not guess can lose marks for "guessing" by having this formula applied to his test results, thereby subtracting some of the marks he legitimately earned. A student who did not study and who guessed his way through the entire exam could beat the formula and get more marks than his knowledge warranted by sheer luck alone (the formula subtracts the "theoretical, long-run" guessing, not the actual guessing). That student's results would be higher than they should giving him an unfair advantage.

The student who does not guess is being unfair to himself. He is not taking advantage of those small bits of knowledge tucked away in his subconscious memory. He worked hard to learn those bits, and should get his reward for that work. Guessing allows him to reap his reward. Table 7-A shows how the scores on an exam could turn out with and without guessing, and with educated guessing.

The examples in Table 7-A are based on the simple multiple choice exam where only one answer is correct, but the rule applies in every case. Make use of your hunches, your intuition, and your feel for the correct answer, and guess. You will be fair to yourself, honest to the testing system (which really is trying to find out what you know), and boost your grades. Every student that I have ever met would rather take home B's than C's, or Passes rather than Fails. Help yourself get those rewards, guess.

	No Guess	Pure Guess*	Educated Guess**
Known answers	80	80	80
Unsure or Unknown Answers	20	20	20
No. tried/No. right by chance	0/0	20/4	20/10
Final Score Corrected for Guessing	$80 - \frac{0}{(5-1)} = 80$	$84 - \frac{16}{(5-1)} = 80$	$90 - \frac{10}{(5-1)} = 87.5$

*Student's guessing produces chance results (1/5x20=4).
**Student uses subconscious memory to eliminate 3 out of 5 choices in each question then guesses answer from the two choices remaining (1/2x20=10).

Table 7-A Exam Scores for Guessing and Not Guessing in a Five Choice Test

Step 5: Review. Look the paper over before you hand it in. Did you go back and answer all of those skipped questions? Did you fill in all the blanks with answers, and match all the matching questions?

The objective exam is prone to a fault that the essay exam is not. Since the objective exam has so many questions it is usually printed on several pages. Be sure your copy of the exam has all its pages; secretaries do have lapses of attention and forget to put pages into a test before it is stapled. Is the full sequence of questions there, in the above example numbers one to one-hundred without any breaks? If the questions run to the bottom of the last page, ask the teacher, "Is question 100 really the last question?" It's your responsibility to see that you have a complete exam.

PACING YOURSELF

Examinations are timed not to make a race out of them, as many students think, but because they must be fitted into a busy semester's schedule. A teacher has only so many class hours to give to exams so they must be completed within a set time. One class period is the most frequently used length of time for an exam, others like weekly quizzes are shorter, and final exams can be longer, sometimes as much as three or four hours. The student has to complete the exam in the time set, and how well he makes use of that time can determine his grade on the exam, and in the long run for the entire course.

Every teacher has heard remarks like these that were said to me just this last semester:

"I didn't have time to finish the last question," said a girl in an introductory psychology course.

"I misjudged my time and had to rush through the last questions," said another girl in a physiological psychology exam.

In giving advice to a young tradesman, Benjamin Franklin reminded him that "time is money." To the student time may not be money, but properly used it can be translated into good grades and the satisfaction of proving that you know your lessons.

The Rules

The rules for using time during an exam are few and logical. They are:

Rule 1

Be on time. Even better, arrive a few minutes early to take care of those last minute details, sharpening pencils, chasing down materials you need, like rulers, calculators, tables, and even taking that last, nervous bathroom stop. Nothing is so distracting in the last minutes of a quiz as an overfilled bladder.

Rule 2

After you have read over your exam (see procedures for essay and objective exams), *divide your time* up amongst the questions and get to work. In a multiple choice exam with a lot of questions, that means get started and work at your top speed until you are finished or until the clock runs out. In an essay exam you will need to evaluate your time distribution more carefully. Two sub-rules govern this: *Sub-rule A* – allot time to questions according to their value in marks, and, *Sub-rule B* – allot time according to your ability to answer the question.

Example: An essay exam has five short questions, and you have fifty minutes to answer them all. The student who is unaware of the above sub-rules would divide his time equally amongst all of the questions, but notice how the marks are allotted.

Question	Marks	Time Allotment z (minutes)		
		(poor)	(better)	(best)
1.	40	10	20	18
2.	20	10	10	12
3.	20	10	10	9
4.	10	10	5	5
5.	10	10	5	5
	100			2 (review)

The first time allotment is poor because the student has not divided his time rationally. He is giving question 1. the same amount of time as questions 4. and 5., which are worth only one-quarter as many marks. The second time allotment is far better since the student is now giving full consideration to the value of each question in scheduling his time. If the student felt that question 2. was going to give him difficulty, and that questions 1., 3., and 5. were going to be easy to answer, he could take time from these latter questions and allot it to question 2. The last column above shows this time division, and also shows that the student is allowing himself a couple of minutes at the end of the exam to look over his paper. Students feel foolish when they loose marks from silly mistakes, like simple arithmetic, or spelling, or forgetting a word. A final review can catch such mistakes.

Figure 7-2 "Alphonse, are you sure we are rehearsing for the right exam?"

Rule 3

Once you have established your time schedule, *keep track of the time.* This may sound like an unnecessary rule, but it is not. Once you become involved in writing your answers you can easily lose track of the time. Clocks and watches are usually hidden from sight; your wristwatch is tucked up your sleeve, and the wall clock is usually out of your field of vision, quite often behind you. There's a simple trick that will help you keep track of the time. Take your wristwatch off of your wrist and lay it on your exam paper. Now the time is immediately before you every moment. You have to keep moving your watch to write your answers around it, so it is hard to ignore.

These three common sense rules will help provide the time stimulus control you need in an exam. Losing marks when you know your stuff merely because you have lost track of the time is a tragedy.

The "Best" Preparation

"What's the best way to prepare for an exam?"

There is a double answer to this question. For long range preparation the answer is to apply as many of your learning skills as you can; for immediate preparation for each examination the answer is *rehearse.* Actors know the value of rehearsal in learning their parts in plays, so let's examine an actor's experience.

It's opening night. On stage the famous stage and screen actor Tony Perkins is playing the part of the psychiatrist in the play *Equus.* The audience is captivated. Perkins' flawless performace grips their attention and for a couple of hours he allows them to leave their own problems and escape into the problems of the character he is portraying. At the end of the performance the audience leaps to its feet cheering and applauding.

Perkins has a problem like any student has. He has to *learn,* his lines, the character he is to portray, stage movements, and put all this together into a smooth polished performance. The student must learn the material in the course he is studying, and then put it all together into his smooth polished performance, the examination.

Does Perkins merely commit his part to memory, then go on stage to give his performance? Of course not. After he has done his memorizing he begins his rehearsals. He will spend dozens, even hundreds of hours with the director and other actors rehearsing his part. Every scene will be tried again and again, until it is perfect. Then, and only then, will he step before his audience and perform.

Learn from Tony Perkins. If you want to have your audience cheering and applauding your examination performances, rehearse. Your audience is the exam grader, usually your teacher. The applause comes in the form of good grades. You want that applause, right? So, let's consider what form rehearsal for exams should take.

Exam Rehearsal

The sequence of rehearsals for a play follow a standard pattern. First rehearsals will be line readings, with the actors sitting on a bare stage, reading their scripts aloud. Next the actors will walk through their parts so they will know what their stage movements will be like. Props, furniture, swords, whatever, will be added in later rehearsals, and finally the dress rehearsal will simulate actual performance conditions with costumes, scenery, and sometimes even an audience.

As you study for an examination, rehearse your part. A student's part requires him to write answers to questions, so if the student is to practice his part he has to answer questions. The student can draw on several sources for questions. Old exam papers are a good source, textbooks often have exercise sections that provide questions on the material in the text, or you can make up your own questions, and this is the most frequently used source.

Old exams are one of the best sources. Ask the teacher if he has any that you can use. Sometimes teachers are jealous of their old examinations and won't give them out. Don't give up, find a student who has taken the course, and ask him for questions. He may have an old exam paper, or if he does not, he may remember some of the questions from a previous exam.

Each teacher has his own individual style in giving exams. Some ask factual questions, others ask problem-solving questions. You have to *know your teacher's style* if you are to rehearse for his examinations properly. If each actor on the stage acted his part in his own way, the result would be chaos. The play's director co-ordinates the individual performances to obtain the smoothly integrated production that the audience sees. The director's style determines the overall performance. A classroom teacher co-ordinates the material being taught with the ability of the students. If the student is to perform well in examinations he must know the teacher's style, just as the actor must know his director's style.

Learning a teacher's examination style is easy. All you need to do is become familiar with the kinds of questions that the teacher asks, that's all. Have you ever noticed that the second or third quiz from a teacher seems easier than the first one? This is because you have become aware of the teacher's examination style, and have adjusted your studying, and your rehearsals to that style.

"Otto has a great exam attitude."

Asking yourself questions about the material you are going to be examined on is your rehearsal. You can do this by yourself, or you can work together with friends. However you do it, just before the exam have a dress rehearsal. Simulate the examination conditions as closely as you can, then *give yourself an examination.*

For example, if your examination is going to be an essay exam, practice essays. Set yourself as many questions as you believe will be on the examination, then without consulting your books write *outlines* for each question. Try to set questions that you believe your teacher will ask. Students can usually make shrewd guesses about exam questions once they are familiar with a teacher's style. Write one answer out in full. This is your dress rehearsal for your essay exam. If you expect a short answer or multiple choice examination with a lot of questions and little time to answer them, practice giving your answers quickly and briefly.

If you have rehearsed well, the next day when you walk into your exam you will have all the confidence of a professional actor opening a play. You will know your "part." Because you have rehearsed it thoroughly you will play it with vigor and delight.

Attitude to Exams

I cannot really advise you on proper exam attitude. That would be like giving you advice on the shape of your nose; there's nothing I can do about it and very little you can do about it. Your attitudes are the result of your entire life up to now, and are very slow to change. I will point out two facts.

Fact one: Fear and anxiety are great inhibitors of behavior. The student who enters an exam thinking, "I'm going to get clobbered. I know I am not going to do well today," probably won't do well. In the psychological laboratory the inhibition caused by fear has been thoroughly investigated.

When people are overly anxious or frightened their behavior becomes simpler, more primitive, more stereotyped. A frightened child at the top of a ladder can only think to hang on tightly, even though the same ladder steps he climbed are there for him to climb down. Sarah Holmes, a student in a perception course of mine, wrote a very sketchy essay exam for me. When we discussed it later she said, "I knew that my final grade in the course was going to be determined by that exam and I was very nervous. I knew my work, but I found it difficult to write answers. Time seemed to be flying, and I only had time to write brief outlines for answers."

Sarah had written much better papers for me before so I knew that she was capable of better work. She had "frozen" on this exam because of her nervousness.

Fact two: Excitement and enthusiasm will carry you over the rough spots. Every athletic coach knows this. In every sport athletes have bad days when nothing goes right. They seem to be all thumbs and left feet. The coach knows that if enthusiasm can be kept high the athlete will get by the slumps and perform well again.

Terry Martin had written a good final exam except for one question. I asked what happened when we next met.

"I just did not know the second part of that answer. I felt I had a pretty good exam going, so I thought, phooey, I'll just skip that part and write what I know!"

His good feeling carried him over a rough spot.

Your feelings, your basic attitude do count in taking exams. You cannot work on your feelings directly. They are always a byproduct of your life. Solid preparation for the exam is the best way to develop a positive attitude.

Exercises

1. Memorize the 6 essay exam steps.

2. Memorize the 4 objective exam steps.

3. Memorize the 3 rules for proper exam pacing.

4. Use the essay exam steps for your next essay exam.

5. Use the objective exam steps for your next objective exam.

6. Properly *rehearse* for your next exam.

6,316 Words

CHAPTER 8 - STUDENT-TEACHER RELATIONS

... The reasonable thing is to learn from those who can teach.

Sophocles, Antigone

> **Summary**
>
> The best student-teacher relations are made when the student actively seeks help from the teacher about the course being taught. The relationship is based upon mutual respect based on work performance by both parties, a professional relationship. An implied contract exists between students and teachers that allows them to use each other to further the learning of the student. Active seeking means that you focus on the courses subject matter, question agressively, seek extra work when you need it, and be sure to reinforce teacher for her help. The help that teachers have given you has changed over your school years from total care in the elementary grades to specialist expertise in high school and beyond. When classes are large be sure that you don't become lost and remain unknown to your teacher. Teachers cannot help students they don't know. You can get help even from bad teachers, but you must take the initiative.

The Best of Help

Are you obtaining the most help you can from your teachers?

This is a key question, and the answer you have for it may determine the quality of your education. You have to decide if you are a passive receiver of teaching, or an active seeker. Jack Pollard and Valerie Cheshire will illustrate the difference between these two types of students.

Jack was a good student. He only missed one class the semester he took the Perception and Sensation Course from me; he was sick that day. Whenever I asked him questions in class he was ready with reasonable answers, indicating that he was keeping up on his reading. His quizzes and final exam earned him a solid B for the course, and his term paper had to be rated better than average.

Valerie was also a B level student, but if I had not known what she was doing I would have called her a pest. After every quiz she discussed her wrong answers with me in exhaustive detail, and would argue her points strongly if she thought she was right. It was a rare class that she did not have a question or two. If I was in a hurry after class I might suggest she read a certain journal article instead of taking the time to answer her questions on a point. After she had read the article, which she always did, she wanted to talk to me about it. By the end of the course I felt that I was teaching Valerie, oh yes, and 20 other students.

I did not ignore Jack, but I could not ignore Valerie. I admired her. She was actively pursuing the teaching she felt she had coming to her, and doing it in exactly the right way. By the end of that course she had a far deeper and broader grasp of Perception and Sensation than most of the other students in the class. This did not show on the grades, because I tested the students on the common knowledge they were supposed to have learned from the lectures and the textbook. Her questioning and seeking took her into areas the other students did not know existed. She made top quality use of this teacher.

Professionalism

The key to receiving top quality teaching from any teacher is to establish a working *professional relationship*. For these years of your life you are a professional student. Our society says that you will be earning your way by obtaining more education. All societies are not this way, nor has ours always been this way. When most of Americans were farmers the children started to work the family farm as soon as their strength allowed them. Many did not learn to read and write, and those who did, minimally so. This same situation exists in a large part of the world today. Our technologically advanced society needs educated citizens, so it puts you to work in your early years obtaining that education. It is your first profession.

If you do your student thing, and teacher does her teacher thing, the professional relationship will work fine. When a doctor gives medical advice to a lawyer for a case the lawyer is trying, they are establishing a professional relationship. Each is bringing his particular expertise to the trial for a common purpose. When you actively seek teaching, and the teacher gives it, a similar relationship is being established.

Professional working arrangements are being stressed here to show you that good teacher-student relations are keyed upon each person's working profession, not on like or dislike.

Students write on their Study Problems List that they can't get along with their teachers. When I query this during their interview I find out that they don't like such-and-such a teacher, or that another teacher did not like them, so they believe. The whole world would grind to a halt if people had to like each other before they could do business with each other.

"Sam's a real bastard, but he's the best lawyer for the job. Hire him."

If I only taught students that I liked, I would be fired pretty quick.

You can still receive first rate teaching from a teacher you don't like, or you believe does not like you, if you actively seek it.

The Contract

Before the steps of active seeking are discussed an underlying assumption of teacher-student relations must be pointed out. You could call it the hidden contract. When you take a course from a teacher you implicitly enter this contract. You agree to allow the teacher to manipulate you in whatever way the teacher feels is necessary for you to learn the course material. These manipulations take the form of giving you lectures, movies, tests, papers to write, and assignments to complete. There is nothing sinister about it.

The other side of this contract is that the teacher agrees to submit to your manipulations to learn the course material. These take the form of you asking questions, and seeking advice, and submitting papers and tests for grading. Again very above board. Students do not use this latter side of the contract enough. They feel if they submit to teachers manipulations that they are being fully taught. WRONG! That's being half taught. Only when the student begins to fully use the teacher is the contract being fulfilled.

Active Seeking

The steps of establishing and maintaining a superb student-teacher relationship are these:

1. Focus on the subject matter being taught. Direct all your question and attention towards the course work. Do not try to establish a relationship on the basis of friendship or outside interests. If that develops, it's icing on the cake.

2. Be an aggressive questioner. Be like Valerie and extend your education into new and deeper areas of the course with your questions.

3. Ask for extra work. I know that sounds like self punishment, but you will see how it works.

4. Reinforce the teacher for good teaching.

Let's expand each of these steps.

The Subject Matter

Students always have a common meeting ground with the teacher, the subject matter being taught. You may be interested in the latest Rock music, playing soccer, your date for that night, and your family, and the teacher may be interested in mountain folk music, long distance running, the book he is writing and his family. From that you might believe you have little in common to talk about, but that's not true. You always have the subject matter being taught. This is the lever you can use to extract fine teaching from any teacher. Use the subject matter to pry good teaching out of him.

"What shall we talk about, Prof?"

Consider the investment the teacher has in that subject matter. In psychology, I spent eight years studying to become a psychologist. I spent hours and hours preparing lectures and discussions for class. I have an enormous vested interest in my subject matter. You can exploit this, and I mean exploit. Whenever you come to me as a student seeking information or explanation on my subject matter I am doomed to give in to you. All my training, my concept of myself as a professional psychologist and teacher, force me to give you what you want, namely teaching in the subject matter.

Aggressive Questioning

In its rawest form teaching and learning are questions and answers. Both parties play. Sometimes teacher asks questions to make students work or think (exams, for example), and sometimes the student asks questions. Both give answers. The more the student questions the more he will learn.

There is no such thing as the dumb questions. Sometimes questions sound dumb and stupid to outsiders, but they never are to the person asking them.

"Duh, what's a two," Igor asks when teacher states "two plus two equals four."

Howls of laughter from the other students. Igor's ears turn red in embarrassment, and that's the last question he ever asks in that class. But how could he know what two plus two equals if he did not know what a two was. Admire Igor for his courage, pity him for his lack of preparation for a basic arithmetic course, but don't accuse him of asking a dumb question. He needed the answer.

Very often after the laughter has subsided and the class has broken up another student will sidle up to the dumb questioner and say, "Hey I'm glad you asked that. I did not know either."

What happens if you don't ask questions, dumb or otherwise? You start to get lost. The teacher assumes if there are no questions that the class is following what is being taught. If you are not, and you don't ask questions, you deserve to be lost. This is disastrous in courses where the knowledge is cumulative, like mathematics. Students flunk algebra because they did not properly learn arithmetic. They let the questions slide.

"Huh?"

That's a good question. How many times have you been listening to a lecture or reading a book, and that question leaps to mind. "Huh?" You should have some sort of an alarm circuit built into you so that whenever "Huh?" happens all of your activity ceases until you get an answer to that question. "Huh?" tells you that you don't understand something. Find out.

Ask questions during class if it is reasonable to do so. If the class is relaxed and informal it is usually reasonable. You can find out about the teacher's policies on class questions early on in the course. It is not reasonable if the teacher is trying to finish an explanation before the class finishes, or if the class has 1200 people in it. Then you ask questions after class. The notetaking chapter tipped you off to writing questions in your notes as they occur to you, so that you won't lose these valuable learning aids.

When you ask questions you immediately establish yourself in the mind of your teacher as a person who is interested, and actively seeking more knowledge. Teachers love to teach that kind of student. Just by asking the question you have started to establish a good relationship, focused on the subject matter.

Extra Work

Seeking extra work sounds like ingratiating behavior (sucking up to teacher!). But if it is done well and in a proper fashion it makes you look like a champ. Here's the wrong way to approach it:

"Teach, I think this is a great course, and you are a terrific teacher, and I would like some extra work!"

Yech! That would be my reaction to that. Pure toady. Look at this approach, instead:

"I'm kind of stuck on this point. I'm afraid I did not follow you yesterday, and the textbook wasn't helpful. Where else can I go?"

Now this I, as a teacher, can relate to. You have a *specific problem,* and you are showing me that you have already tried to solve it for yourself (you read the textbook). Now you are appealing to me for an alternative route. You are not asking me to go through the whole explanation that I did yesterday all over again. You are not asking me to do more work, you are offering to *do the work yourself* (. . . can I go?").

The three key points in this approach are: 1. specific problem, 2. previous work, and 3. willingness to do more work to solve your problem. You knock down all teachers defenses with that kind of triple threat approach.

Reinforce the Teacher

Teachers need reinforcement to continue teaching. No reinforcement produces extinction. Teacher stops teaching and becomes a lecturer, or some other kind of low animal. Reinforced teaching produces more and better teaching. Only students can reinforce teaching. Be sure you do.

Success is the best reinforcement for both students and teachers. If teacher is succeeding in answering your questions, explaining difficult points to you, or helping you with extra readings or assignments, let her know that they are helping. A simple "thanks" goes a long way. Even better, *show the teacher how her help has worked.*

Let her overhear you tell another student, "that last example really made the point for me. I was in a fog until then."

Or you could mutter after receiving the answer to a question, "Oh yeah, now I see how that works. I can also see how it would work in that other situation." Showing the teacher that her help is making you think will delight her.

The more you reinforce the teacher this way the more she will be willing to help you. She may even volunteer help when you have not asked. Then you know you've got it made. Just keep the reinforcements flowing. (See Chapter 17 for a full explanation of reinforcement.)

You have to be honest about such reinforcements. Don't give them if they are not earned, but don't miss the opportunity to give them if they are earned. Sometimes students play games with the reinforcement technique.

George, the teacher, ignored Sue, the student, in class. He was not being mean, he just preferred to talk to other people in the class. Sue decided she was going to use reinforcement to *make* George talk to her. Over a few weeks, every time George's eyes fell on Sue as he was lecturing, she nodded her head in understanding, and flashed a gorgeous smile. It worked. Soon these reinforcements of hers had George lecturing right to her most of the time. Is this OK?

Maybe yes, maybe no. If George knew the game being played, and realized Sue was seeking attention, and gave it to her, that's OK. But if he did not, and Sue knew he did not, that's sneaky manipulation and it's not OK.

An experiment was conducted in a California school system to train students to get help from teachers by reinforcing them. The students were shown how to reinforce good teaching behavior in an acceptable way, by "thank you's" and "I sure appreciate the help." One of the students trained was Jess, 14 years old, 185 pounds, and vicious. He had taken after an assistant principal with the leg he had torn off a chair. Jess was not getting any teaching, because the teachers were scared stiff of him. Also, he had the personality of a bear with a toothache. Jess was trained to smile (in front of a mirror, would you believe?) and to say his "thank you's" in a proper fashion at the right times. An observer in the classroom kept track of the number of times the teacher gave aid to Jess, and as the weeks and reinforcements piled up, so did the teaching help.

To prove to Jess that it was the reinforcements that were getting him the help he needed and wanted, he was instructed to stop them for a week. The observer charted the results, which showed a dramatic drop in the assistance given to Jess.

Reinforcement used to gain the teaching help you need is a useful, successful, and ethical technique. Use them.

Specialist Teachers

You learned that teachers are there to help even before you went to school. Mom and Dad were your teachers in our pre-school years, and you went to them for all kinds of help. When you started into elementary grades you naturally transferred your help-seeking to your teacher. You spent the whole class day in her room and you got to know her well, and she knew you well. You went to her for all kinds of help. She helped you learn to read and write and add and subtract. She also acted as judge in your squabbles. When Mom was not there you treated her just like Mom.

In our later school years the system changed. The teachers were specialists, and you became a nomad. You moved from room to room during the day to seek the classes of the specialist, the English, Math, or Physical Education specialist. The relationship changed. Now you had to know half a dozen or more teachers, and to make that job more difficult you saw each one for only an hour a day. On the other side the teacher now had to teach about 100 students, whom she only saw for one period a day.

The basic relationship remained the same. The teacher was there to help and the student seeks help. The relationship is not as close as it was in earlier years and requires more active seeking on the student's part. In high school the teacher's attention is divided amongst many more students. Not all of them need help to the same degree or at the same time. The student must take the initiative more and more.

This separation of teacher and student can be carried to extremes. In college the teacher may not even get to know your name.

The Anonymous Student

If you go to a large state university you will sit in a lot of large lecture classes. For a teacher who really wants to teach, any class over 25 students is large. Class sizes of 100, 300 or even 500 are not unusual in large universities. The teacher cannot possibly know that many students well, so he lectures to a crowd of nameless faces. Even so a few students always stand out of that crowd.

The student who always has sharp questions stands out. The student who tops the classes in tests and exams stands out. The trouble maker stands out. The beautiful student stands out, as does the student who is blind, or crippled. These students bring themselves to the teacher's attention by being exceptional in some characteristic. Teachers want to teach individuals, not herds, so they are glad when they can identify an individual student in some way. It's worthwhile to be identified.

The advantages of not being an anonymous student, one of the herd, are many. The teacher is more likely to give you attention and time if he knows you. You will work harder for a teacher who knows you than for a distant indifferent lecturer. When your papers and exams are being graded there is an advantage sometimes if the teacher can place your face with the name on the paper. If he knows you even a little he may understand better what you are trying to say on that paper. The quality of your education improves when you study with teachers, instead of taking courses from lecturers.

Don't be the anonymous student. Apply the subject matter rule. Seek advice on the course material, ask questions, discuss ideas with the teacher.

Don't be intimidated by the large class. You may have to do your questioning at the end of class, or in the teacher's office by appointment. Respect his time if he has a large class, and don't feel he can devote hours to you. A few minutes now and then, especially early in the course, can mark you as a worthy student in his mind.

Rotten Teachers

We all get a bad teacher sooner or later. They come in all shapes and sizes. A few that I have experienced:

1. The intimidator. He ran his classes through fear and was big enough and mean enough to enforce his rule.

2. Super dull. He read his lectures from notes. He could go an entire class without once looking up at the students.

3. Ms. Like me, like me! She was so concerned that her students think well of her and like her that she was a wishy-washy teacher.

Avoid the bad teacher if you can. Very often you are stuck with him. Even bad teachers can be useful. Your strategy must be to look the teacher over carefully and decide how he can be useful to you. He does have some expert knowledge and it is up to you to dig it out. Don't give up. You may not get as much good advice as you would from a better teacher, but you will get more if you keep trying than if you quit on him completely.

Exercises

1. Select a part on one course that really interests you. Ask the teacher for extra reading on that part.

2. Use the three step approach for seeking extra work at least once this week.

3. Once again, choose one class and make a point to ask at least two good questions during that class.

4. Choose one teacher, possibly one who does not pay much attention to you, and start to reinforce that teacher for attending to you. "Thank you," smile, nod, "I understand," can all be used to reinforce. Keep this up for at least a month and watch the teachers behavior towards you change for the better.

5. Do all of your teachers know your name? If so, fine. If not, do something about that. NOW!

3,449 Words

SECTION IV

THE STUDY HABIT

Students with good study habits take school work in their stride. They get their study assignments done punctually and always seem to have lots of time for fun. The rules for developing a study habit are laid out in the next six chapters. Habits are behaviors you don't have to think about or concentrate upon. Today you walk and talk easily. When you were a baby you had to concentrate very hard to learn both of these habits. When your studies become habitual, they become easy. Would you like to know the value of a good study place, and how to use time? Would you like to concentrate on your studies better, and learn how to cope with boredom? Would you prefer to work with good motivation rather than none at all? Read on!

CHAPTER 9 – A PLACE AND A TIME

> **Summary**
>
> You must have a special place to study, and work there consistently. The place should be free of distractions and have the right social setting. Your work will very soon become "conditioned" to this place, so that the walls will "urge" you to work. Similarily you must schedule your study times regularly. Regularity in your life is easy to follow; constant change is frustrating. Both regularity of place and time will shortly produce the study habit that generates good grades and learning excellence. The ideal way to start a habit is to do it and never make exceptions. Reality tempers this ideal with conflicts, distractions, and old habits which interfere with the new ones. You can start a new habit abruptly, or by slowly building it into your life. You can follow three clear rules when you find yourself backsliding from your new study habit; never quit completely, go through the motions, and trick yourself into working.

A STUDY PLACE

A Unique Work Place

You are to have a unique study place. It should be somewhere that you consider to be ideal as a study place. Different people will have different needs for the *perfect study place*. Consider these students of mine:

>Marguerite Jaspers is an only child and has a room of her own at home. She is easily distracted by other people, and needs solitude and quiet to study.
>
>Janice Floyd grew up with five brothers, a sister, her parents and a grandmother, all in one house. She loves to be with people, even when she is reading or preparing assignments. She works best when people are around her, and easily returns to work after being interrupted.
>
>Carl Poole reads with his stereo-earphones on.

As you can see the perfect study place will be something special for each individual. What are your special requirements?

One requirment that every student's study place must meet is *uniqueness*. That place must be used for study exclusively. It is not a place to read magazines. It is not a place to relax and file your nails. It is not a place to talk to your friends, in person or on the telephone. It is not a place to eat or drink. It is not a place to build model airplanes, work on your stamp collection or whatever your hobby is. IT IS YOUR STUDY PLACE!

This is the place where you will work at your lessons. In no sense will it be a place for recreation. If you want to take a break, relax, or have a snack go somewhere else. Does your present study place meet this uniqueness requirement? If it does not, change it. Don't try to salvage it by using it only for study from now on. Scrap it and find another. It is beyond salvage. Why so? Because you have conditioned yourself to bad habits in that place.

Place Conditioning

Conditioning is a psychologists technical term for automatic learning. In its strict scientific sense it means learning under a controlled laboratory procedure. The word has crept into our everyday language to mean any learning achieved through automatic repetition. The key word is *automatic.* Conditioning is not learning you think about, and conciously set out to obtain. Conditioning happens to you automatically when a stimulus and some behavior of yours are reinforced together. (See Chapter 17 for examples of reinforced learning)

When you become conditioned to a place, all that means is that some behavior of yours automatically occurs when you are in that place. You automatically drive when you are seated behind the wheel of your car. You rarely go through the motions of driving when you are seated in your bathroom. If you were asked to wait in a basketball gymnasium with a ball in the center of the floor you would probably shoot a basket or two to pass the time. If you were asked to wait at the corner of Main Street and Center Avenue during rush hour, you probably would not shoot any baskets even though a ball and basket were provided. You might wonder who the nut was who left a basketball on the manhole cover in the center of all that traffic.

Our behavior does become conditioned to places. We wear our bathing suits at the beach, not in the classroom, even though the classroom is hot enough to excuse wearing a bathing suit. You talk differently in the classroom than you do when you are out with your friends.

"Can I leave now, Mrs. Jones?"

"Hey Charlie, let's split, eh?"

Different behaviors go with different places, and you learn that difference. To build a study habit you make use of this fact. You want study and school work conditioned to your study place. You want your books in that study place to whisper to you, "read me, read me." Your pens in that place should murmur "write beautiful words." The desk top should command "concentration," and the very walls of your study place demand that you "WORK! WORK! WORK!"

The way to develop such conditioning is to work at the same place often, and do nothing but work there. As you succeed in completing your lessons day by day the place will become associated with your work. Working there will become easier and easier, because of this conditioning. You will have learned that work is the appropriate behavior in that place, just as shooting baskets is easy to do in a gym.

Some places are better suited to study than others.

The Horrible Example

Over 75% of the students I have talked with use their bedrooms as a study place. The college students use their dormitory rooms, the high school student their own rooms at home. If these students had deliberately set out to choose the worst possible study place, they could not have been more successful.

The Law of Stimulus Control states that people and *places* in the world around us exert control over our behavior. By using a bedroom as a study place students are ignoring this important principle of learning, and suffer for it. Students are confused when I condemn bedrooms as work places for they seem to have so many of the ideal physical characteristics that students cannot see the psychological flaw. Here is a dialogue from one of my classes as I let the students discover for themselves what is wrong with bedroom studying.

"So, you study in your own room, eh, Paul."

"Yes, sir."

"You complained to me the other day that teachers gave you boring assignments. I believe that you said they put you to sleep."

"Right."

"What do you spend the most time doing in that room, Paul?"

"What do I do most....? Oh, sleep, I guess."

"Would it be fair to say that you spent from six to eight hours a day sleeping in that room, and that represented at least 70 percent of the total activity you do in that room?"

Paul, slowly and with raised eyebrows, "Say, that's right."

I then reminded Paul and his classmates of the behavioral conditioning that a few exposures to a basketball gym can produce.

Then I say, "If you spend nearly a third of each day every day performing one kind of behavior in one particular place, the stimulus control developed must be awesome. "Paul, what are the walls of your bedroom practically shouting at you to do every time you step inside the door?"

"Go to sleep," Paul admits shaking his head.

That's why *bedrooms are rotten work places.* One student objected strongly to my condemnation of bedrooms as study places. She said she did all her work in her room and never felt sleepy. I knew that she was a real workhorse, and probably spent a great deal of time in her bedroom working, so I asked her how well she was sleeping lately? She said "not too well" claiming pressure from exams and term papers. I looked at the class and a few students were smiling and nodding their heads. They got it, even though she didn't. The stimulus control of her room was for work, not sleep.

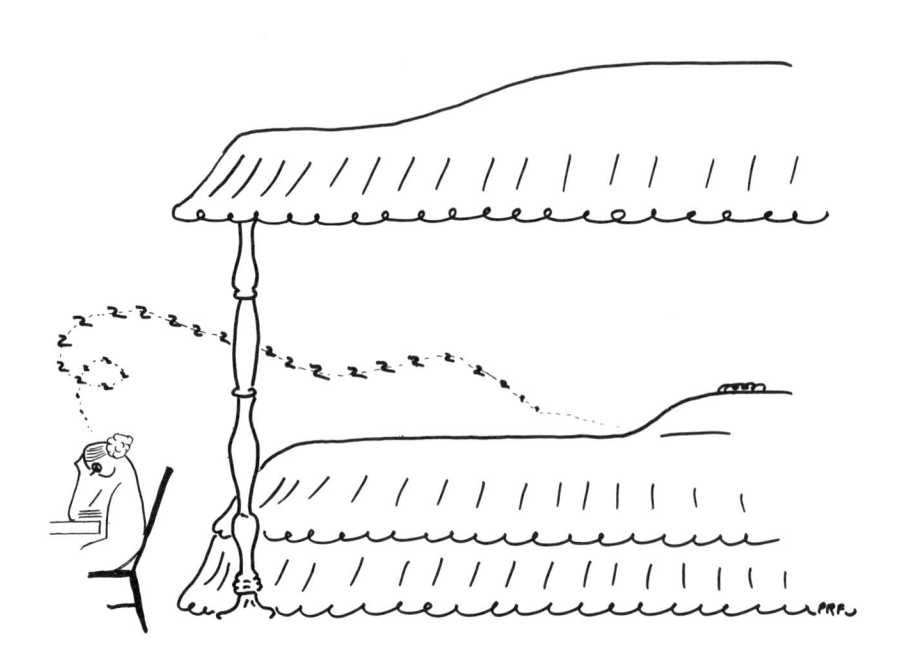

The Physical Side

Not much to say here that isn't obvious. The only reason for saying at all is that occasionally I find students working under poor physical conditions when they don't need to, so here goes.

Have a good light. If you have a desk lamp a 60 watt bulb is best, a 100 watt bulb is too bright. The bulb should not shine directly in your eyes. Bright light and fluorescent lights can be irritating over several hours study. A reminder that right handers should have the light coming from their left side, and left handers from the right so that their hand does not shade their writing.

Use a straight backed chair, not a padded arm chair or a swivel chair. Both of the latter types encourage poor posture which is tiring after an hour or so. A chair without arms is better than one with arms, and the chair legs should allow your thighs to rest on the seat with your feet flat on the floor (basketball centers and shorties take note). You're going to spend a lot of time in that chair over a semester, so make it work for you, not against you.

Your desk does not need to be expensive or gorgeous, but it does need to be large enough and the right height. Sitting with your belly up to the desk with your back comfortably braced by the chair's back, your hands, wrists and forearms should rest comfortably flat on the desk top. If your forearms don't touch your desk it is too low. A few old magazines under the legs will fix that. If you have to push your elbows away from your sides to get your arms flat on the desk it's too high. Saw the legs off, get a taller chair, whatever, but fix it, or you will begin to suffer from that dread student disease, the 11:00 p.m. kink in the neck.

When I say large enough I mean just that. To get a desk the right size I use a door placed across a couple of filing cabinets. On this I can place:

two telephone books	a small bookcase holding 19 books
an address book	my desk lamp
a card index file	an IBM selectric typewriter
a stack of file trays	a large desk-blotter-calendar
a telephone	two ink pads
a three-hole punch	a holder for 6 stamps
a postage scale	an assorted collection of 19 books and journals
plus staplers, tape	stamp holders, and working space

You may not need all that stuff, but I do. Running along side my desk I have another bookcase, and of course the four filing drawers supporting the desk-top are full of files and other goodies. The point is, *I don't have to go anywhere to get anything I need.* It's all there. Your work place should meet that criterion as well. One of the big advantages of having an imposing work place like mine is that people treat it with respect. They know that when I am sitting there, I AM WORKING. Conversation nearby drops, and the talkers move off when I sit at my desk. People don't casually move pieces of paper I leave on my desk, because they know it is MY WORK.

One of the tricks of having a successful work place is to generate that respect for it with your family and friends. When you are at YOUR WORK PLACE, you should be afforded all the courtesies of a monk praying in his cell. You should get reactions like:

"Martha, could you call back later. He's at his desk."

or " Excuse me son, could I borrow some paper?"

or "Yeah sure, sis. I'll turn the radio down. Right away!"

Wouldn't that be marvelous?

Common physical distractions to avoid if possible are window drafts, blasts of hot air from a furnace vent, TV noise, other noisy machinery like fans, fridges, or concrete mixers, and so on. Be comfortable but not so comfortable that you fall asleep. Studying in bed is a mistake. Physical distractions are usually easy to take care of, but not so people distractions.

The Social Side

To study with people around or not to study with people around, that is the question (with apologies to Bill Shakespeare).

You have to figure that one out for yourself.

You have to discover whether you are a Marguerite, or a Janice or a Carl, all mentioned at the beginning of this chapter. If you need people around you, fine. Some students can only study in the crowded study halls of the school library, "The Zoo." On the other hand one student I knew studied in the library stacks under the Treasury Reports for Virginia for 1896. Nobody bothered her, not even the spiders visited that section.

If you like people near you, but not so near that they distract you with their presence or sounds you will have to arrange that. At home you can drown out distracting people noises by quietly playing the radio or stereo (Carl's trick). Tune in to a station that plays *anything but* your favorite music. It's supposed to be a background masking noise, not your center of interest. If you decide you want some company for a moment, you can step out and talk, then back to your work place to work — the best of both worlds, privacy and company.

A STUDY TIME

When Harry Truman was a young man he was a farmer. Like most farmers he arose at 4 a.m. to start his days work. When he became a U.S. Senator, then Vice-President and finally President he still got up at 4 a.m. President Truman knew the value of a good routine.

Your studying can be improved by developing *regular time habits* as well as having a regular work place, and for the same reasons, convenience and conditioning.

Chapter 10 will show you how to manage your time in considerable detail, so I'll be brief here.

Set regular times for study, just as you have regular times for sleeping, eating, classes, jobs and all the other important events in your daily life. Plan your study times so that they don't conflict with other things you want to do such as sports, TV watching, or camel riding. Avoid leaving your studies until last thing before you go to bed at night. Study requires concentration and an alert mind, not one fatigued by the days excitements and frustrations. A short, regular study time each day, Monday to Friday inclusive, is far superior than two long ones.

Now I'll let you in on the secret trick of using that study time. Are you ready? Even when you *don't* have anything to do, (that's right I said don't) go to your study place for a few minutes and make yourself do some work. Review a lesson, re-work a few problems, read ahead in your textbook. Why do this? When the hands of the clock reach your study time each day you want to react like a racehorse to the starting bell. You want to develop a reflex to go to work. A reflex? That's too tame. You want to develop a driving passion to go to work. Wild horses and steel chains couldn't keep you from starting your work.

Every time you go to your study place at your study time, you increase your conditioning. When you don't go, you actively decrease your conditioning (it's called extinction, see Chapter 17). Even if you don't do much work the success of being at your study place on time will strengthen your study habit.

That's the secret to developing a solid study habit that will ease the path for your education for years to come.

HABIT FORMATION

The Ideal

The secret of developing a powerful study habit is no secret at all. Study at your study place at your regular study times and never make an exception.

Sometimes your life depends on behavior that occurs without exception. The person who has not developed the habit of stopping at stop signs or red traffic lights, or driving on the right side of the solid yellow lines is a natural customer for a grave plot salesman. Our lives do not depend on most of the habits we develop, and so we make exceptions. Every time the exception is made the habit is weakened.

The Reality

Our lives are full of conflicts, distractions, and old habits that interfere with our new ones. A super TV program is scheduled at the time you planned to write that term paper — conflict. Just as you settle down to read for that book report your boyfriend or girlfriend calls on the telephone — distraction. The track coach shows his star miler a postural fault that is costing him energy. The athlete can correct it as long as he concentrates, but when his attention shifts he goes back to the old habit — interference.

Despite these problems you can develop new habits, you know that. All

I am going to do here is state the two basic methods of habit formation and describe the best situations in which to use them.

Method 1

This is the ideal all over again. Start your habit and never make an exception. Much of the time this is the toughest way to start a new habit. Drug addicts call this method "Cold Turkey." (One of the symptoms of kicking a heroin habit abruptly is a clammy, goose-bumped skin like that of a turkey just out of the fridge). Starting a habit abruptly and not making exceptions runs into all of those problems we mentioned earlier.

The world does not change just because you have decided to start a new habit, and the world keeps prompting you to continue your old habit. After all you spent months and even years developing the old habit, and you have conditioned it to a lot of stimuli in the world. All that stimulation keeps urging you to continue your old habit. An instance of this, at the age of 44 I decided to change my handwriting, which was almost illegible, even to me. I strove to learn a fine Italic style of writing, and even took lessons. But, every time I had to write something fast I kept slipping back to my old style, or to some weird mixture of both styles. I could not avoid the exceptions.

There is one life situation that you can use the Cold Turkey method easily. When you have a large change in your life style you create a natural opportunity to change habits quite easily and suddenly. When your life style changes you have to learn a lot of new habits, and for a little while your environment encourages the beginning of such new habits. Consider these examples:

1. You change schools. You meet a lot of new friends, all of your teachers are new and the place is different. Most of these people don't know you and your old habits, so here's a good chance to start fresh with a new batch.

2. You leave home to go to college. You not only have a new school environment, but you have left your home environment as well. You really can become a new person if you wish. The danger here is that you have lost all your anchors and you can develop a lot of bad habits. This is the time when many students lose what study habits they have made, and end up having to take a course like the Learn-to-Learn Course to relearn what they have lost.

Other large life changes which would allow you to easily make abrupt changes in habits would be changing jobs, changing careers, getting married, or even getting divorced, if it should come to that. You can also use the abrupt method of habit formation when the change in your life is significant but not as huge as the ones described above. Take a course. When all of the people around you are classmates interested in developing the same new habit, your habit development is much easier. Learn French Cooking, automobile tuneups, or a new philosophy. Take a course.

Method 2

The alternative to abrupt habit change is gradual habit change. This method is usually the most practical. It allows the exceptions, with the understanding that they will become fewer and fewer as the habit develops. That is really how my new handwriting came about. This is how most of your new habits will develop. To use this method requires patience and the realization that a failure today does not mean you will never succeed. You also must be satisfied with small gains, piled one on top of the other. The abrupt method shows instant success, or failure. This "slow'n sneaky" method gives you semi-successes, and half-failures. Neither of these last two results are satisfying, but you can live with that if you see progress (see Chapter 12).

Let's say you have decided to use the Readrite system of study. Your old system consisted of reading and re-reading the textbook, and your notes. When you start the Readrite system you will find that you probably read too much and don't take enough notes. That's your old system interfering with your new habit formation. *Rule number one of this method is to start small.* You may have to limit your reading to single paragraphs, but it will start to develop the sub-habit of alternately reading and writing. After you have established this read-then-write pattern you can begin to use it in more meaningful chunks.

YOUR DADDY'S IN THERE
COOLING HIS BRAIN.

Rule two of the gradual method of habit formation is to reinforce your new habit every step of the way. You must do it successfully and feel rewarded for doing it (see Chapter 17 for the full use of reinforcement). This rule is most important. The method requires a long campaign before the new habit is solidly established. You must feel that the habit is being rewarded and strengthened as you go or you will quit. Can you imagine trying to learn to play the piano if you could not hear, or were totally tone deaf. You would never know if you struck the right notes and were making beautiful music or a horrible noise. You have to have positive feedback to see if you are succeeding. Records of your progress is one way of assuring yourself that you are progressing (again see Chapter 12).

The gradual method of habit formation will work if you are willing to progress in small, even partial steps, and succeed each step of the way. You must receive feedback from your learning if you are to achieve those successes. You must also know what to do when your new habit comes a bit unglued.

Backsliding

Most of our new habit formation is like a man heaving a large boulder up a muddy hill. For each four steps upward, he slides back three. Such backsliding is very discouraging. Many attempts to form new habits die with this discouragement.

"I can't pronounce the French r's. I'll never learn that language!"

"My new grip isn't working! I missed a dozen putts today."

"I must not be cut out to be a salesman. I haven't sold a thing all week."

There are three little tricks that will carry you over such slumps in your performance:

1. *Never quit completely.* As long as you are performing some part of your habit there is hope. If you quit completely there's little chance of starting up again when times get better. How do you keep a habit going when your really down?

2. *Go through the motions.* Be satisfied with minimal performance. If you were a runner and you were too sick to run, take a walk at the same time you would ordinarily run. If your day was so busy that you were going to have to skip your regular study time, just sit quietly in your study place for a minute. If your golf putting has become disastrous, be satisfied with bogeys for awhile, the birdies will return.

3. Sometimes we can get better performance out of ourselves if we *trick ourself* into working.

"I'm not going to run at all today", says the sick runner. "I'll just jog a lap of the track." After that one lap the runner feels a bit better, so he does another, then another, until he finishes most of his run. If he had planned to run five miles, he probably would not have run at all. He tricked himself into doing some running, and ended up doing more than he expected.

"I'm too tired to do all these math problems. I'll just try one to see how they are done." And one can lead to another.

Backsliding is discouraging, but it need not be terminal. Bide your time and better days will be ahead.

The Laws

Stimulus Control — regular places and times use this law to its fullest.

Gradualness — the second method of habit development emphasizes the effectiveness of starting small and slow and building gradually.

Reinforcement — absolutely necessary in the building of habits.

Repetition — only through repeated practice can a strong habit develop.

Specific practice — if you can avoid the exceptions your habit will build faster and be stronger.

Activity — all habits require action. 'Nuff said.

Exercises

1. Decide whether you *need* isolation or people or some combination of these for a study place.

2. Choose a unique study place.

3. Have all your study materials at your study place (See page 131).

4. Choose *one* study skill and start to apply it to your work (See the Action Plan in *Appendix* H).

4080 Words

CHAPTER 10 - USING TIME

*Dost thou love Life? Then do not squander
Time; for that's the stuff Life is made of.*

Benjamin Franklin, Poor
Richard's Almanac 1746

Summary

The secret of using time is knowing where your time goes. Time is the major resource that you have at your disposal. Estimating how your activities use time shows you that the largest part of it is spent in routine maintenance activities, like eating, sleeping and travelling. Your optional time is distributed throughout the day and needs careful planning to extract the best use out of it. Before you start to plan you measure how your time is spent. The rules for planning your time are 1. plan in advance, 2. write your plan, 3. write your committed times in first, 4. write in your study hours according to a mini-max system, and 5. leave empty time slots. Don't ignore small scraps of time. Make your plan work for you. Don't be dominated by it, and amend it when it needs amending.

Introduction

A student needs time the way a banker needs money, an industrialist needs factories, and a politician needs people. Time is your major resource. You must guard your time the way Wells-Fargo guards its cash and bullion. You must spend your time with all the care of a corporation cost accountant. Your time is more valuable than money. You can always earn more money, but you can never earn more time. Once an hour is past you can't retrieve it.

In all human affairs there are only three resources: materials (which includes money), people, and time. You don't need many materials to be a student. Once you are in school a few books, some paper and pen, and you are ready to work. Consider that a fighter pilot needs a million dollar aircraft and the equipment to back it up to do his job. As for people, it helps if you have good teachers and inspiring fellow students, but it's not your job to gather them together. The school system does that. The one resource you are responsible for is your time.

Time like money can be spent haphazardly, but don't expect much result from such spending. Businesses succeed by carefully budgeting their dollars; they are masters at collecting and spending money to end up with a profit. You don't need to collect time, it's there already, but you do need to spend it. The profit will be your education. This chapter will show you how to budget your time wisely in three easy steps: 1. Discover where you are spending your time now, 2. prepare a flexible plan to budget your time, and 3. follow your plan intelligently, constantly bringing it up to date.

KNOW WHERE YOUR TIME GOES

The first step in making good use of your time is knowing how you are spending it now. You have to know this so that you can make the correct adjustments to let you do all you want to do. This sounds simple enough, but it is going to require some work by you. If you are going to design a workable, useful, even enjoyable schedule for yourself you have to know in detail what your days are like.

The passage of time requires no effort on your part. We don't have to physically work to make it pass, or spend any money. Because of this we are very casual about our use of time. We only really pay attention to time passing when an urgent event demands it. With fifteen minutes to catch your plane your taxi is stalled in traffic, and then you notice how fast the second hand moves. Other than crises like that, we really could not care whether it is 9:00 a.m. or 9:15 a.m. See how well you can answer the following questions about everyday events:

1. How long did it take you to eat breakfast this morning?
2. How much time did you spend in cars today?
3. Can you tell me within 15 minutes how much time you spent on your studies this last week?
4. Do you know how much time you spent in class this last week? Don't figure it out. Have you kept track of class time?

Eating, travelling, studying, and classes are all big time consumers in your life as a student. Do you really know how much time you spend on these matters?

Most of our daily lives are taken up with routine matters. We are not as badly off as cows who spend 95 percent of their days either eating or sleeping, but a large proportion of each day is pre-scheduled. Use Figure 10-1 to estimate how much of your week is spent on the items listed.

Item	Each Day		Per Week
1. sleeping (at night and naps)	_____	x 7=	_____
2. eating (all meals and snacks, including preparation and cleaning up)	_____	x 7=	_____
3. classes	_____	x 7=	_____
4. personal (baths, hair, laundry, dressing, and so on)	_____	x 7=	_____
5. travel (to and from work, between classes, driving, walking, biking)	_____	x 7=	_____
6. exercise (sports, walking, riding or biking not in 5.)	_____	x 7=	_____
TOTALS	_____	x 7=	_____

Figure 10-1 Estimated Weekly Time Expenditure

The six items in Table 10-1 are "must" items. We must eat, sleep, work (or study which is the same thing), look after ourselves and travel about. We do each one of these every day. If we let any one of them go too long our lives suffer. Leave out item 4 for a few days and people won't get into elevators with you or ride with you in closed cars. Go without 1 or 2 too long and your body shrieks "ENOUGH!"

This exercise will show you two things. First, you have only the vaguest idea how much time you spend on even routine matters, let alone special events. You can figure out roughly how much time you spend on each item (8 hours a day for sleep is easy), and then do the arithmetic to find your weekly expense on that item. But, if you had to bet that your estimate for each item was accurate to within 30 minutes for the week would you wager $500 on it? Students do every semester. Every time you sign up for a course you invest a lot of your time, which is worth quite a lot to you, and a lot of your money or your parents money. The bet is that you will have the time to do the work for that course. Is it a good bet?

Second, your total for the week probably comes to between 108 and 128 hours for those six items. It's startling how much time we spend each week just staying alive. Notice that I have not included study or recreation in that list. If you want to go to football games, or watch TV, or read your textbook you will have to do it out of the remaining time. There is a big chunk of time left over, somewhere between 40 and 60 hours. That looks like plenty of time to do homework and have fun as well, and it is. Some students have an item 7 on their time expense list, the job they need to work at to support themselves while they go to school. That job can cut 20 to 40 hours out of the "time left over," and they still find time to study and have fun. There seems to be lots of time, so what's the problem?

The problem is that the time left over does not come in big chunks, it comes in little bits scattered around. You have to locate these bits of time, identify them as usable, and then use them.

The Time Sheet

You must *measure your use of time, find out exactly where you spend time.* To do this you need a clock or watch, a pen and a recording sheet. Recording sheets are located in Appendix K at the very back of the book. Take one out and tape it to the inside cover of your notebook. Now you are ready to start measuring.

The scale of your measurement is up to you. You can get bogged down if you try to record every little event in your day and how many minutes it took. I suggest you choose some major categories like the six listed in Figure 10-1, plus categories for study, recreation, and work. Keeping track of how much time you spend in these eight major items will be plenty. You could even work up a number code or abreviation system to save you a lot of writing (1. is sleep, or S is sleep, and so on). Jot your code down the side of the sheet. Start your sheet in the upper left with the time you wake up, and conclude the day's recording when you go to sleep. In between these times record when you change from one activity to another. (See Figure 10-2)

Time	Activity	Time
8:00	breakfast	
8:15	drive	
9:00	history class	
10:00	math class	
11:00	break	
12:00	eat lunch	
12:20	wash car	
1:00	lab	

Figure 10-2 Activity Record

The time sheet will give you a *true picture* of how you are spending your time. No estimates here, or foggy guesses, just the facts. You will discover how much time is spent on the necessities of sleeping, eating, classes and so forth. You will discover exactly how much left-over time exists, and *where it is*. You will be in a position to make an intelligent plan to use your time well.

You may be thinking right now that you can skip this first step and make a schedule for yourself right away. Here's fair warning. If you try to schedule your time without knowing the reality of how you actually spend time, you will build conflict and frustrations into your plan that will defeat it. From long experience helping students organize their time I can confidently predict that your schedule will fail. Not only will it not work, but you will abandon it and give up the idea of time management altogether. You will be back at square one.

MAKE A PLAN

Flexibility, that's the key to successful time planning, flexibility.

Airlines can run on fixed schedules, people can't. (Now that I think of it airlines aren't so hot at scheduling either). You have to leave a lot of elbow room in a good time plan. You have to be able to change it quickly to take into account the unexpected event, without destroying the plan completely.

Too often schedules become some kind of monster that haunts us. We look at the schedule and it says, "You've gotta do this, you've gotta do that, gotta, gotta, . . .". The plan should work for you, not you for it. A good time plan is like your car. When you need it it is there. When you want to go somewhere it helps you get there. When you don't need it, it sits patiently waiting for you until you do need it.

Four Planning Rules

1. Make your *plan in advance.* That's not quite as silly as it sounds. Deciding at two in the afternoon you will study French tonight, because your date for that evening fell through is not really planning. That's rolling with the punches. Making your time plan a day in advance is reasonable at first; later you will want to do it a week in advance.

2. *Write your plan.* Head carried plans are unreliable. Use the time sheets and write your plan for the next day or week. Scotch tape it to your notebook or the bathroom mirror. The mirror display will let your family know what you are going to be doing. In a short while they will consult your weekly plan before they plan things for you to do. That's nice, no hassle. The written plan is necessary for you to follow through on the final step discussed in the next section.

3. A time plan has the hours of the day running down one column with the activity for each hour written beside it. Write in the hours from wake-up time to lights out, then write the day's planned activities beside the appropriate hour. *Write in the fixed items first.* These are activities like classes, meeting, sporting events, appointments, or dates that you are commited to.

4. Write in your *study times.* Be specific about this. Don't just block out an hour or two and write "Study" beside it. Write what you will be doing: "Spanish Grammar," or "Chemistry problems," or "study-History exam." To do this well you need to know how much time you will spend that week on a particular subject. This will vary from week to week depending on the demands of your classes and your reading. Use a system of minimums and maximums (Mini-max) to give you flexibility in planning your study time. The system works like this:

Mini-Max

a. Decide on how little work you can get away with on a subject and come up with a grade, or some standard satisfactory to you. For example you might find that two hours a week in an easy course was good enough for a C or a B or whatever you wanted. Jot that figure in the margin of your time sheet, "Course A – 2 hrs."

b. Decide how much you can afford to spend on that course to meet a higher standard – greater understanding or maybe an A.

c. The first figure is the minimum and the second figure is the maximum. Schedule the maximum. Find time slots and plan to study the maximum time you have allotted for that subject. Where does the minimum come in? That comes in when your rich uncle Harry visits you for three days and takes you out each evening. It also comes in when you get a galloping case of the Lithuanian green virus. It is your flexibility factor. Each week you *plan to study up to your maximum* allotted times, but if for some reason you cannot, your planning is a success if you *meet your minimums.* This way you avoid building unnecessary failure into your planning. If you plan for the best, the maximum, you will make it often enough to improve your grade. One thing that is perfectly predictable is the unexpected. You have to plan for it. The mini-max system of scheduling allows this.

5. Leave lots and lots of *empty slots* in your time plan. Don't be compulsive and fill up every hour of the entire day with some planned activity. We all need goof-off time. We're not computors that run perfectly at all hours. The empty slots will add more flexibility to your plan. They give you places to move activities that suddenly won't work where they are.

Scraps of Time

Richard Burton was a famous British explorer, soldier, diplomat, and writer of the 19th century. He was the first Christian European to see the inside of the holy city of Mecca, which he did by disguising himself as an Arab merchant. His intimate knowledge of the Arabian language allowed him to pull off this coup, and it also allowed him to be the first man to translate the Arabian Nights into English. He became famous for his explorations in search of the headwaters of the Nile River.

Burton was a gifted linguist. During his life he learned to speak 23 languages. Later in his life he was asked where he had found the hours of time to study, since he had pursued a tremendously active career. He flatly denied spending hours at study. His method was to write on a scrap of paper each morning some words of vocabulary, and a grammar rule or two of the new language he was working on that day. Whenever he had a few minutes break during the day, say between appointments or at lunch, he would pull out this scrap of paper and study for a minute or two. Twenty-three languages learned a few minutes at a time!

A little arithmetic will show how useful a few minutes each day can be to you. Ten minutes a day, every day for a year mounts up to 3,650 minutes, that's about 61 hours a year. How much time is that? It is enough to watch 30 full length movies, and buy popcorn as well. It's the same as a week and a half full-time work. If you consider that a semester-long college course has 38 classroom hours, you could take that course and have time left over to read a 500 page textbook. Ten minutes a day, that's all.

Your day has lots of time scraps scattered throughout. A lot of these scraps (your breaks) you use as a breather between your active periods. You need those breaks, but maybe you can turn one or two to good advantage, to your studies.

The best kind of work to do in short time periods is routine, repetitive work. School work is full of such jobs, like memorizing vocabulary for language courses, learning periodic tables for chemistry, or working problems in mathematics. Since they are so routine they don't require much deep thought or warmup. You can flip open your notebook and work at them in any spare moment you have during the day. Such routine tasks can be boring if tackled in large blocks. An hour of vocabulary memorization can generate a real hatred for the language. Nibbling away at such work, a few minutes at a time, gets it done painlessly.

How much time do you spend each week waiting, waiting for a friend, waiting for a class to begin or waiting for a ride. Waiting times are useful scraps.

Make them do double duty, work at your studies while waiting. Travel time can also serve as double duty time. One student I knew used a 20 minute bus ride to and from school each day to study his Latin, a course he was not too fond of. That was the only time he studied Latin vocabulary. If you are not driving, you can do the same.

There's a trite old saying that goes, "If you want to get a job done, give it to a busy man." It's true. Busy people have learned to use their time efficiently. He will squeeze a job into 15 minutes a day, and quickly get it done.

Occasionally the time scrap is a large chunk of time. Occasionally students have free hours between classes. Work some study into those hours. In college the classroom you have been in for the last 50 minutes may empty and remain so for the next hour. Stay in your seat and work. Since you have just finished a class in a particular subject work on that one. You are all warmed up to it.

The Working Day

We need time to rest and play and lie on our backs to gaze at the clouds drifting overhead. These rest hours allow us to work more intensively during working hours. One of the big surprises to industrialists of this century was the discovery that people would produce more in an eight hour day than they would in a twelve hour day. We need time to recharge our personal batteries.

You need to schedule rest and recreation times as well as work times. Do this by having a clearly defined working day. Too often students let their work day drag on and on until late in the evening. They poke away at it and make it last most of their waking hours. There is "nothing so fatiguing as the eternal hanging on of an uncompleted task," said William James the great American philosopher and psychologist. Your studies will become a burden to you unless you restrict them to certain hours.

Work your working day, whatever it is, and when it is over put your work out of your mind. You can quit your studies at 5 p.m. like a factory or office worker does his job if you budget the time during the day. I have known dozens of college students who pay their way by working at jobs. They *have* to leave their studies to earn a living. If they can divide their days into school time and job time so neatly you can divide yours into study hours and recreation hours. Set yourself a clear-cut studying day and when it is over, enjoy your life.

Use the Plan

Now that you have the written plan you can use it. This plan is not a blueprint that must be followed to the last dotted "i" and crossed "t." The plan is a suggestion to yourself for an intelligent way to spend your time, and profit the most. Follow the plan as closely as you can. You have spent some valuable time creating this plan, so it deserves a serious attempt on your part.

But good time plans, as I said before, are like automobiles. They need maintenance from time to time. When your plan breaks down, fix it and go again. Don't abandon it the first time it sputters. When you are able to follow the plan, that's a success and you should record it. A check mark alongside the hour will do it. At the end of the week you can see what works by noting what you checked, and you can see what did not work. That should let you build a better plan for the following week.

Calendars and Little Black Books

Keep a calendar on which you can note pending events like exams, papers due, parties, beach weekends, birthdays, and so on. Consult your calendar each week before you prepare your time plan for the following week. Keeping a long range calendar will allow for a little long range planning. You don't want to discover 48 hours in advance that you have an exam, a paper due, and a laboratory report due all on the same day. If you had noted each of these items on your calendar, you would have lots of advance warning.

Little black books carried in pocket or purse aid our feeble memories. You may believe at the time that you will remember the due date of the History term paper, but a note in the little black book is more certain. The little black book will transfer useful facts back to your desk calendar and onto your weekly schedule surely and safely.

This chapter has taken you a long time to read and digest. You won't have to spend much time putting it into practice. You may not think you need any of this. So be it. At your age I thought I was immortal, now I'm not sure. Sometimes you get very busy, and knowing how to spend your time profitably is a useful skill.

The Laws

Gradualness – There are no final time plans. You work on them bit by bit until you perfect them to your liking.

Reinforcement – When you plan in writing you can look back at your plan to see how successful it was. You can detect its weaknesses and correct them. You can shape a better plan.

Active Learning – Time planning makes you *think*. It also gives you the power to control your own time. You have control. You act and the results follow.

Stimulus Control – Runs all through your planning. You use clocks, forms and pens to measure your time spending. You use the forms and your pen again to plan, and you use your calendar and forms to follow and correct your plan.

Practice (specific) — From the very beginning you make yourself aware of the importance of time to you. You measure time, you allot time, you use those times. It is your major resource and you must heighten your awareness of its value. Time planning will promote that awareness.

Exercises

1. Use figure 10-1 to estimate your weekly time usage of must items.

2. Estimate how much optional time you have per week.

3. Use time sheets to keep track of how you spend time for a day, or a week.

4. Copy the schedule forms in the Action Plan (page 291), and plan your activities for one day. Use your plan, then at the end of that day see how well you kept to your plan.

5. Make another plan for the following day, ammending your plan to take into account the errors of your previous day's plan.

6. Memorize the five planning rules.

7. Memorize the three steps of Mini-Max planning.

8. Choose some activity that you could profitably do in small scraps of time, and do it in small scraps. Identify as many small time scraps in each day as you can.

9. Buy a wall or desk pad calendar, and a small notebook to carry with you.

10. Post your time schedule on the fridge or on the bathroom mirror.

3,838 Words

CHAPTER 11 - CONCENTRATION

"I had no special sagacity, only the power of patient thought. I keep the subject constantly before me and wait until the first dawnings open little by little into the full light."

Isaac Newton

Summary

There are five steps in training yourself to improve your concentration: 1. Catch your concentration slipping, 2. Promise yourself a break, 3. Work intensively at your task for a *short* period of time, 4. Take your break, and 5. Return to work. This training works because of two motivational factors: Your attitude towards concentration improves as soon as you are aware that you can do something positive about it, and since you permissively allow yourself the occasional break while you work, your work is less oppressive. You can also improve your concentration on long dull tasks by working on them in short spurts. If you work on a task quickly your concentration will be better than if you dawdle along. Set deadlines to complete your work, and make them real by involving other people in your dealines. Perfect concentration is possible, and you can achieve it with patience and work.

Introduction

"I have trouble concentrating," said Brenda Holmes, age 17.

And Brenda is not alone. Eighty percent of the Student Problem Lists include poor concentration as a major study problem. What can be done about this?

If you ask your friends or teachers or parents you will get a lot of free advice like this:

"You've got to buckle down, get a grip on yourself."

"Its just laziness. You could really do it if you wanted to."

"Find a nice quiet place to work."

"Try harder."

The advice is well meant, and some is useful ("quiet place"), but a lot of it asks the student to use will power he does not have. If you are told to try harder to do something you cannot do, you become frustrated and confused. You need to be shown how to do it.

This chapter will show you several ways to improve your ability to concentrate on your studies. Concentration is a skill which can be learned. First you will see how to train yourself to improve your concentration, then you will see various techniques you can use to help concentrate.

Training Yourself to Concentrate

This training has five steps:

1. Work until your attention wanders
2. Promise yourself a break, then
3. Work intensively for a *short* time period
4. Take your break
5. Return to work

In step one, your attention can wander several times and you will not be aware of it. During concentration training held in class students would look out of the window, smile at the teacher, glance across the aisle at a friend, yawn, and look at their watch all within a couple of minutes, before they became aware that their attention was wandering. It is quite normal for a student to lose track of his work several times when he first starts to practice before he catches his wandering attention. Do not let this concern you, because you will improve with practice. Within a few days you will catch your mind wandering the first time it happens, so be patient and don't become discouraged.

As soon as you do become aware that your mind has moved away from the task at hand do step 2, promise yourself a break. Since any job that you cannot concentrate upon is uninteresting, the most effective reinforcement is a negative one (see Chapter 17); take a break. Get away from your work for a short time. You can double the strength of the reinforcement if you do something you like during the break (consult your positive reinforcement list or the one in Chapter 17). DO NOT, take your reinforcement at the time you notice that your concentration has failed. You don't want to reinforce that failure; you do want to reinforce improved concentration. That's where step 3 comes in. When you discover that your attention has wandered away from your work, and have promised yourself your reinforcement, then turn back to your work briefly. The work that you do during these next couple of minutes, plus the reinforcement that you will take at the end of this short work stint, are the crucial steps in the training. Since reinforcement strengthens the behavior that is performed just before the reinforcement occurs, that behavior should be well done. You don't want to strengthen lackadaisical work, sloppy work, half hearted work, so *work hard*. If you were memorizing French verbs say the next five verbs ALOUD, write them down, use them, then take your reinforcement. If you are solving mathematics problems, strive to complete the problem you are working on accurately and quickly. Then take a break.

Reinforce Extra Work

Students usually object to this going-back-to-work step.

"If I cannot concentrate how can I go back to work?", they ask.

You can because you know that this next work stint is going to be brief, and you will be taking a break at the end of it. Efficiency experts in industry call this the coffee-break effect. When these experts measure work output they find a rise in performance just before coffee breaks, lunch hours or quitting time.

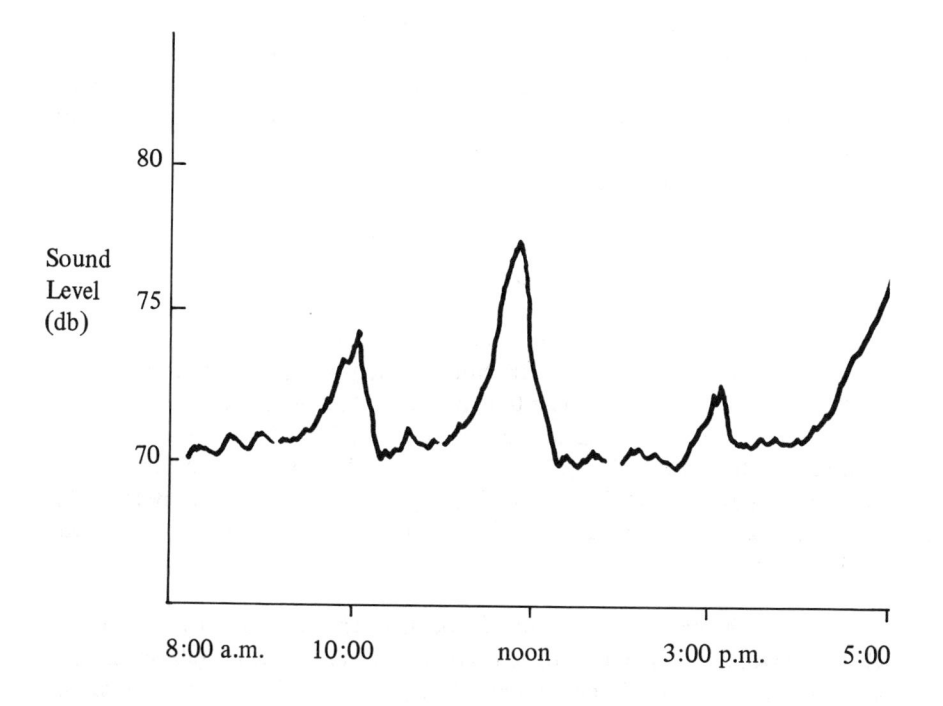

Figure 11−1 Sound levels in a typing pool measured throughout the day. The level indicates the amount of typing being done.

When workers know that the work period is going to end shortly they work harder to complete their tasks. If you know that you will be leaving your studying in a couple of minutes, you will find that you can buckle down to it again quite easily for that short time period.

The key to this intense work period is its brevity. If you are reading be sure that you do not read more than a couple of minutes, finish the paragraph you are on, or the section if you are near the end. If you are working problems in mathematics, chemistry or biology, complete the problem you are on, or if you have just finished one, start another. If you are writing, compose another sentence or two. In all cases try to give your work the maximum attention possible for those few minutes. Then, take your break.

The break may take two forms. You can switch jobs completely and work at another task you prefer more. For example, if you were reading history, and have a book report due in English, your break could be a half hour reading *Lolita*. That's a long break. If you want a short break, then leave your study place for a few moments, drink a coke, then settle back to work. Watch out for these "short" breaks, they can get away from you and s-t-r-e-t-c-h out to incredible lengths. Table 11–A shows the results of a class exercise showing the times students spent working before their attention wandered, and the amount of time they took on break before returning to work. Notice how many students took a break longer than the work period. If you are aware of this potential hazard you will be able to control it.

Then, go back to work, step 5.

The Concentration drill is not an instant cure, nor is it a cure-all. You must use the drill consistently to benefit from it. At first the drill will seem to be laughably inefficient. One student told me that at first he seemed to be on a permanent break, and had to work a long time to finish his Spanish (his poor concentration subject). He admitted that he did get his work done and that it was more fun my way than this old way of trying to force his attention. Because the intensive work step is steadily being strengthened by reinforcements, concentration does improve.

Although this drill will improve your concentration on any subject you choose to work on – and it is important that you choose a single subject and not do several at once – it will not necessarily improve your concentration on all tasks. You could become a super concentrator in chemistry, but still be a day dreamer in your social studies. Do not despair. You will improve your ability to train yourself to be a high powered concentrator. After the first two or three successes you will find that you can improve your concentration on any task within a few days, instead of a few weeks.

Table 11–A *Concentration Drill Practice, Learn-to-Learn Course July 1975**

Student	Work	Break	Work	Break
Mitsy	3'10"	3'40"	4'10"	4'45"
Mark	3'45"	4'10"		
Jeffrey	3'55"	3'	2'40"	5'25"
Dale	4'10"	3'		
Rusty	4'10"	2'50"	3'45"	4'38"
Wanda	4'10"	2'20"		
Kelly	4'10"	2'45"	4'20"	3'10"
Lucy	4'25"	2'55"		
John	5'05"	2'15"		
Diane	5'05"	2'10"	5'20"	3'20"
Jeff	6'	1'40"		
Ellen	6'	1'		
Hughes	6'15"	1'45"		

*The numbers show the amount of time in minutes (') and seconds (") that the student read their books, and took a break.

Successful Concentration

The steady application of reinforcement to a behavior strengthens that behavior, and this is so with concentration. In the long run the reinforcers will improve concentration, *if you keep doing it.*

Concentration training has a couple of motivational pluses that will help you use it. First of all, once you decide to try the drill you will have adopted a new positive mental attitude towards improving your concentration. You will have dropped the old outmoded idea that concentration has to be forced if it isn't working. You know that concentration is a habit, a skill, and if you have not developed the habit yet, you can. As soon as you realize that learning to concentrate on, say, the geography of Russia has to be learned, you can learn that skill like any other. Students experience a lifting sense of relief once they discover this fact, and they quickly develop a positive attitude towards this work.

Second, training allows you to be permissive with yourself. This is the second important motivational boost. We all like to indulge ourselves occasionally. When we find that we cannot concentrate the drill allows us to leave the work, to enjoy ourselves for a moment. That's nice, something to look forward to. Compare that technique with the old force-your-attention-back-to-the-work approach. In this latter method you punish yourself for trying to concentrate. Forcing yourself back to study boring material is punishing. The laws of reinforcement tell us that you will be worse off if you use punishment, so let's not use it. The little break you take is like the pressure escape valve on a pressure cooker. When dull work builds up a desire to flee from it, a small break fulfills that desire and allows us to continue.

That's how concentration training works. Now let's see what else you can do to improve your concentration.

Break it up, keep it short

Anyone can concentrate intensively for a brief time. That's the secret of step three in concentration training. Take advantage of this fact. If you have a long, boring task to do, break it up. Work at it in short spurts. Teachers use this trick to help them concentrate while grading papers. Forty papers all written on the same topic can be tedious. If they are read in half-hour batches, with breaks in between, concentration stays high.

The duller the task, the shorter the work session — that's the rule. Another rule has to do with how fast you are working.

Speed Tightens Concentration

If you want to concentrate better, work faster.

If you want to tighten your attention on your reading, speed up.

If you want to study more efficiently, beat the clock.

Going faster really improves your concentration in lots of things. Consider this example. Drive down a country road at forty miles an hour. You can look at the apple trees blooming, watch a buzzard circle overhead, and still drive safely. Speed down this same road at 85 miles per hour, and you have to concentrate on your driving. You don't have time to pay attention to the scenery, just the road.

You don't need to study at breakneck speed to concentrate, but working within a set time will help focus your attention. If you think you will need 30 minutes to learn a section of your book, note the time and try to do it in 25 minutes. A little time pressure helps.

If you find your book dull and your mind drifting off the page, do a Speed Drill (see Chapter 4). The drill will pick up your study speed, and the increased flow of information to your brain will force it to pay closer attention. If working fast in short work sessions is still not giving you the concentration you want, then set time goals the way your teachers do.

Deadlines

"Your papers will be due by the end of class next Monday. Late papers will be penalized one letter grade," - *a teacher assignment.*

Teachers set time limits for work. They know that if they don't, students will take forever to get assignments in. Students accept such time limits as one of the realities of school work. They realize that without those time limits they would procrastinate more in their work.

The world famous economist C. Northcote Parkinson described this kind of behavior in his law "Work Expands to fill Time". If you have a lot of time you will use it. If you have a little time you will use that. He tells the story of an elderly retired lady who took an entire morning to mail a post card. She had to select the card, and looked in several stores before she found the one she wanted. Then she composed her message over tea in a tea shop. The stamp required another trip to the neighborhood post office. By way of contrast, a busy executive grabs the standard printed card, writes his message, and tosses in into the company mail basket. Time taken, 50 seconds. The lady had all that time to use so she happily filled it with a task that could have been done in a few seconds.

The message for you is if you think you have lots of time to do your work, you will take lots of time. When you feel that you have lots of time you don't feel the need to concentrate intensively on what you are doing. The quality of your work suffers because of this lack of concentration.

Newspaper reporters know the value of working to time limits to improve the quality of their work. They must have their writing done by a certain time each day if it is to be printed in that day's paper. In the newspaper business this time limit is called the *deadline.* Stories that miss the deadline are dead and don't get printed that day or any other day.

Calgary Herald reporter Bill Dodge tells this story. "I wrote a feature story on the weather that took a week to finish. On the day I turned it in I also wrote a story on a fatal train-car wreck. The wreck happened only a few minutes before deadline, so I had to work intensively and fast. As I typed each page the copy boy tore it from my typewriter and ran it to the editors. When the paper came out I read both stories. The wreck story was better written than the feature story. It was clearer, and more understandable."

The pressure of a deadline can improve your concentration and the quality of your work. The *deadlines must be real.* Teacher's term paper deadline is real because there is a penalty if you are late. Deadlines have to be set by the world. If you want to set a deadline for yourself you must make it real. If you set yourself a goal of completing a job by four o'clock today, and nothing happens if you don't get it done, that's not a deadline.

If you set a four o'clock deadline to finish studying a chapter, then call a friend and ask him to allow you to teach it to him at four, you have created a deadline. The penalty is real. Your friend will be annoyed at you if you don't keep your appointment, he has other things to do. You will appear unreliable in his eyes, and foolish in your own.

The secret of setting deadlines for yourself to improve your concentration is to involve other people in your work. "Dad, if I finished this section of my term paper tonight would you read it?" Teachers give quizzes during the semester to force students to keep up in their work. You can force yourself to do better work by setting deadlines, which involve other people. The method is straightforward:

1. Choose the task you want to get done.

2. Pick a reasonable time to do it -- shorter is better than longer.

3. Involve other people in your deadline. Hand your work in to them, discuss it with them, have them criticize it or grade it.

Physical Activity

Any physical activity you do while studying will improve your concentration. I don't mean dribble a basketball while you try to read your textbook, I mean activity directly related to the study.

Study too often means that you sit still, showing about as much activity as a lump of cheese in the fridge. Your brain is used processing dozens of bits of information each second. Sitting slows down this process, and because your brain is not involved enough in what you are doing it flutters off like a butterfly into a daydream. Concentration is lost.

Using a pen as you study provides some physical activity, focuses your attention to the task, and provides immediate feedback on how you are doing. Say your French vocabulary aloud is better than just thinking to yourself. You can't check your pronounciation without hearing it. Working problems is a better way to learn mathematics and science than reading by itself, because you work with your pen and paper.

Any activitiy you do with your hands, mouth or your body will increase your concentration. *Be active.*

Learned Laziness

If you can train yourself to concentrate, it follows that you can train yourself to be lazy, to have a wandering mind, or to have a short attention span. Students really do this, as the following tale shows.

Jack was busy failing most of his classes in the second semester of his sophomore year at college. He had a good first semester as a freshman but ever since then his grades had been going downhill. He was put on probation at the end of the fall semester, and unless he improved his work the school was going to expell him. I was his academic adviser, so I was trying to get at the cause of his poor work.

"I just don't seem to be able to concentrate on my studies any more," he told me. "I had good study habits when I first got here, but somehow I have lost them."

"Can you give me a particular example of your poor work habits," I asked him.

"Sure. Last night I was trying to write a term paper – not one of my favorite jobs – when a friend asked me out to a party. I went. Just like that. It does not take much to yank me away from my studies."

"Oho," I thought to myself, "here may be a cause."

A few more questions showed that Jack had a booming social life. He had lots of friends, and enjoyed being with them. I asked him if his example was typical, and he said yes, that was happening to him all of the time.

If you look at the example Jack gave in terms of the Law of Reinforcement, you will see that he gave himself a double reinforcement for *quitting* his work. He got a negative reinforcement when he left the term paper (avoiding work he did not like), and a positive reinforcement for quitting when he went to the party with his friend. Since Jack said that example was typical, he had very likely done this dozens, if not hundreds of times. He was training himself to be a quitter.

Reinforcements work automatically. They don't have to be planned to do their job. You run the risk of training yourself to be a quitter, as Jack did, if you don't become aware of that possibility. Whenever you leave a task you don't enjoy you automatically give yourself a reinforcement for quitting. If you let that happen a few times too many, you will learn to be lazy. You will start to avoid your studies more and more.

The cure for learned laziness is awareness. Now that you know that you can train yourself to be lazy, don't let it happen. Instead of reinforcing yourself for quitting, reinforce yourself for working. Use concentration training to help you develop perfect concentration.

Perfect Concentration

Perfect concentration is hard to achieve. We all can do it for short periods of time, but our attention soon wavers and is drawn away. A few people have developed their power of concentration on a particular subject matter to a high degree. Isaac Newton, the 18th century scientific genius, claimed that concentration was his chief ability. The British mathematician, Alfred North Whitehead, could concentrate on his mathematics so thoroughly that he could shut out the world around him for hours at a time. His good friend and collaborator Lord Bertrand Russell tells of his remarkable powers of concentration.

"One hot summer day when I was staying with him (Whitehead) at Grantchester, our friend Compton Davies arrived and I took him into the garden to say how-do-you-do to his host. Whitehead was sitting writing mathematics. Davies and I stood in front of him at a distance of no more than a yard and watched him covering page after page with symbols. He never saw us, and after a time we went away with a feeling of awe."

Great athletes such as golfer Jack Nicklaus, racing driver Richard Petty, or quarterback Joe Namath are all credited with having superb powers of concentration, and this is one of the strengths that makes them great. You can develop your power of concentration given enough time and the right subject matter, and the proper training. If you want to achieve such power, work at your concentration training each day, use the various techniques suggested above, and you can have perfect concentration.

The Laws

This chapter gives a classic example of the practical application of scientific laws to a human problem.

Gradualness – You are not urged to instantly use your will power, whatever that is, to force concentration. You are shown a training method which will dramatically improve your concentration over time. Steady application of this training has turned weak concentrators into students who can focus their attention on their tasks for hours.

Repetition – The training is not a one shot affair. You need to repeat the five steps whenever your attention lapses. The more you repeat it the better your concentration will become.

Reinforcement – Step 4 uses both the techniques of positive and negative reinforcement to strengthen your behavior. This is the crucial step in the training.

Active – Step 3 insists that you work *intensively* before you take your break. You don't need to work long, just hard. The harder you work in this step, the stronger your concentration will become.

Stimulus Control – Using the clock to time your work, and asking friends to help make your deadlines real and is practical use of this law.

Practice (specific) – In all the techniques proposed in this chapter you are told to behave in the way people do behave when their concentration is high. You work fast, you work towards a goal (your deadline), you take positive steps whenever your concentration lapses.

Exercises

1. Memorize the five steps of Concentration Training.

2. Choose a *dull* book to read, and when you catch your mind wandering do the five steps.

3. Repeat 2.

4. Plan to use Concentration Training routinely on one subject you are studying.

5. Record on graph paper the amount of time you study before your mind wanders. Plot time in minutes on the vertical axis and study sessions 1, 2, 3, and so on, on the horizontal axis.

6. Use a watch to time the length of your breaks during one session of Concentration Training.

7. Estimate how long it will take you to do a homework assignment, chop a few minutes off of that estimate and try to finish in the shorter time.

8. Start setting deadlines on homework assignments. Set one today.

3,930 Words

CHAPTER 12 - RECORD KEEPING

> **Summary**
>
> The Learnometer forms at the end of this book will record the development of your study power. Record your daily activity to improve your learning efficiency. You will also keep records of your reading speed, learning efficiency, study problems, chapter tests, and even what you are doing each hour of the day. Each of these records is explained in this chapter. The chapter concludes with an explanation of why record keeping is essential for successful behavior change.

STUDY POWER RECORDS

Introduction

The first five sections of this chapter explain the record keeping required to successfully complete the 15 day plan. These records will show you your progress every step of the way. You can use these records to eliminate your weaknesses and rejoice in your strengths. The records are:

1. The Learnometer
2. The Study Problems List
3. Chapter Tests
4. Reading Test Records
5. Weekly schedules

The Learnometer

Tear out the last Learnometer (Appendix K) to look at it as you read this section. You need a daily record to show your progress in study power. This record should provide you with instant feedback on how you are doing, yet it must be simple to keep. The record must be portable, and at the same time provide permanent and objective evidence of your daily performance.

A lot of experimenting went into the perfecting the Learnometer as just this kind of record. The Learnometer is a checklist. Your record keeping consists of checking the correct space, jotting down a time, or writing a word or two to describe what you did. You can carry it in your looseleaf notebook and use it throughout the day. What could be simpler.

166 *Record Keeping*

The Learnometer appears to be complicated with all those numbered items and criss-crossed lines. Yet, after you have completed one or two you will see how easy it is to keep, and how useful it will be to you. You will note that the instructions at the beginning of Appendix K explain how to fill out the Daily Summary, and what each of the 29 items is about. Take a few minutes to read over these instructions now.

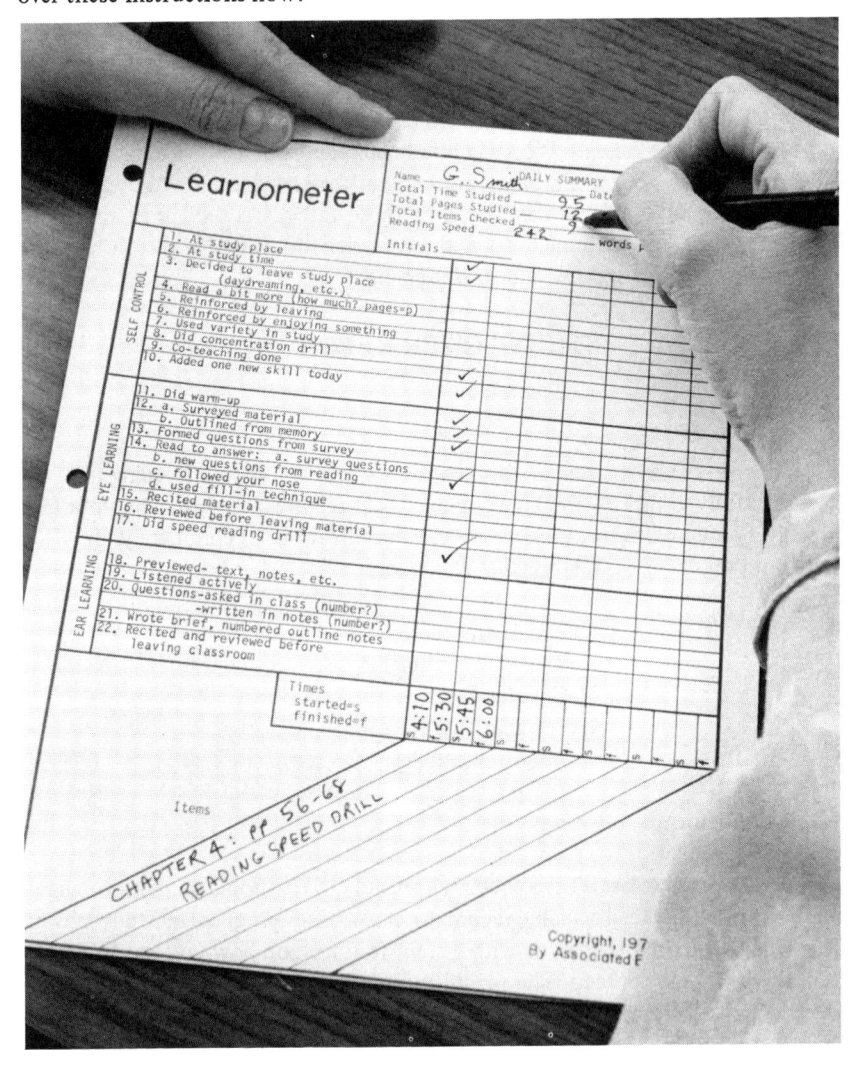

Figure 12 - 1 The Learnometer shows the student daily progress in acquiring study skills.

Done? OK. You can see that the 29 items are a miniature of this entire book. These are the learning skills you need to be an efficient student. To try to explain each one of these skills here would be trying to explain the whole book in a couple of paragraphs. I can't really do that, and you would choke on so much information. As you complete each day of the plan you will discover new items to be checked.

The First Day's Learnometer

I will lead you through the first day's Learnometer to get you started. Day one of the 15-day plan instructs you to find a study place and a study time. After you do this, check items 1 and 2 on the Learnometer. If you stick to the plan you will have checks opposite these items each day for the next 15 days. If during that time you miss doing either one of these items, don't check it. This is your record, so keep it accurate.

These two items will be the only two you will check today. As the days of the plan go by, you will find more and more checks on each day's Learnometer, as you learn and practice more and more skills. This increase in the number of checks marks your progress. The more you check the better student you are becoming. Make your checks large and impressive. A black or red felt-tipped pen makes super checks.

Next, the plan for day one tells you to complete the Study Problems List in Appendix B. Do that, and note what time you start this task and what time you finished it. Write "Completed Study Problems List" in the left diagonal line in the *Description of Activities* Section. At the top end of this diagonal space enter the time you began this task in the block marked *s* and the time you finished in the block marked *f*. You are starting to record how long it takes you to do your work.

At first students find this time recording a pain. *IT MUST BE DONE!* Remember that power is work done in time. One of the ways to develop study power is know how much time it takes you to do your work, so that you can improve on it. For example, if it takes 10 minutes to read a page in your textbook today, and 12 minutes tomorrow you know that you are not reading as fast. You can do something about that. If you don't know how long it takes you to read you may never become aware of the problem and you won't improve.

By now you realize that you should have recorded your start and finishing times for reading this chapter and the introduction to the book, but you did not. That's OK. You have to start somewhere. Write that you read those two chapters in the next two diagonal lines. Finally, record that you completed the first reading test. That completes the first day's Learnometer, except for the Daily Summary.

The last thing to be completed each day is the Daily Summary. Fill it out as instructed. You compile the summary from the body of the Learnometer and from a few other sources. You can calculate the number of minutes you worked at your studies from the *Times* section at the bottom of the form. Subtracting start times from finish times and adding all of them together for the day will give you that figure. Always record your total time in minutes, not in hours and minutes. The *Description of Activities* section will let you count how many pages you studied each day. Count the number of check marks and record that figure (you want the total number of *check marks*, not the number of items checked).

You will have a reading speed to record only on the days you calculate that figure. Today you will have one because you completed the First Reading Test. Get that figure from the reading test scoring sheet. Your study speed is always much slower that your reading speed because you do many more tasks while you study. The number of words in each chapter is given at the end of the chapters in bold face print. Knowing that fact and the amount of time it took you to study a chapter will allow you to calculate your study speed and record it.

The *Initials* space is a key item on this form. In that space you have a teacher, a parent, a friend or a fellow Study Power student write their initials each day. Having to face another person each day and showing them your work provides you with powerful motivation to do it well. When you do a good job you want to share your success. When you make mistakes, public exposure makes you correct them, fast. Showing your learnometer to another person benefits you both of these ways, and will give you a chance to discuss your new-found skills. The intials are your record of this meeting.

Your Learnometer recording is off to a good start. Complete Learnometers as accurately as possible each day for the next 15 days. Tear them out of the back of the book and put them into a section of your note book. Fill them out throughout the day as you use your skills. Don't leave your recording until the end of the day when you are tired and have forgotten half of what you have done. A check mark only takes a second, a time recording five seconds, and an activity description a quarter of a minute. These few seconds will reward you with instant feedback on your progress, and the satisfaction of seeing the good work you are doing.

The Learnometer is the key record of your progress in developing your study power, but it is not the only one.

The Study Problems List

This list (Appendix B) will be the first of several before-and-after pictures you are going to take of yourself, so to speak. You are going to list all of your study problems, everything. Have a lemon party for yourself. At the end of the 15-day plan you are going to inspect that list again, to find out if there are any problems left unsolved. Ninety-eight percent of all the problems listed by students in the Learn-to-Learn classes have been solved by the end of the course. I suspect you will find this to be true for you also. The list will show you this fact in black and white.

Chapter Tests

By developing your study power you will learn skills that will be useful to you for the rest of your life. Every course you take from now on will benefit from your skillfulness as a student. In a way this book is like a book on Parachute Jumping; you don't want to miss any important points, because those points could be needed later on. This is one book it will pay off to learn 100 percent, like the parachute book. That's what the chapter tests are for.

Each test allows you to see if you have mastered the important points of the chapter. If you miss a question you know that you need to go over that section once again to learn it properly. The chapter tests also record the *knowledge* you have learned or failed to learn. The Learnometer records the *application* of this knowledge, what you do with it. These two records will give you a clear picture of your increasing study power, day by day.

Reading Test Records

These records provide another before-and-after picture of yourself. The first reading test measures your reading speed, your learning, and your learning efficiency before you start the 15-day plan. The second test measures your abilities half way through the 15-day plan, and the last test does it again at the end. You record your data on the Scoring Sheets.

Weekly Schedule

Chapter 10 shows you how to manage your time efficiently. The weekly schedule is the record of this time management. Time is the most precious asset you have as a student. You have to learn how to spend your time to your best advantage. The Weekly Schedule is a valuable time management training aid. This record is discussed in detail in Chapter 10.

ADVANTAGES OF RECORD KEEPING

The following sections will show you some good reasons for keeping records. Records are kept of every important human activity. Courts keep records of trials, verdicts, sentences and judges decrees. Schools keep records of students courses and their grades. Parents and doctors keep records of the illness

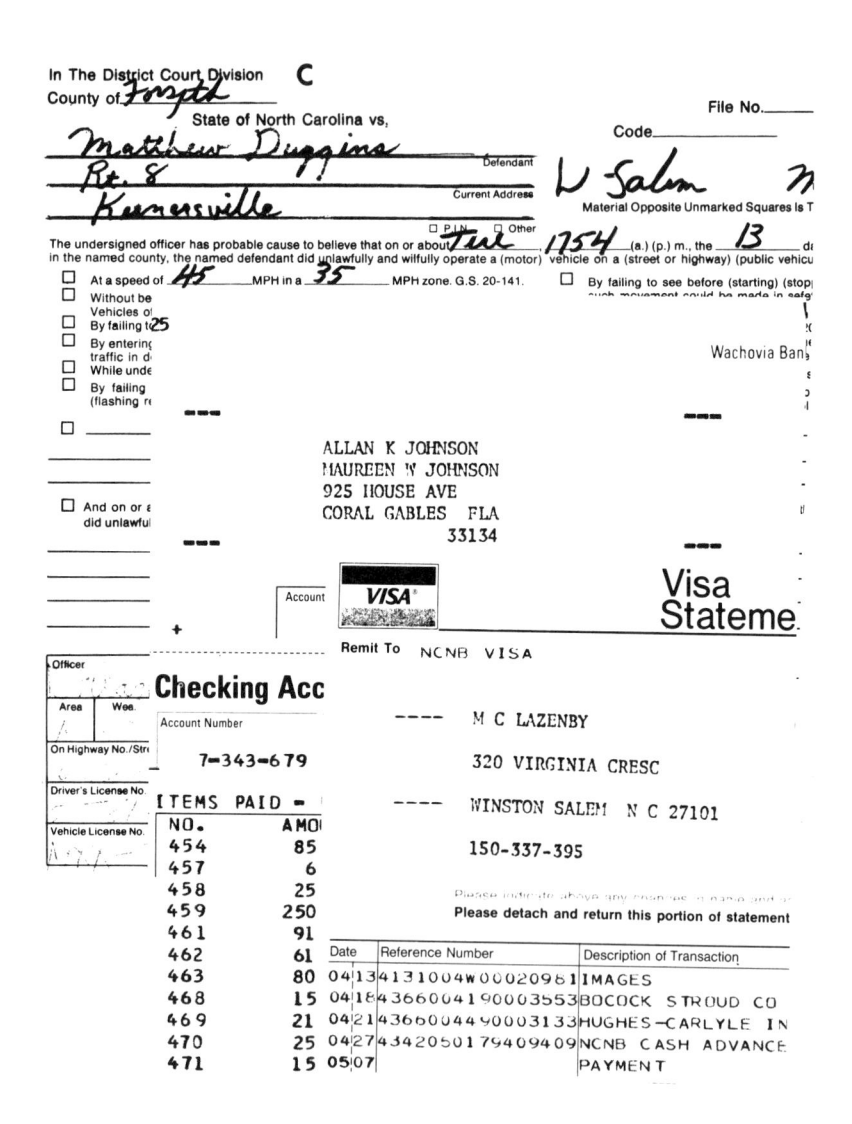

Figure 12-1 Some personal records kept for us by others.

of children as they grow up. Athletes and teams keep records of performances so that the athlete can improve on them.

As a student you need to keep records so that you can improve your craftsmanship. To be a better student you need to know how good or bad you are now, and how you performed in the past so that you can strengthen your weak skills and maintain your strong ones.

Before you read the next section fill out the personal Records Questionnaire on the next page. It will help you follow the remainder of this chapter.

Personal Records

We all keep personal records of who and what we are, and what we do. Sometimes we laboriously write the record ourselves (diets), sometimes others keep the record for us (school attendance), and sometimes we merely make a note of a fact for future use (a dinner date). No matter how it is done we all realize that record keeping can be valuable to us. Scientists are the super record keepers. In their work they record facts in exhaustive detail and with incredible accuracy. It is this passion for record keeping that has advanced science to the high position it holds today in our society.

The three parts of the Personal Records Questionnaire will give you an idea of the value certain types of record keeping have for you. The questions in part A can be answered by just about everyone. Out of a hundred people given this questionnaire 86 answered all four questions quite accurately. These are the personal statistics and information that we all keep in our heads. The questions in part B of the questionnaire are also well answered, although not all the questions apply to everyone. When a question did apply to a person they were able to give a good answer; 80 percent of the applicable questions were answered, which is comparable to the results of part A.

When these same one hundred students answered part C the results were very different from the first two parts. By far the most frequent answer (94%) to these questions was "don't know." None of these students had taken a study skills course. There must be a significant difference between part C and the first two parts.

Your Statistics

First of all, personal statistics are valuable to individuals in our society. By the time a person is adult he has been asked the first three questions of the questionnaire dozens of times. His weight and height were properly recorded by his parents and the school nurse many times. The importance of these numbers was impressed upon us at an early age, so we began to carry them around in our heads. When we bought new shoes our foot was carefully measured, our foot size determined, and the correctly fitted shoe purchased. The importance of correctly fitting shoes was emphasized to us by our parents, shoe sales clerks, our doctors and teachers in school, so that number was carefully recorded in our memory. Dentists and the teachers of health in our schools harp upon the need for regular teeth check-ups if they are to stay white and sound. Our youth oriented culture values a brilliant smile. For this reason we buy millions of tons of toothpaste each year, and hundreds of miles of steel wire to straighten crooked teeth. We also can remember when we were at the dentist last time.

We remember the information sought by the questions in part A of the questionnaire of its importance to us. Keeping this kind of record is a modern idea. If you asked Americans of the 17th century the same questions they would not have been able to tell you these facts. In the days before the mass production of standard clothing sizes there was no point in knowing this information. When only one man in one hundred could visit a dentist regularly, and the rest visited only when they needed to have a tooth pulled or filled, the idea of regular check-ups did not exist.

Secondly we keep track of the information sought in part B, because we would like to improve our performance in these areas. If you only worked ten hours for pay last week and want to make more money, you might ask the boss for more time. In North Carolina and many other states you can lose your driver's license if you accumulate too many points against yourself. For that reason people who have collected some bad driving points are usually a lot more careful than they were before. If you are trying to save money, or just live within your means you keep close track of what you spend. At the end of the month you balance your check book (your records) against the bank statement (their records), to make sure you have not overspent. If you have, your records will tell you where and you can correct it, you hope. Similarly you can improve your typing speed or your weight loss if you are dieting by knowing what you are doing now. The hourly time card, the points record on your drivers license, or your checkbook are useful records that help you improve your behavior.

Student Records

The difference between the students answers to part C on the questionnaire and the first two parts can now be explained. Students do not see any value in keeping track of their reading speed, or where they studied, or how often they took notes from their reading. They do not believe that keeping such records would help them become better students. The same student who would record his time in running one hundred yeards to the nearest one-hundredth of a second so that he could improve his sprinting, would not see the purpose in recording his reading speed. *This is a serious mistake.*

Personal Records Questionnaire

Answer as many of these questions as you can from memory.

PART A

1. What is your weight to the nearest pound? _____ pounds

2. What is your height to the nearest inch? _____ inches

3. What is your shoe size? _____

4. When were you last at the dentist? _____ months _____ year

PART B

1. How many hours did you work for pay last week? _____ hours

2. Do you have any points against you for speeding, illegal parking, any traffic infractions? _____ points

3. Did you spend more or less money this week than last week, and how much? $_____

4. How fast can you type? _____ WPM

5. What was your grade point average in school last semester? _____

6. How much weight did you lose on your diet last week? _____ pounds

PART C

1. Before you bought this book did you know what your reading speed was?   Yes, _____ WPM   Don't know_____

2. How many times a week were you in your study place last month?
1._____ , 2._____ , 3. _____ , don't know _____

3. Last month, how often did you take notes from your reading?

   1. _____ , 2._____ , 3. _____ , don't know_____

4. Did you do a warm-up before you studied yesterday?
Yes_____ , no_____ , don't remember _____

5. How many study skills did you improve on this week?

   1._____ , 2. _____ , 3. _____ , don't know_____

The Problems of Recording Behavior

"How much butter is there in that bucket?"
"How well does that girl sing?"

Most people would have little difficulty in finding an answer to the first question. They would take the bucket to the nearest scale and weigh it.

"You've got eight pounds of butter," they would tell me, and would probably think I was a little simple for not doing that myself.

But the second question would either draw an opinion, "Pretty well," or "lousey," or a puzzled look when they discovered that I wanted some kind of measurement of her singing. How do you measure a song?

Some human behavior seems beyond measurement, and in one sense it is. Great artistic works defy measurement. Michelangelo's painting of the Sistine Chapel, or Rodin's famous sculpture "The Thinker," cannot be measured by any scale known to man. Great humanitarian works such as Ghandi's march to the sea which aroused a whole subcontinent against their British rulers are so vast in their impact on human affairs they defy any attempt at quantification. Yet much human behavior can be measured, and these measures recorded. Even the singing ability of a girl can be turned into useful quantities.

If our songstress should hit a few sour notes during a singing lesson her teacher might ask, "How often did you practice last week? How long have you sung each day?"

The teacher knows that the amount of practice done has an important bearing on the quality of singing. The teacher might also ask, "What songs did you practice," and be indignant if the girl only practiced easy songs that she knew well. Most skills improve only if the student constantly reaches further than she can perform now.

The teacher asked, "how often," "how long," and "what" exactly did the singer sing. Counting, timing, and accurate description form the basic measuring systems of the behavioral scientist. They must also become part of the daily work done by any student who wishes to improve his learning skills.

The basic skills a student has to develop to improve his study power can all be measured by one of these three measuring systems. Reading speed can be measured by timing how long it takes to read a passage in a book, and then computing how many words per minute the passage was read (timing and counting). The amount of time spent at your study place is a good rough estimate of how much school work you are doing. Counting the number of times you went to that study place each week can show you how strong a study habit you are developing. These measures of behavior do not need to be elaborate any more than weighing a bucket of butter needs to be difficult. They do need to be done systematically if the student is going to become efficient at his work.

The Value of Recording Your Behavior

There are two reasons that you should keep a record of your day-to-day performance of study skills. One reason has to do with perception and the other with learning.

How can you tell if you have improved at a skill if you can't see the improvement? During the learning period of any skill there is a time of conflict and frustration when the student cannot see whether he is making any progress. In tennis, it is difficult to hit the ball over the net and keep it in the playing court when you are a beginner. After playing and taking lessons for a few weeks the student may lament that he is worse than when he began. The tennis instructor can see the small but significant improvements that the student has made, because of the instructor's experience and skill. The student may not be aware of these gains, so the instructor's encouragement is very important to keep the learner going.

The same holds true for learning skills. If you are fortunate enough to have a teacher to guide you during the first hard weeks you will persevere and overcome the hardships you will experience. If you don't have a teacher to point out your gains, then you must show them to yourself. In order to see the small gains that you will experience at first you *must keep accurate records!*

Let's take one skill, the use of a study place as an aid in strengthening a study habit and question a student about it.

"Did you use your study place the last two weeks?"
"Sure I did," the student replies.
"How often did you use it?"
"Oh, let's see. I usually study every night from Sunday to Thursday, so I must have used it at least five times a week."

The student does not really know how often he went to his study place, he's merely figuring it out based upon this five-night-a-week assumption. See how he handles the next question.

"Did you increase the use of your study place from the first to the second week?"

176   Record Keeping

"Gee, I guess not. Weeell, maybe I did, but I'm not sure."

I have asked many students similar series of questions, and the results usually come out as you have just seen. The next step is to ask the student to produce the records that he has been instructed to keep day-by-day, and actually count the times he used the study place. When students discover that they were at their study place one or two more times the second week than the first week, they are pleased and encouraged. Yet, when they relied on their memory of the past two weeks they were unsure of any improvement. They could not perceive it.

Accurate, tangible daily records will give you the necessary perceptual information to judge your progress. If you see you are making progress you will continue; if you don't see any progress you will quit.

Records as Reinforcement

When you succeed at your learning skills you want to go on and improve your performance even more. Success reinforces your performance and strengthens your skills. Chapter 17 discusses such reinforcement. For the

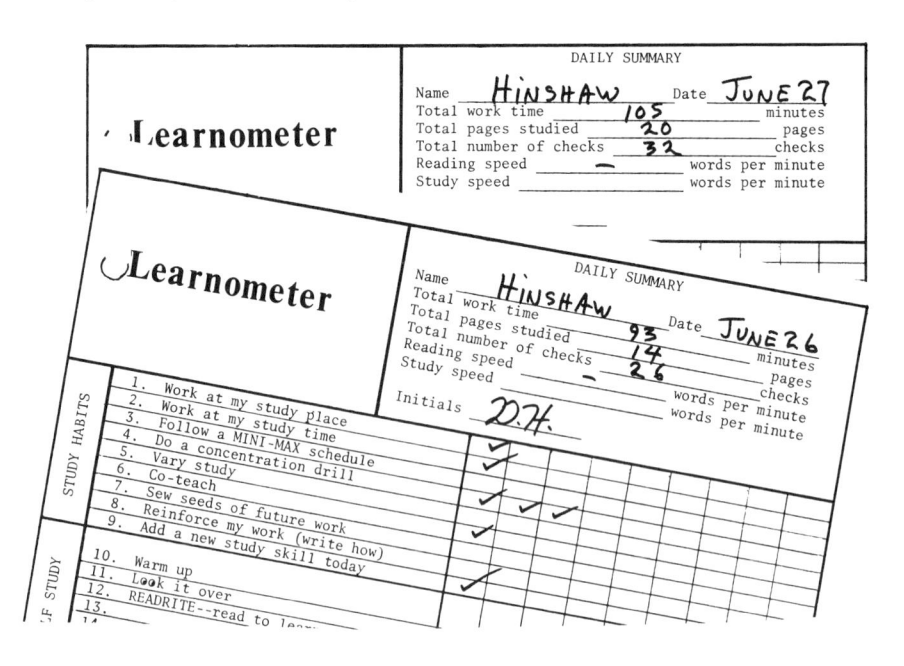

Figure 12-2 Learnometer Daily Summaries

moment all you need to know is that *reinforcement is absolutely essential for efficient learning.* Your records give you that reinforcement.

Every time you check off a skill on the Learnometer you can see your own success and strengthen that skill. Each gain in reading speed recorded on your Reading Speed Record encourages you to improve further. When the reading tests show that you are learning more in less time, you can't help but become excited at your own craftsmanship. These records form a positive feedback loop; the more you succeed the more you want to improve.

Without these records you are left in the never-never land of uncertainty.

"I think my study habits have improved."
"My reading speed is better now than last month, but I'm not sure I have improved in the last couple of weeks."
"I don't seem to be getting anywhere."

Compare those remarks to these:

"I was at my study place, at my study time, every day but two last month, and that was an improvement of four days over the previous month."
"This week I read 425 words a minute. Last week's rate was 420, and last month's was 390!"
"I have 12 percent more checks on my Learnometer this month than I had last month."

Keep records on your learning skills. They will make you look so beautiful!

The Laws

This is a technical chapter dealing with the 15-day plan, so the application of the laws will not be discussed. Can you see which of the laws are put to use in keeping the Learnometer?

3836 Words

CHAPTER 13 — FIGHT BOREDOM WITH VARIETY

"Variety's the very spice of life."   *WRONG!*
William Cowper, 1785

"Variety's the very bread of life."   *RIGHT!*
The Author, 1981

> **Summary**
>
> Boredom is a common study problem. Scientists have researched boredom with fascinating results. Even single cells of your nervous system "turn off" when their stimulation lacks variety. The brain will deny the very existence of object whose stimuli lack sufficient variety. If the brain is totally stimulus deprived it fills the void with its own imagery and we hallucinate. When the world becomes dull to the normal waking brain it also produces images, but we call them daydreams. In both cases the brain is reacting normally to abnormal dullness. The solution to such dullness is to add variety to your life. Vary the stimulation you receive, and your actions.

"If I want to enjoy a daydream I just have to sit down to my studies," a cynical student told me during an interview.

She was complaining that her studies bored her. She felt that if her work was more interesting she would work harder and get better grades. She was not alone, for boredom regularly crops up on the Study Problem Lists. It is a common student study problem.

Boredom — What Is It?

Boredom is the feeling we have when the world appears dull, uninteresting and monotonous. This feeling irritates us and we would like to avoid it, so we try to stay away from boring activities. Boredom can be frustrating if we must continue a dull job. The job has to be done, we're bored, so we become angry at the spot we're in. We feel helpless. Even worse sometimes we feel guilty.

"I suppose I really should be interested in Math. Dad's an engineer," said one student.

"Mom says if I am bored it's my fault, " another student grumbled.

The daydream is a major symptom of boredom. At the end of this chapter you will find out exactly what a daydream is, and how to cope with boredom. Since the practical solution to boredom was partly included in the chapter on concentration (11), the presentation of this solution will be delayed until we have explored the nature of boredom.

The Nervous System

In 1785 science had not even begun to research the nature of boredom, so Mr. Cowper can be excused for calling variety the spice of life. Today we know that variety is the very bread of life. Variety is essential to the normal functioning of people. By variety we mean the moment to moment variations in the stimulation people receive and the actions they perform. Science has discovered that without normal variety the nervous system does some pretty weird things.

Let's examine what happens to the basic building block of our nervous system, the cell called the neuron, when it is deprived of varied stimulation. Figure 13-1 shows the reaction of a frog's skin neuron to the stimulation of pressure. Your skin is peppered with such neurons which tell the brain what is pressing on the skin, where the skin is being pressed and by how much. The top curve in the figure shows how a small probe like the tip of a ballpoint pen was pressed into the skin twice and then released. The bottom line shows the electrical activity of the neuron to the pressure. The short vertical strokes on this line are the electrical messages the neuron is sending to the brain. Where there are no strokes the neuron is not sending any messages.

Notice that the neuron only sends messages when the probe is being actively pressed into the skin. When the probe is held steady, even though it is pressed deeply into the skin, the neuron stops sending messages. Effectively the neuron is saying to the brain, "nothing is happening here." Messages are sent only when there is a *change* in pressure (variety). Human subjects also report pressure sensation on the skin only when pressure is increasing or decreasing.

This property of neurons, called *adaptation*, is a general property of all sensory systems, not just pressure receptors. The same phenomenon can be demonstrated for sight, hearing, warmth, cold, and even pain. Furthermore, not only the neurons of your sensory systems react this way, but neurons within the brain itself adapt (that is, stop sending messages) to continual unvaried stimulation. The property of adaptation is a general property of your nervous system.

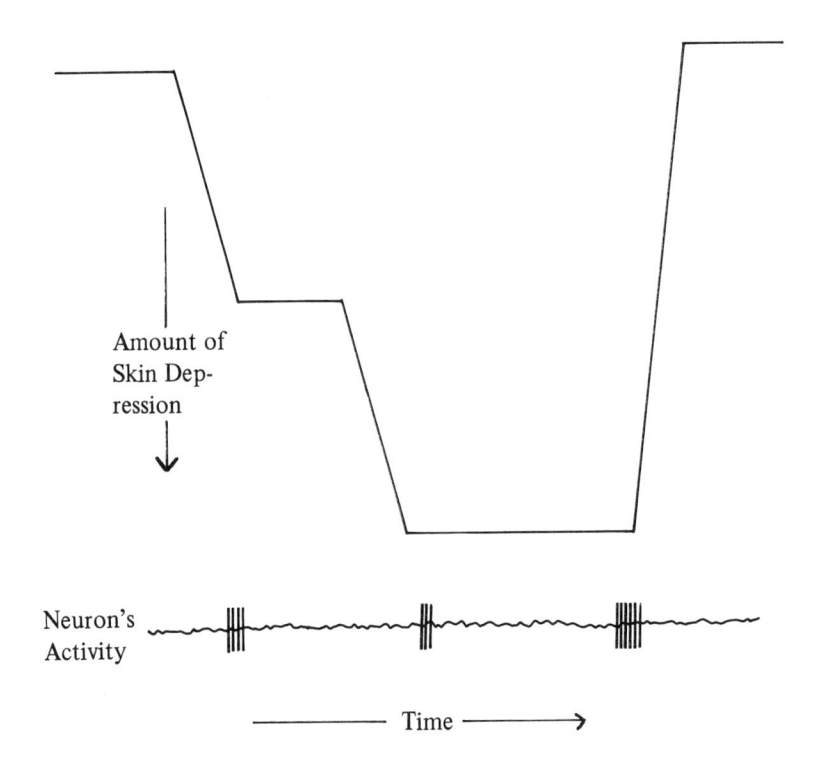

Figure 13-1 The reaction of a single sensory neuron to changes in pressure on the skin. (After Nafe and Kenshalo, 1958)

See The Brain Adapt

You may not yet see the relevance of this discussion to your boredom problem, so let me show you the brain adapting.

When your eye sees something in the world it sends messages to the brain which the brain interprets. Your eye sees black marks on white paper here, and the brain interprets those marks as being letters and words, and the brain assigns meanings to those words. If your eye looks at a stimulus without sufficient variability to it, the brain scans the message it is receiving and says "there is nothing there." That's about what the pressure sensitive neuron was doing when the pressure was held steady.

Figure 13-2 will demonstrate the brain making this interpretation.

Boredom Demonstration

Look at the sharp left circle with one eye. (Cover one eye with your hand and look at the circle with the other). Fixate your gaze firmly on the black dot in the center of the grey circle and slowly count to 15. Don't blink. Observe what happens, namely nothing. The sharp grey circle remains easily visible against its darker grey background for the whole 15 count.

Repeat the above procedure for the blurred grey circle. Notice that as you start to count, the blurred grey circle is clearly visible against the background, but as the count goes on it disappears, and you appear to be staring at a dark grey square without any light grey circle on it at all. If this did not work for you, switch eyes and try again. If it still does not work, you are probably not holding your gaze firmly fixed on the center black dot. Try again.

Once you can make the blurred circle disappear try this variation. As soon as the circle has disappeared shift your gaze to the black X. You will see the circle pop back into view.

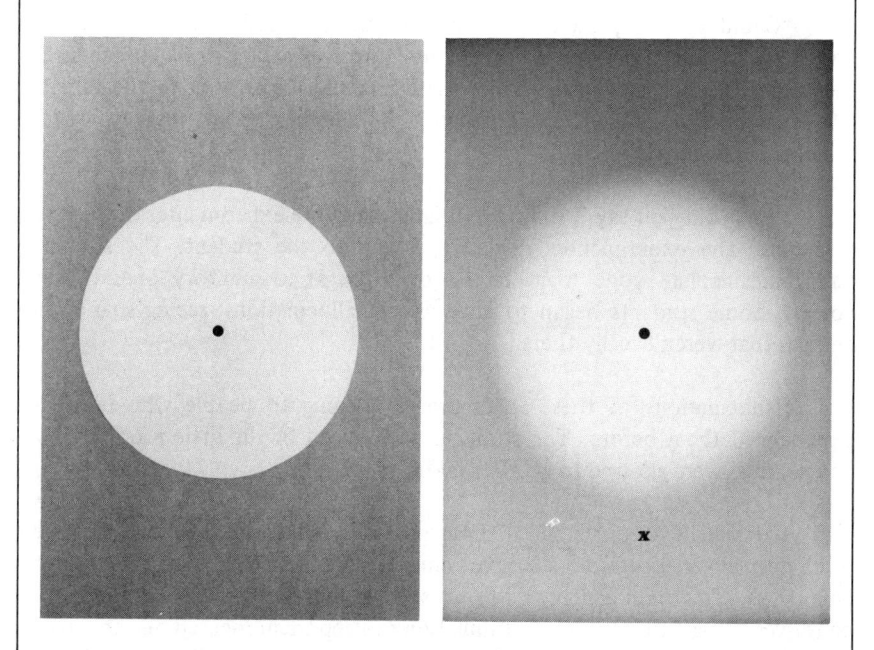

Figure 13 – 2 Demonstration of visual adaptation (Adapted from Cornsweet, 1970)

Effectively the brain is saying, "I'm not getting enough varied stimulation here, so I declare there is nothing there." By blurring the edge of the circle I denied the brain sufficiently varied stimulation for it to give its normal interpretation, "there's a circle there."

Are you convinced that the brain can do some strange things when denied its normal varied stimulation? If not, the next example should convince you.

Stimulus Deprivation

What if I stopped your whole world from varying, instead of just a small circle on a piece of paper? Scientists have tried this experiment, with incredible results.

Students at McGill University were asked to lie as still as they could on a bed in a small soundproofed room. Over their eyes they wore frosted goggles so that all they could see was a film of milky white, no edges (like the blurred circle), and scarcely any color. The room was soundproofed and the gentle hiss of a ventilator fan masked any noise they made breathing or shifting around on the bed. They were asked to remain in this room as long as they could, days if possible, but few remained long.

"Could you do something about the bugs in here," a student asked. He had been in this room for several hours, and was asking the experimenter's help through the intercom system that connected the room to the outside. The experimenter could find no bugs, although the student insisted that he felt them crawling on his skin.

"What did you say," the student later asked the experimenter through the intercom. The experimenter denied speaking to the student. The student's hallucinations had gone from tactile ones (bugs) to auditory ones (unseen voices). Some students began to have visual hallucinations, seeing shapes and animals that weren't really there.

Hallucinations of these kinds are frightening to people who have not experienced them before. The students wanted out of the little room, and, of course, they were allowed to go after taking some tests.

The McGill scientists had demonstrated that if the brain is fully deprived of all normal variation from the environment, (stimulus deprivation), it begins to hallucinate. The brain generates its own stimulation. Our complex brains cannot go for very long without proper stimulation to keep them focused on the outside world. If this stimulation is denied, as in the experiment, the brain fills this void with images of its own which we call hallucinations.

> OF COURSE THERE'S NOTHING IN THERE WITH YOU

Does this have anything to do with you? You don't hallucinate during your studies, or do you?

Daydream Defined

The daydream is the brain's way of filling a dull spot in the day. Your senses are not deprived of stimulation, but the input the brain is receiving is monotonous (how about the 20th French Vocabulary word), and is not providing enough stimulation. The brain then starts to produce images exactly as it did in the above experiment. Since you have a normal sensory input of the world around you, you don't interpret those images as hallucinations, you just call them a daydream.

If it seems that I am stretching the point between you at your desk, and the student in the isolation room, remember that boredom is relative. Things that you find interesting, a friend might not. I suspect that you would find a ride in a modified stockcar around the Charlotte Speedway at 190 MPH interesting, exciting, even terrifying, but not dull. Yet Richard Petty, 100 laps into a 400 lap race on the same speedway, might not be too fascinated. He would be alert and concentrating on his driving, but occasionally he might wonder what he was going to eat for supper, or what was going to be on TV that night. Your excitement is his ho hum.

The brain is using the same process to produce both hallucinations and daydreams. In the former case the images are sensory and appear to be happening out in the world instead of in that student's head. It was the lack of sensory input that the brain was compensating for. In your case the images are internal and you interpret them as being a daydream. In both cases the brain was desperately trying to compensate for the lack of varied information it was receiving.

The problem suggests its own solution.

Variety Beats Boredom

Many of the steps you can take to cope with boredom have been covered in Chapter 11, Concentration, but I will go over them once more.

1. Vary your work. If you find that you are getting bored with math problems, switch to English. If you keep two sets of work handy, you can fight off boredom for hours by switching your work every time you find your mind wandering.

2. Vary your actions. Even if you keep on working at the same material you can vary what you do. In the Readrite technique you vary your actions by Look-Overs, reading, notetaking, and self testing. Instead of just reading the book you have four separate jobs to cycle through, and this variety will help maintain your interest and attention. If you have been reading for awhile, change and work problems, or write. Sitting still too long is pretty dull. Get up and move about. You can study vocabulary while you walk around the block.

3. For especially dull subjects keep your work sessions short, so that you can maintain interest. You can hold your attention to even the dullest subject for five or ten minutes if you know that you will be finished at the end of that time.

4. Racing drivers know that driving becomes a lot more fun if it is done fast. Take a tip from them. When the job becomes dull, work faster.

5. In class, use notetaking and questions to give variety to lecture.

Dull work creeps into our studies sooner or later. It's unavoidable. Don't give in to boredom. As you have just discovered there are ways of fighting it. Don't feel guilty about being bored with some of your studies. The feeling of boredom, that nothing is happening, is your normal reaction to monotony. You react that way from your neurons on up. Cope with dullness in your life the way your brain copes with dullness in its inputs. Get active.

Exercises

1. Study with the books for two subjects open on your desk. Switch your work from one subject to the other every 15 – 20 minutes, or when your mind wanders.

2. During a dull class take notes intensively.

3. Use scraps of time (see Chapter 10) to work at dull repetitive tasks (memorization of any kind).

2,025 Words

CHAPTER 14 - MOTIVATION

> **Summary**
>
> Motivation acts in a cycle whose parts are your needs, your actions, and your goals and incentives. Needs are generally increased by depriving yourself of the thing you need, like food, or money. Since you cannot deprive yourself of schooling, you cannot increase your need for schooling that way. Your motivation to study is better manipulated by changing your incentives or goals. Goals should be concrete and immediate so that you can achieve the success that will raise your motivation. How you act towards your studies also determines your motivation. Acting *as if* you were well motivated towards subjects where your motivation is not high, can change your feelings about them. Learning itself is not directly effected by changing motivation, although your performance is. Better attention and more work will increase your learning, and these behaviors of yours are effected by your motivation.

The Motivation Cycle

If you understand the true nature of motivation then you are in a better position to improve your own motivation. Figure 14 — 1 shows the basic motivation cycle. Motivation is not a simple drive that makes you go when it is operating, and stop when it is not. Motivation has three parts:

1. *Needs* exist inside of you. Hunger, desire for attention, curiosity and a need for fine music are examples of such needs. Some of your needs are biological, like hunger, thirst, and sex. Other needs have been learned and become included in our personality, for example, a love of fine music, a desire to own land, the need for money.

2. The *actions* you take or don't take in answering these needs are part of the cycle. You may be hungry, but how do you satisfy that hunger? Do you eat hot dogs or caviar? Do you snack when your hunger arises, or do you hold off and stuff yourself at mealtimes? If you are curious about your new neighbors, do you go to meet them immediately, or wait until you can arrange for a proper introduction? These actions form an indispensible step in the cycle and are always directed towards incentives or goals.

3. *Goals and incentives* serve a double purpose in this cycle. They serve as the focus for our motivated activity, and by satisfying them we reduce our need. Imagine that while driving to the beach one weekend your stomach contracts in hunger pangs. Right away you start to look for a restaurant (Goal 1.), when you find one you enter and look for a menu (Goal 2.) and a waitress to take your order (Goal 3.). When your food (Final Goal) arrives you gulp it down, and your stomach stops growling. Your need has been satisfied, your hunger motive drops to zero, and another motivation re-instates itself, driving to your beach holiday.

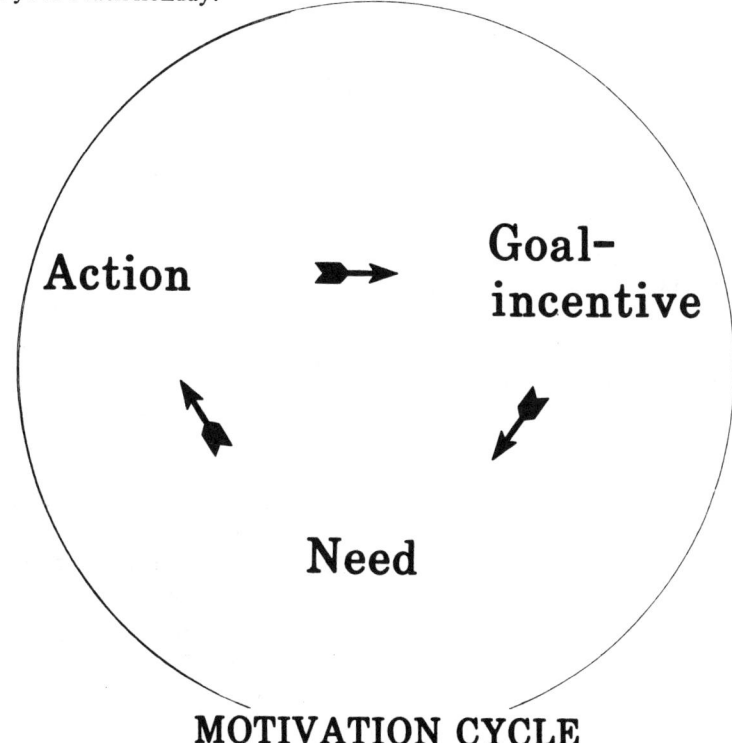

Action ➡ **Goal-incentive**

Need

MOTIVATION CYCLE

Our behavior is always motivated. We are always acting in one motivation cycle or another. Sometimes several needs exist at once, and our behaviors can be complicated in fulfilling these needs. It is quite possible to watch the movie at the drive-in, eat pizza, and kiss your girlfriend, or boyfriend all in the same minute. Working on several motivations at once can be challenging.

Notice the way the cycle operates. The need generates specific action. If you are hungry you don't go and turn the stereo on, you head for the fridge. Needs *energize* your behavior and direct it to the correct goals. If you are not hungry you have no desire to go to the fridge, none of your energy is used to that end. Your hunger not only gets you moving, but it selects the behavior you will perform. Being hungry automatically elimates behaviors such as typing, ballroom dancing, or reading Playboy, and selects behaviors such as looking for food, opening fridge doors, making sandwiches, and so on. Not only does the need select the behavior, but it also determines what goals and incentives you will attend to.

A starving man is not interested in listening to Beethoven's fifth symphony. A sailor home from six months at sea does not want to go to a lecture, he wants to find a girl to take out.

You might assume from all of this that establishing a strong need is the key to successful motivation. That is one-third true. Needs are only one of the three parts of the motivation cycle, and are the most difficult for the student to manipulate.

Deprivation

The standard way of testing for a need, and for establishing one is to deprive yourself of something. Deprive yourself of food for 24 hours and all you can think of is FOOD, FOOD, FOOD! No question there, we have a strong need for food, one of the strongest in our make-up. We have even stronger needs than that. Deprive yourself of water of any kind for a few hours, or deprive yourself of air for sixty seconds. How about those needs?

Deprivation can also be used to test whether you have a real need for something. If all the wallpaper was removed from your home and you did not have a strong urge to go out and buy wallpaper, you have no need for it. Your mother might start looking at wallpaper catalogues, discussing the prices with salesmen and visiting wallpaper stores. She has a need for wallpaper. Fathers know that one of the best ways to get sons and daughters to go out to work is to cut off their sources of money. In our society virtually everybody has a need for money, and jobs are the most ready source.

The general rule is that the more you are deprived the greater the need, within limits. If you are deprived of food, water or air for too long you die, and you have no further need for them. Yet within these limits the longer you go without these substances the greater will be your need. This is also true for acquired needs like property, money, music and good clothes.

A good example of acquired need deprivation is teenage materialism. Teenagers seem to want things in a large way. They want a car, or a stereo or money, and parents sometimes are driven to a frenzy over their demands. Teenagers are usually poorer than adults. They don't have as much money or property as adults do, so their need is high. Dad and Mom have the house, and all the clothes they want, and the boat, and the car. Their son or daughter see all their things, compare it to what they have, and want such things for themselves. Relative to their parents they are deprived.

Scientists have discovered in laboratory studies that behavior can be finely controlled by the amount of need deprivation. If you want a person to work harder at a task. you deprive him more of the incentive he is working for. He'll work harder. On the other hand, if you satisfy a person's need completely he won't work for that type of motivation at all. If you have just finished gorging yourself at a banquet, you lose interest in food. You might even find some offer of a delicacy nauseating.

School Motivation

The average American high school student is satiated with schooling. He has been at school for better than half of his life. School is free and compulsory. He is not deprived of either schooling or learning. This makes it difficult for him to develop a need for more schooling. You would predict that if you could deprive him of schooling his motivation would improve, because his need would rise. This is true.

Some students have their schooling interrupted before they can complete it. They have to leave at an early age to help support a family, or go to war. When these people return to school they return with high motivation. My personal experience was with Vietnam veterans, young men who were drafted and had a break in their schooling between high school and college. Some of the best motivated students I ever knew were these veterans.

Historically people who have been deprived of the opportunity of schooling, become the most fervid supporters of public education when it becomes available to them. At the turn of this century a wave of immigrants from eastern Europe came to America. In their homelands these people, mostly peasants, had no free schooling available to them or their children. When they discovered the public schools in this country, they leaped at the opportunity to educate themselves and their children. Again, deprivation produced high motivation.

You can see the dilemma that the American high school and college student has. One way to increase motivation would be to leave school, but that is not acceptable either to the student or his parents. Increasing the need for education by depriving yourself of it is not a practical manipulation. You have to work on other parts of the motivation cycle.

Goals and Incentives

Incentives are the rewards you strive for in your life. Recognition, attention from loved ones, fine clothes, money, food, sex, all of these are incentives. They can also be called our goals, although we think of these two concepts as being seperate. A goal is something we strive for, and an incentive is the reward we presume we will receive if we achieve our goal. They can be one and the same thing: your goal might be to save $500 from your summer job, and obviously that is the incentive as well. Generally defined, goals and incentives are the things and events in the world that you will work for.

Your motivation can be strongly influenced by incentives. If your father wanted you to work harder at your studies, he might encourage you with these words:

"If you make the honor roll next semester, I will buy you that Italian sports car you have been asking for."

That could act as a strong incentive for you to work. Another kind of incentive is illustrated by these incidents:

The writer who re-writes the short story for the 25th time, although he knows that such perfection will not earn him any more money.

The secretary who re-types a letter because of a single mistake.

The mother who sews late at night to make her daughters first ball gown fit perfectly.

The amateur pilot who flies his sport plane with all the care and accuracy of the professional airlines pilot.

The machinist who strives to work to closer and closer tolerances on every job he does.

The incentives for these people are the satisfactions they get from doing the job well, and succeeding in reaching their goals.

The sports car is an example of an *extrinsic* incentive, while the last five examples show *intrinsic* incentives. Extrinsic incentives come from outside the job you are doing. Money, praise, and recognition from other people are examples of extrinsic incentives. Intrinsic incentives are built into the task itself. Success at doing the job is the universal intrinsic incentive. Both kinds are useful, and can be helpful to you in maintaining your motivation to study.

For goals to realize the benefit of intrinsic incentives they must be *concrete* and *immediate*. There is not much incentive value in the goal of becoming an artist or a doctor, someday. If that is your long-term goal, you have to translate that into goals for today.

"What must I do today to work towards my long-term goal?" is the question you must ask yourself.

Even the most ambitious goal can be broken down into a series of specific sub-goals. Americans might have wanted to put a man on the moon, but that had to be translated into specific goals, like "We nee 4000 quarter-inch steel bolts." You may want to make an "A" in Social Studies, but you have to translate that long range goal into, "how many hours shall I work on Social Studies this week, and what shall I do." If your goals are clearly set and realizable, you will maintain high motivation by the feedback you get from achieving each of those sub-goals. These small successes will accumulate and give you a good feeling about your work. Since you are succeeding in your work you will want to do more; success breeds success.

Action Motivation

Your motivation to study can be improved by what you *do* about study. Inaction will not help your motivation. Not working at a task decreases your motivation. The longer you put off a disagreeable task the more awful it appears.

You can improve your motivation towards a specific course of study by the kinds of actions you take. A real-life example will show this.

Bill Frantz was taking a course in economics and one in anthropology. He needed both of these courses for his degree. He loved anthropology, and loathed economics. His grades at mid-term showed it, he was failing economics and getting A's in anthropology. He asked my advice, and I then asked him a series of questions, about anthropology.

Do you do any extra reading?

Do you attend any special lectures or seminars?

Do you discuss the subject with your friends?

Do you ask questions in class, or after class?

Do you do more than the weekly required textbook reading?

He answered "yes" to all of these questions. I then repeated the series for economics, and he answered "no" to them all. I suggested that he make a plan to start to do these things in economics. His inaction was hurting his motivation in that course. We worked out a plan for the next two weeks, after which he was to report back to me. When he reported back, he admitted that there were some aspects of economics that interested him. At the same time he was taking on these extras, he had developed a regular work schedule for the economics course. He passed the course. He did not love it, but he was working at it steadily, and he had stopped hating it.

Bill was making use of a discovery of social psychology to change his motivation by his actions. This discovery is called by many names, but we shall use the name Balance Theory. Simply stated Balance Theory says that you cannot believe one thing, and do another. You cannot tolerate the internal conflict this produces for very long, and shortly either your beliefs or your behavior will change.

For example, you could not believe that you loved animals and at the same time beat your dog every day. Very quickly you would either stop beating your dog, or you would decide that you hated dogs. Here's a closer-to-life example. A man is buying a new car and has narrowed his choice down to the Volkswagon diesel Rabbit and the Honda CVCC. The Honda salesman calls him at home that evening, and that tips the scales. He buys the Honda. Up to that point he liked both cars equally well. After he has bought the Honda he begins to notice things wrong with the Rabbit that he had not noticed before, it did not accelerate too well, or start easily on cold days, and it had a peculiar smell. All of these points convinced him he had made a good choice.

What he was doing was restoring his system to balance. He had liked the Rabbit fine before he rejected it in favor of the Honda. His rejection and his liking for the car were in conflict, so he started to resolve it by changing his beliefs about the Rabbit. He could just as easily have resolved it by buying a Rabbit, but that option was not open to him. This resolving of the conflict between belief and action is called *dissonance reduction.*

Bill Frantz's feelings about the economics course and his inaction were not in conflict. But, when he started to do the same kind of actions for economics that he was doing for the course he loved, he was in conflict. Since I would not let him stop his actions, his beliefs about the course changed, producing better motivation.

This technique of changing your own motivation is very powerful, and you can do it. I call it "As if" psychology.

"As If" Psychology

The rule for using the "As If" technique is: *To improve your motivation act as if you were well motivated.*

That rule is like the golden rule in that it is easy to state but can be tricky to follow. Let's develop the use of this rule by example.

The first step you have to take to improve your motivation using this technique is to identify the kind of behavior you might have if you were well motivated. You need to look around you to find a similar situation which you like, enjoy, and work hard at, and examine your behavior under those closely.

One of the most skillful users of As If psychology was a salesman by the name of Frank Bettger. In his prime Bettger sold one million dollars of life insurance a year. One day a younger salesman watched Bettger successfully sell a term policy to a businessman.

"Frank, how can you be so enthusiastic about selling that term policy. It's like any other term policy sold by any other company," the young man asked.

Bettger replied, "I can sell with enthusiasm, because I have it. But I did not always have it."

Bettger went on to tell how he almost failed selling insurance. He was ready to quit one day, when he decided to shoot the works. He had nothing to lose, so he sold a businessman as hard as he could and mustered all the enthusiasm he could. It worked! He sold the policy. When he carefully analyzed his own behavior, he figured out that it was the enthusiasm that made the difference. The next sale he sold "as if" he was really enthusiastic about the policy, and it worked again. He kept on doing it, until one day he discovered he had become genuinely enthusiastic about selling insurance. Acting enthusiastic about insurance selling for so long had changed his outlook so that he had become enthusiastic.

Enthusiasm is important for a salesman. Some other kind of behavior may be more important to you in improving your learning motivation. For Bill Frantz seminar attendance, the extra questions, and the discussion were the important behaviors. You must identify the positive behaviors that you can use to help you shift your feelings. Generally these behaviors are the extras you do. The extra work (what kind?), the extra writing, or reading, or discussing you do. Look for them and start to do such extras in the area where your motivation is not the best.

Awareness and Action

Now that you know about the motivation cycle you are in a better position to do something about your own motivation. Motivation can be improved by three approaches:

    a. Directly changing your needs by deprivation. This is not very practical for most of us.

    b. Setting concrete goals you can achieve, thereby receiving the successes you need to continue work, and by arranging incentives for achievement.

c. Using "as if" techniques, to indirectly change your needs, and produce better quality work.

You should also be aware that learning can go on just as well when you are poorly motivated as when you are highly motivated.

Learning and Performance

Psychologists make a distinction between learning and performance. Performance is what you do, and learning is what you store in your head — a potential for future action. Psychologists know that motivation affects performance, but not learning. This is quite a different view than is held my most students.

"Oh, boy, if I could only get motivated I could learn so much better!"

Teachers hear this lament almost daily from their students, and it is true in its basic idea, but false in its major assumption. This assumption is that learning itself will improve with increased motivation. This is not true. The renowned psychologist, Bugelski of New York University has a superb classroom demonstration to show just this fact. Here's how it goes.

"I am going to have you learn a list of eight words," Bugelski tells his class. "Since this is a short list, I am going to mix in another eight words that you are not going to have to learn, so the total list will be sixteen words long, got it?"

"After I say each word you are to repeat it aloud three times. For example, if I say 'apple' you say 'apple-apple-apple' out loud, and so on for all sixteen words. "Furthermore, you are only to learn the odd-numbered words, that is the first, third, fifth, seventh words, and so on to the end of the list. You are *not* to learn the even numbered words, but you are to repeat them back to me out loud just like the odd numbered words that you are supposed to learn.

After he has checked to see if the class has any questions he starts the list.

"Word number one is 'grasshopper'."

"GRASSHOPPER — GRASSHOPPER — GRASSHOPPER," the class chants in unison. They do this for the whole list, then Bugelski pulls a fast one.

"All right," he says, "Write down as many of the words as you can, *both the even and odd numbered words.*"

The students are indignant at this sudden change in the rules.

"You said we had to learn only the odd-numbered words," some angry person will exclaim.

"It's my game," Bugelski replies. "I'll play it the way I want. Now write down as many of the words as you can remember."

Muttering under their breaths the students write the words.

When all the words that the students wrote down correctly from memory are counted a truly amazing result appears. The students remember just as many even numbered words as they do odd numbered words. To the average student this is an astounding result. As far as he could see all the people in that class were motivated to learn the odd words, and not the even words. Since the list is long it would seem that students would concentrate their learning on those odd words alone.

The rule that comes out of this can be stated, "equal performance on tasks of equal difficulty will produce the same learning for both tasks, regardless of any differences in motivation." This rule refutes the old idea that better motivation produces better learning. The rule says that it does not matter that a student hates Spanish and loves mathematics; if they are of equal difficulty for her she will learn as much of one subject as the other *providing that she works equally hard at each subject.*

Motivation, Performance and Attention

If the above rule is true (and it is) then why have we all formed this strong impression that being well motivated makes learning easier, that we learn faster and better with good motivation? We all have a wealth of experience that seems to support this impression, such as this following experience.

Ten-year old Betsy loves school. She dashes eagerly out to catch the bus each schoolday, and goes home every afternoon filled with rich experiences, and a warm sense of accomplishment. Her classmate, Diane, is a reluctant student. She mopes about her classrooms all day, and looks forward to the afternoon bell with eagerness and relief that another day at school is finished. Both have the same IQ's and Betsy brings home excellent report cards, while Diane's are mediocre at best.

You can probably think of two or three personal experiences just like this that seem to show better learning with better motivation. This better learning is an *indirect* result of this motivation, not a direct result. Motivation affects performance, not learning, but of course better performance, harder work, produces better learning.

If Betsy looks forward to her arithmetic as an interesting challenge, she may work two or three more problems each day than Diane does. In a months time she will have forty to sixty more problems worked than Diane, and this extra work will have produced better learning of her arithmetic. *More work produces more learning,* and better motivation tends to produce more work.

Are you convinced? No? I don't blame you. It still sounds too simple, doesn't it? You, just as I do, feel that the work done by a well motivated student is qualitatively better than that of a poorly motivated student. Again, you are right. Here's an example.

Kurt and Michael were learning to type. Miss Johnson, the junior high school teacher, had just demonstrated the typing of a page of manuscript, and the students were practicing. Kurt's paper was finished sooner and had fewer mistakes than Michael's paper. Both had typed a page, so both had the same amount of practice, and both boys were about the same size, maturity, and physical co-ordination. Why the immediate difference in their typing?

Kurt really wanted to type. He wanted to write for the school paper and realized that typing would be a big help. Michael was taking typing because his mother had told him it would be a useful skill. When Michael was asked what he had just learned from the teacher he was able to give a good summary of the teacher's instructions. He hadn't missed anything, and he had tried to put those instructions into practice. Kurt had also learned the instructions, but with a difference.

"I noticed that Miss Johnson's typing was very rhythmical, almost musical in its cadence. She sat very straight in her chair, yet seemed to be relaxed. I tried to do those things when I practiced," Kurt said. Kurt had paid very close attention, not only to what Miss Johnson said, but what she did, and the subtleties of how she did it. His better motivation made him *attend* to the details better than Michael did.

Attention! Better motivation produces better attention. Attending closely can become a habit, and once such a habit is well learned it becomes the multiplier in every learning situation from then on. The student who can attend more closely to his learning over the days, months and years of schooling will gain an enormous advantage.

The girl who wants to be a biologist like her father will start to notice the things he does at his work at an early age. Her brother who wants to be a rock guitarist will not.

The boy who wants to make the high school football team as a running back will see the fakes and moves made by defensive players, that his butterfly collecting brother does not see at all.

The husband and wife who love each other will be aware of changes in mood in each other, that they will not notice in even their closest friends.

To learn well you must be aware, and motivation fine tunes this awareness.

Don't believe that you cannot learn well if you are poorly motivated. You can. If you work at your lessons steadily you will learn. On the other hand, the advantage of being well motivated is that you attend better to your lessons, and you work at them harder. It is better to be well motivated, but poor motivation is not an excuse for poor learning. If you are learning badly then look at your behavior, and solve that problem first.

4,368 Words

SECTION V. THE LAWS OF LEARNING

The learning and study skills described in the previous four sections of this book show you what to do to develop study power. This section shows why you do it. The six laws of learning described here are major learning laws discovered by science in the last century. They are natural laws of human behavior, in the same way that the law of gravity or the laws of friction are natural laws of physics. Such laws describe how the world works. There is a double advantage for you to learn these laws. First, you will see the reasons behind each of the study skills. These skills follow these laws closely, and for that reason you will succeed if you use them. Second, by understanding the laws behind the skills you will be able to apply your study skills in new situations. The student with a deep understanding of what he is doing when he studies will benefit much more than a student who merely knows a cookbook set of rules.

CHAPTER 15 - GRADUALNESS

Learn at the right speed, not too fast, nor too slowly

> **Summary**
>
> Learning is governed by the structure and operation of our memory system. We have a short-term memory, which is used to hold small amounts of information temporarily until it can be transferred to long-term memory. The transfer is accomplished by using the information. Once this information is in long-term memory it is held permanently. Short-term memory is stored by the continuing electrical activity of the brain, whereas long-term memory is stored as a physical structure in the brain. Forgetting from short-term memory is fast and is caused by the changing of the electrical activity. Long-term memory forgetting is caused by interference from information already stored. Learning too quickly builds up inhibition which causes forgetting. Each task must be properly paced to be learned efficiently.

Introduction

These last three chapters will show you some of the facts and theory behind the laws of learning underlying the skills taught in this book. If you are a practical person you may feel that these chapters are not necessary, and that all you need to know is how to learn, not why you must learn that way. On the contrary, if you are a practical person these chapters are of great value to you.

The skills you have learned in the previous chapters can be used for most learning, but you will find learning situations where these methods don't fit perfectly. No method can cover all situations. Learning these skills without understanding the underlying principles is like learning to cook solely by following recipes in a cookbook. If you have one recipe for a cake, you can make that cake just fine, but if you don't understand why you are using baking powder, eggs, flour, and so on, you will not be able to improvise, nor will you be able to figure out the fault when something goes wrong. If the cake turns out flat and heavy, and you understand that it is the action of the baking powder that gives a cake its loft and lightness, you can correct yourself next time.

Another analogy will show how knowledge of basic facts and theory can be practically useful. A week ago a Volkswagen stalled in the middle of an intersection crammed with 5 p.m. traffic. I asked the driver what was wrong, and he he shook his head and said, "It won't go." I know a little mechanics, so I tried to start it. Shortly I had figured out that he was not getting any spark. A wire from the coil to the distributor had come loose, so I re-attached it, and sent him on his way. Easy for me, impossible for him. He did not understand the way the machine he was driving worked.

He did not know anything about the laws of electricity, or mechanics, or hydrodynamics. As long as the car worked he could drive it. When it did not work he had no idea how to get it going again. Also, he was not achieving the best use of his machine. I could see at a glance from the dirty engine, and by the way the brakes felt that he was neglecting the car and eventually this was going to cause more breakdowns, poor performance, and loss of use.

What could be more practical than learning enough about *how* a car works so that you can get good service from the machine, and be able to figure out what is wrong when it does not work? The same reasoning applies to you as a student. What could be more practical than knowing enough about your learning and memory so that you can get good use out of them and be able to figure out what is wrong when you have trouble learning or remembering?

We'll start our discussion on the scientific basis of learning and memory with a look at the structure of your memory.

Memory Structure

In your brain you have at least two different kinds of memory (see figure 15-1), a short-term memory and a long-term memory. These two memories serve different purposes and operate differently. The short-term memory holds information temporarily, while the long-term memory is for permanent storage. You might hold a telephone number in your short-term memory for a few seconds while you dialed it, but then you would forget it, because you would not need it again. You would store new words of the English language in your long-term memory because you would use them over and over again in your life.

The figure shows that information to be learned flows *through the short-term memory* into long-term memory. This figure is an adaptation of a theory of memory functioning by two research psychologists, R. C. Atkinson and R. M. Schiffrin (1968). Their theory summarizes a vast amount of research data and shows how the different parts of memory work together. Each of these parts will be considered in turn.

Short-term Memory

Let's take an item of information and trace it through your memory

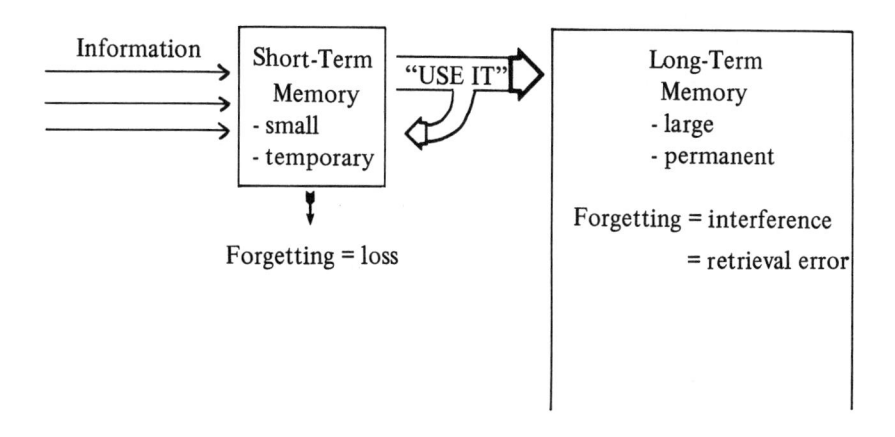

```
Information  →  Short-Term    "USE IT"⇨    Long-Term
             →  Memory                     Memory
             →  - small                    - large
                - temporary                - permanent

                   ↓                       Forgetting = interference
                Forgetting = loss                     = retrieval error
```

Figure 15-1 The human memory system. (Adapted from Atkinson & Schiffrin, 1968)

system. When you started to learn to drive a car you had to learn that the pedal you pushed on the floor to make the car go was called the accelerator. You heard your mom or dad or driving teacher call this pedal by that name but you did not pay much attention the first time you heard it. Then came your first driving lesson.

"To drive off you put the car in gear and gently depress the accelerator."

You look blank and ask, "Depress the what?"

Patiently your driving instructor points to the floor and says again, "That pedal is the accelerator."

"Accelerator, accelerator, accelerator," you mutter to yourself as you drive away from the curb.

You have now taken that bit of information and plugged it into your short-term memory. By muttering it to yourself you keep it going in short-term memory. Items stored in this memory do not stay there very long, and have to be actively kept there by rehearsal. Scientists are not yet sure how long information is held in short-term memory, but it probably remains there for *a few seconds on up to an hour* at the most.

Lloyd and Margaret Peterson, a husband and wife team of research psychologists, demonstrated the very short-term storage we have for lists of alphabet letters (Figure 15-2). Demonstration 1, based on the Peterson's experiment, will allow you to see for yourself how briefly you hold information in your short-term memory. Their experiment showed that you forget almost all of the letters you put into short-term memory within 20 seconds. This is amazing when you consider that their subjects were asked to remember only three letters of the alphabet at a time.

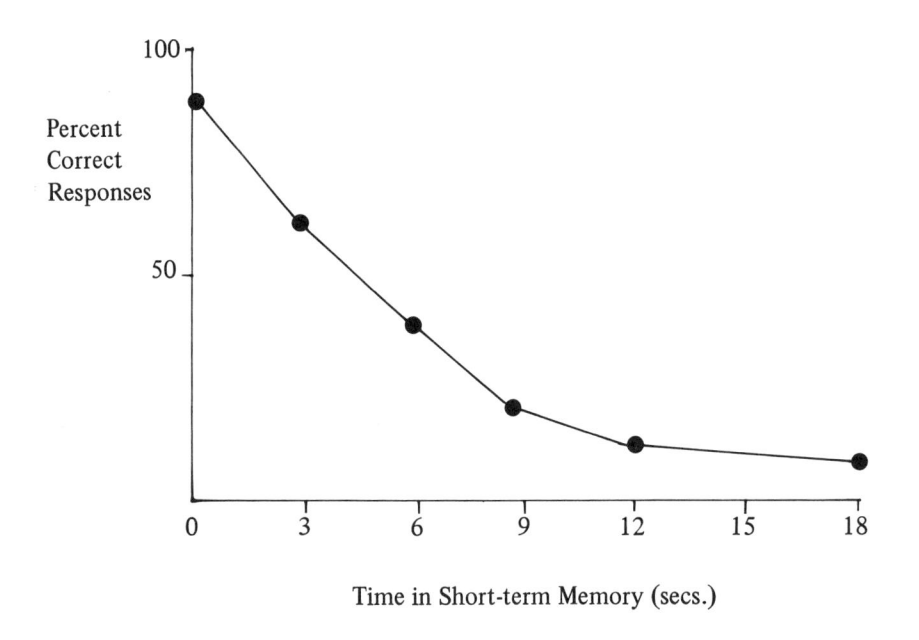

[Graph: Percent Correct Responses vs. Time in Short-term Memory (secs.)]

Figure 15-2 Recall of three letters when rehearsal is stopped (Adapted from Peterson and Peterson, 1959)

If your driving instructor was a clumsy teacher he might have said, "So you don't know what the accelerator is. Let's learn some parts."

Pointing as he spoke he began to say, "That's the accelerator, that's the choke, that's the clutch, that's the carburetor, . . ."

"Wait a minute!" you say. "I can't remember all that at once. Slow down, please."

You have discovered that your *short-term memory is small.* This memory has a very limited capacity for information. It has to be fed slowly so it can process the information. The capacity varies slightly from person to person, and from time to time, but seven items seem to fill it up most of the time. Demonstration 2 will let you find that out.

Short-term memory does not seem to be much of a memory, does it? It can hold only a few bits of information, and unless you keep rehearsing them they will disappear within a few seconds. Why do you have such a feeble memory anyways?

We need a temporary memory. We need it to allow us to remember the words at the beginning of a sentence so that we can form a sensible ending to the sentence a few moments later. We don't want to remember those beginning words forever, just until the sentence is finished. As you walk into a room you look at the chair you are going to sit in, turn your back to it and sit. Silly as it may sound, you have to remember that the chair is there after you have turned around so that you can seat yourself properly. Every moment of every day we are barraged with information that we need to use for a moment or two, but do not need to store for a long time. That's the purpose of short-term memory, to hold information temporarily.

Have you ever read a paragraph, felt that you understood it and knew what was in it, but a few moments later could not remember any of it? I'm sure you have. It happens to all of us. I call this the *student's illusion.* You have the illusion of learning, because your short-term memory is holding that paragraph temporarily. You have this feeling that your work is done. Not so, as you will see shortly; if you have not used this information in some way it will be quickly lost from your short-term memory.

Interestingly enough, when engineers started to build high speed electronic computers they discovered that they needed short-term memories in them. They had to put these short-term electronic memories, called buffers, between the outside world and the computer's main permanent memory storage, or the machine would not work efficiently. They had re-discovered nature's short-term memory.

How is the short-term memory storage connected to the long-term storage?

Use it or Lose it

As Figure 15-1 shows you must use the information to move it into long-term memory. The figure also shows that if you use the information (rehearsal is a form of usage) you will replug it back into short-term storage and extend its life there.

If every bit of information held in your short-term memory automatically went into long-term storage as well, you would not need your short-term memory at all. Why have two memories that are doing the job of one? You need a criterion to decide what information to take from short-term memory and store it in long-term memory. The criterion is so simple it is elegant. Only useful information will be stored in long-term memory. You decide what is useful by using it.

Short-Term Memory Demonstration 1.

Have a friend read the letter-number sets to you out loud one set at a time; time your performance for about 20 seconds. As he reads each pair, you repeat the number out loud and count backwards from that number by three's as fast as you can, again out loud. At the end of the time try to remember the letters.

Example: Your friend says, "QSX 231."

You say, " 231, 228, 225, 222, 219, . . ." and so on until the 20 seconds is up. Then you try to remember the letters.

Try doing half a dozen sets in a row. You will probably remember the letters for the first two sets, then watch what happens. Try doing it for a shorter time period, say 8 seconds, and compare the results.

MKR 321	GQZ 570	XMH 131	DJH 882
NPB 148	XDB 979	NQK 726	QCN 317
CXJ 389	FHJ 937	BJG 523	DJZ 549
QZM 973	XBN 726	ZMK 837	BFM 105
CSF 117	FJC 610	SZQ 865	CGJ 324
PJZ 433	RBM 978	CFP 442	XKB 940

When you drive to school in the morning you see dozens of car license plates, but you don't need to remember them so you don't bother to learn them. You do need to know your own license number, if only to fill out credit card sales slips when you buy gasoline so you use it. You say it to yourself when you first get the license; you write it down. This usage stores the information in long-term memory. If you don't use it you lose it quickly from short-term memory.

The rule is simple. What you use, you remember. What you don't use, you forget. That is a solidly established scientific fact. It also makes sense. Why clutter up our brains with a trash pile of useless information?

Long-term Memory

Long-term memory is a vast, permanent storage. Here is where you keep all the information you will need in the future to live your life successfully. You store your entire language in there, all the words, all the rules of grammar, all the subtle shades of meaning of those words. Here is where you keep the programs that move your body to work, to play, to sing and to weep, to run frantically or to rest calmly. Any skills you have learned are stored in here. We don't know its size. As far as we know nobody has ever filled their long-term memory, even if they kept learning for a hundred years. Your long-term memory seems to have infinite capacity.

Information stored in your long-term memory is held there permanently. Once stored, it is not lost.

"Aha, I gotcha!" you say. "If my long-term storage is permanent, why is it that I forget information I have stored in there?

No argument about the forgetting, but if you can wait until the next section you will see that forgetting in long-term memory happens, even though the information is still stored there. Patience.

Long-term storage is a permanent structure in the brain, whereas short-term memory is a temporary electrical signal of the brain. Scientists have demonstrated this in a number of ingenious ways. If a hibernating animal, like a hamster, has its body cooled down to near freezing temperature, it goes to sleep. When its body is cooled, the electrical activity of the brain stops, yes, it stops. You cannot measure any electrical activity there at all, even though the normal warm and awake brain of the hamster buzzes with electrical signals. When the hamster is warmed up again, it awakes, scampers around its cage, and remembers. Any information the hamster has stored in its brain before it was cooled is still there. If it had learned to run a maze before chilling, it would remember how to run it after chilling.

If you take the same little fellow and disrupt the electrical activity of its brain with a large electrical shock, you will destroy its short-term memories, but not its long-term ones. Long-term memory cannot be an electrical signal, so logically it should be a structure.

Think of permanent memories as photographic prints or phonograph records filed in the brain, and you will have some idea what is meant by a permanent structure. Short-term memory, on the other hand, is like the electrical signal flowing through the wires of your radio, producing music and words. As soon as you turn off the electricity the music is gone, and no record is left behind.

Short-term Memory Demonstration 2.

Have a friend read each of the sets of numbers below one digit at a time slowly. When he finishes the set, you repeat back the digits in the order they were given. Note how many you get right in each set.

Example: Your friend says, " 2 3 7 8."

You say, "2 3 7 8," or as many as you can.

After you have done the left hand sets this way, do the right hand sets, but this time you say the numbers in reverse order. See if you can figure out what has happened in short-term memory terms.

357	873
5837	6724
09768	21869
163752	597682
2795403	2139467
14250361	41263078
397452860	814029875

What kind of a structure in the brain is long-term memory? We are not sure, but we are getting some clues. Most brain-cell structures are built of *proteins,* also proteins catalyze the production of structures. It is pretty safe to say that without protein no brain structure could be built. If the hamster's brain is injected with a protein poison like puromycin, it cannot produce any protein for a few hours. If during those few hours the hamster is trained in a task he will learn it temporarily, but not permanently. Without the proteins to build the memory structure long-term memory storage cannot happen.

To summarize, short-term memory, because of its small size and temporrary storage, acts as a bottleneck in the processing of information. Once the information is used and stored in long-term memory a structure is created that will keep this information for you the rest of your life. But, you still can forget.

Forgetting

When you can't remember something which you know you have learned you say you have forgotten it. You forget from both of your memory storages, but the manner of the forgetting is different for each storage.

Short-term memory forgetting is simply a *loss of information*. The facts are not stored permanently, and in a short while they are gone. Since the short-term storage is electrical in nature, it is reasonable to believe that the electrical signal fades out, or is replaced by more recent signals. Either way, it is lost. When you forget the telephone number you have just looked up, before you dial it, it is really gone, so you had better look it up again, and rehearse it while you walk to the phone.

In long-term memory the information is not lost; it is still there in storage, but you pull out the wrong "file." When you are asked the date of the American Revolution and you say, "1861," you have pulled out the wrong file. You went looking for the Revolution's date in your long-term memory storage and grabbed the file with the date of the Civil War. Practically the result is the same: you have forgotten the proper date. You have these two dates on file, and the Civil War date has interfered with your attempt to recall the date of the Revolutionary War. This is called *interference forgetting*.

Since the 1930's a growing body of scientific evidence points to interference forgetting as the major form of forgetting in long-term memory. Every time scientists tried to prove that information was being lost from long-term memory, they failed. The information remains, and causes forgetting by interference. When you consider all the information you have stored in long-term storage, it should not surprise you that occasionally one piece of information interferes with another piece being recalled.

Perhaps another example of interference forgetting will help you see how it happens.

The first racquet game I learned to play was badminton. After playing it for years I tried to learn to play tennis. I had a difficult time because every stroke I made with the tennis racquet used the badminton technique, and it did not work. Power strokes with the badminton racquet are done with a flexed wrist, but the tennis racquet is heavier and requires a firm wrist. My memories of how to play badminton were interfering with my tennis learning. I never did learn to play tennis very well.

Another kind of forgetting is caused by changing stimuli from your environment, but that properly belongs in the next chapter.

The more distinctive your memory files are the less likely you are to suffer from interference forgetting. When you learn any fact you must learn it clearly and distinctly from any similar facts you may have already stored, or may store in the future. That sounds much more difficult than it is. In practice you distinguish one fact from another by comparing them and noting the differences and similarities. You also note the context that the fact is imbedded in. Using *comparison*, and *developing relations* between isolated bits of information is the style of the intelligent, efficient learner. That person is labelling his files carefully, to minimize interference forgetting. This careful filing takes time.

You can see that the structure and functioning of your memory system demands some time to do its job properly. You have to feed information to it slowly or you overload the short-term memory. You can usually tell when that is happening, you feel strained and even confused by too much happening, too fast. Once an item is in short-term memory you need to use it some way to move it into long-term storage. You can learn (that's the name we give to this *transfer* from short to long-term memory) by simple repetition, saying a vocabulary word over and over again, or kicking a soccer ball over and over again until you do it right. But if you make your repetitions meaningful by comparing your new fact with others that you already know, or looking at your new fact in as many ways as possible, your long-term memory will be filed better. You will be less likely to forget it through interference.

Learning Inhibition

Before we leave the topic of learning and memory let's discuss a couple of interesting facts about learning that indicate that gradual learning has advantages over crammed learning.

Figure 15-3 shows the learning curves produced by students in a motor task in a four (4) day period. They learned the task a bit more each day. Notice that as they start learning each day their performance is higher than it was at the finish of the previous day's work. They seem to be able to do better at the beginning of each day than they did at the end of the previous day. Strange! To understand this jump in performance at the beginning of each day's work you need to understand response inhibition.

To explain this jump, scientists use the concept of *inhibition*. As the subject in this experiment works at the list on each day, he develops an inhibition, a resistance to further work. He is not tired, but his brain is effectively saying to him, "Enough, I don't want to do any more of this." This causes the person to make mistakes, thereby lowering his score at the end of the day. The next day when he is fresh, the brain is not inhibited so his performance at first does not have mistakes, and you see the jump in the curve. This inhibition against continuing with a repetitive task suggests that you should space out monotonous work so that you can refresh yourself between bouts.

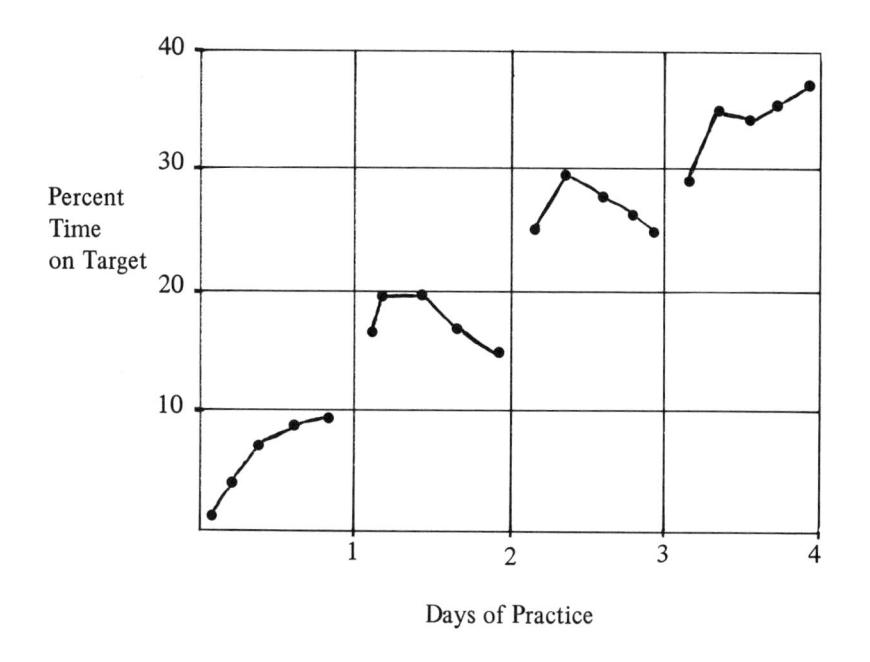

Figure 15-3 Their learning curves show the jumps in performance that the rest between days work can cause. (Adapted from Kimble and Shatel, 1952)

Learning Speed

Other experiments show that for learning facts there is a "best" learning speed. This speed will vary from task to task. Trying to learn too quickly produces a lot of the inhibition, and you make a lot of mistakes. This means that the facts are not properly labelled when they are filed so you forget them. This is a lot of wasted effort, and very inefficient learning. Exam cramming is an example of such learning. You seem to be able to hold the crammed information for a brief while, but it is soon lost and has to be re-learned.

Learning too slowly can be inefficient also. Sometimes it is better to work at a complex learning task for a long solid block of time. If the learning requires that you understand involved relationships, you need to struggle through the material all at once to find that understanding. Spacing out that kind of learning can be inefficient, because you have to have such a long warm-up each time you work to pick up where you left off.

The rule is to go as fast as you comfortably can. Don't dawdle over your studies, don't rush at them, pace yourself.

The Law of Gradualness

All of the scientific facts and theory discussed here point out that learning can't be rushed. You need to pace your learning to do it correctly. This is the law of gradualness.

3,970 Words

CHAPTER 16 - STIMULUS CONTROL AND SPECIFIC PRACTICE

Learning stimuli = remembering stimuli (Stimulus Control)

Learn it as you'll use it (Specific Practice)

Summary

Early experiments showed that animals can lose the learning they have achieved if they are distracted by outside stimuli. Scientists now control for this by training animals and people in specifically constructed rooms that totally control environmental stimulation, the technique known as stimulus control. When you are trained to a particular stimulus, you react better to that stimulus than to any other stimulus. Also, if the background environment is changed between learning and later recall, your recall is degraded. Because we react so sensitively to changes in stimulation, the law of stimulus control states that the stimuli should be the same for learning and later recall.

Similarly the actions you take when you learn a task should be the same as the ones you will take later when you try to remember what you have learned, the law of specific practice. Experiments demonstrate that forgetting is higher when two similar responses are stored in memory to the same stimulus, than when the responses and stimuli are very different. Athletes make use of this law by training themselves as closely to competitive conditions as possible.

STIMULUS CONTROL

Pavlov's Dogs

The dog was starting to condition to the sound of the bell. When the bell was rung the dog started to salivate. It was learning that the bell was a signal for food.

Suddenly the door opened and a medical student walked through the laboratory. Tail wagging slowly, the dog watched him pass. When the dog was tested again with the bell he did not salivate, nor the next time, and barely the third time.

The researcher called a halt to the experiment for the day. The dog had "de-conditioned." The experiment was part of the pioneer learning studies of Professor Ivan Pavlov, the Russian Nobel prize-winning physiologist. Professor Pavlov made many important discoveries, one of which was the need for *stimulus control* during learning experiments. The slightest distraction could ruin a day's work. Generations of behavioral scientists since the time of Professor Pavlov's early experiments at the turn of the century have confirmed this finding. Learning is a delicate process, vulnerable to any variation in stimulation from the environment.

By stimulus control the modern researcher means taking total control of the animal's environment while it is learning. This is accomplished by using some elaborate and expensive apparatus.

Scientific Apparatus

The Skinner Box is an apparatus widely used for learning experiments. I am going to describe this apparatus so that you will see the extreme degree of stimulus control that scientists have found necessary for learning experiments. The better the control, the faster and smoother the learning is.

The apparatus shown in Figure 16-1 is a Skinner Box. Every possible sense modality is controlled, sight, hearing, touch, and when necessary smell and taste. The sounds that the animal hears are controlled three ways. First, the whole apparatus is placed inside a sound insulated box so that the animal is shielded from any noise made in the laboratory by the experimenters, other apparatus, or other animals. Second, to be doubly sure that the animal is not distracted by any noise seeping through the sound proofing, a small ventilator fan provides a background hum . Third, the experimental sound stimuli, tones, clicks, buzzes, or whatever the experimenter wants to use are fed into the box via an electronic speaker system. This system regulates the timing, intensity and quality of the sounds used for experiments in milliseconds, decibels and fractions of frequencies. The only sounds that the animal can hear that the experimenter does not control totally are those made by the animal itself.

The same degree of control is imposed on what the animal can see. The light in the box is constant, no light enters from the outside, and the stimulus lights are regulated with the same degree of care that sounds are. Even the amount of food that the animal eats as reinforcement is carefully measured out.

By controlling the animal's environment this way the experimenter can easily train it. For example, a pigeon can be trained to peck a lighted key 5,000 times an hour for food with a few minutes' training.

The stimulus control that is so successful with dogs and pigeons also works for people. Scientists don't put people in boxes, but they do construct special rooms in laboratories to achieve the same effect. These rooms will be soundproofed, carefully lighted and the experimental task will be as carefully regulated as it is for the animals. The general rule applies here as well, the more carefully the stimuli are controlled, the easier it is for a person to learn.

Look at the stimuli that effect your behavior in your everyday learning. Are they helping you learn or are they making it more difficult for you to learn? By using stimulus control you can increase your learning efficiency.

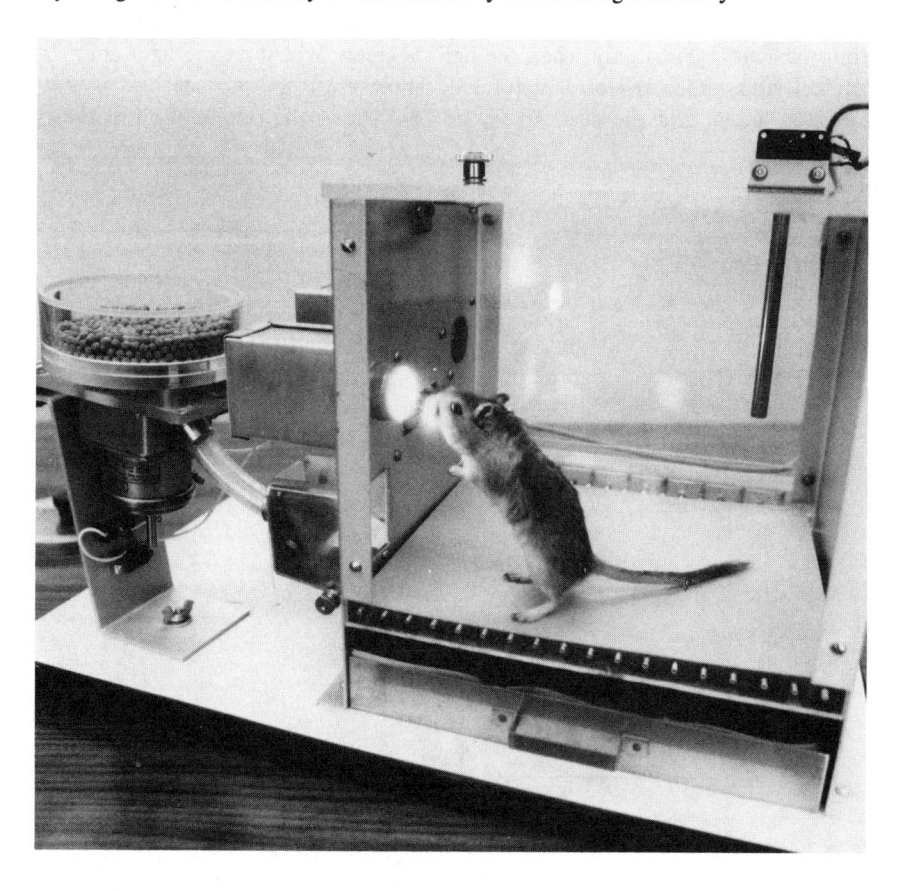

Figure 16-1 A Skinner box for Gerbils. The animal has learned to press a lever for the food when the light turns on.

Stimulus Generalization

By using the Skinner Box the experimenter controls the experimental stimulus to a high degree. If he was training a pigeon to peck a key lighted from behind with a green light, he would control the wavelength of the light. He would use a special machine called a monochrometer to produce a green light that was constant within a few wavelengths throughout the experiment. The intensity and the timing of the light would also be controlled.

Once the pigeon has been trained to peck the key to that particular shade of green, he will peck fast whenever the light is turned on. Figure 16-2 shows that if the wavelength of the light is changed the bird does not peck as much, and if the color is changed enough the bird almost ceases pecking entirely. This is called *stimulus generalization*. You must understand that the pigeon is given reinforcements (grain) only when the light is green. Whenever the light color is changed from green the bird is not fed. These are tests . . . the bird is also tested on green, and the curve in Figure 16-2 shows the results of all of these tests.

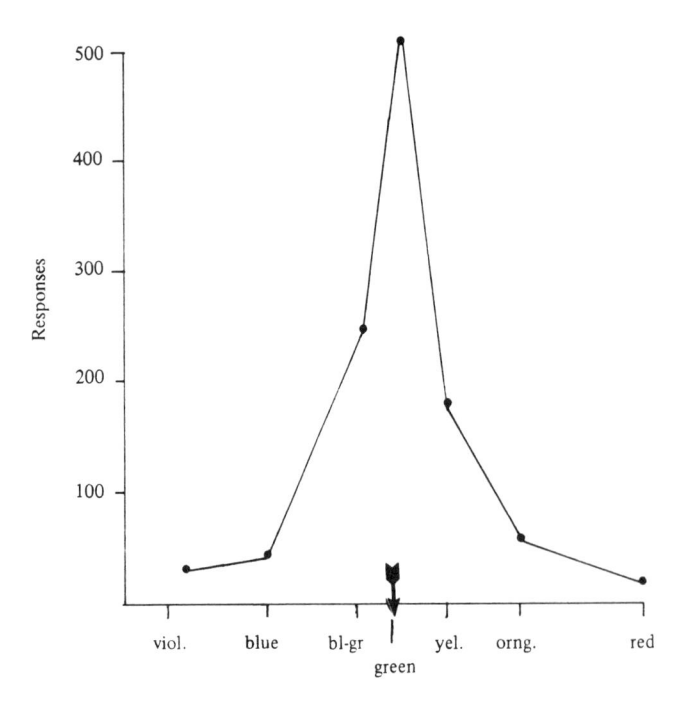

Figure 16-2 Stimulus generalization curve for a pigeon trained to peck at a green light (↓) (Adapted from Guttman and Kalish, 1958)

People also show stimulus generalization. You will respond to stimuli other than the one you were trained on, but your responding is less. You will jump, clap and cheer when your high school band plays your school fight song, but you will show mild interest when they play another school's fight song. If you learned that World War II started on the 7th of December, 1941, you could probably give the date quickly if someone asked you, "When did World War II begin?" But, if they phrased the question, "What date did the second great war of this century start," you might hesitate slightly before you tentatively offered an answer. The stimuli of the second question are not exactly the same as the ones used when you learned the date, so your response is weaker.

Stated positively, *the law of stimulus control says that the closer the stimuli used when you learn a response resembles the stimuli you will use when you remember, the better remembering will be.* This is the basic reason for exerting stimulus control. You want to avoid changing stimuli between learning and remembering, so you control them. An extreme example of this would be the student who does all of his study for a course in the room he will take the exam in. That will be good stimulus control, but that is not really necessary. There are limits to which you need to carry this principle.

Context

The stimuli from the world of a learning person can be divided into two sets, the stimuli that are pertinent to the learning task and those that form the background or context. When you learn that **H+** is the symbol for hydrogen, that letter and the plus sign are the pertinent stimuli, and everything else is context. The remaining words on that page of your chemistry book, the room you are sitting in, even your stray thoughts all form a context for the stimuli of **H+**.

Changing context between learning and remembering will also degrade your remembering. One experiment had people learn a list of words in a well lit classroom. Half of the people learning these words were tested in the same classroom a day later, the other half were tested in a dusty, poorly lit attic. Another group learned in the attic, and were also divided into attic, classroom test groups. The groups that were tested in the same room they learned the words in remembered more words than those who were tested in another room. It did not matter whether the same room was the attic or the classroom. Changing context between learning and remembering caused forgetting.

My own research has shown that changing contexts can cause forgetting in short-term memory as well.

Stimulus Control

When you learn anything, the stimuli you sense during learning form a key that will help you retrieve the proper response from your memory when you try to remember. If the *retrieval key* is duplicated perfectly at the time you remember, you cannot help but unlock the correct response. If the key is changed by changing the pertinent or contextual stimuli, then you run a greater chance of forgetting.

The most general way of stating the law of stimulus control then becomes:

The more learning stimuli resemble remembering stimuli the better you will remember.

This law of learning is applied in dozens of ways in the study skills you have learned from this book. It is an important law to use. For example, when you study from a book test yourself, because the test questions you use will be stimuli in tests given by the teacher. Or again, when you learn a new sport skill, it is important to learn it in the same context as it will be used, with the same equipment. It is better to practice your golf swing with a real club and ball on a golf course or driving range, than doing dry runs in your office or living room with a broom.

Behavioral scientists divide learning tasks into the two parts, the stimuli and the response. So far in this chapter we have spoken of the effects of varying the stimuli. Let's consider the response.

SPECIFIC PRACTICE

A prime goal of learning is to make remembering as easy as possible. In the most general sense remembering means any kind of information retrieval from your long-term memory. This would include being able to recall the facts to write an essay in a history exam, or being able to recognize a face again, or being able to perform the proper movements in skills of all sorts. Your long-term memory is the storage for all this information and you want to be able to find it easily.

The previous sections stressed that keeping the stimuli the same when you learn and remember will aid remembering. In this section the rule is: keep the responses the same when you learn a task as when you remember it and you will remember it better. This is the *law of specific practice*.

The stimuli serve as the key to unlock the correct file in your memory to produce the information. That information is going to produce some kind of response. You can only get out of storage what you put in.

Athletic coaches have known for centuries that the training an athlete does must be specific to the sport. You cannot develop general speed, or strength or endurance. A bike racer who could race 50 miles within a couple of hours could not run half that distance in double the time. Marathon running and biking use very different sets of muscles and skills. The heart, lungs and circulation of both the runner and the biker would be equal to either task, but the leg muscles and nervous system would not.

The racer who trains for 100 meter or 200 meter sprints must train very differently than the track athlete who runs 3000 meter or 5000 meter races. The sprinter would do a little long, slow distance to build up a base of general fitness, but he would spend his most serious training on speed work on the track. The 5000 meter man would spend 90 percent of his running on long, slow distance, and only a small fraction on speed work. Yet both are runners.

After the basics have been learned in any competitive sport, the best practice becomes competition itself. This gives the participant the chance to use his skills exactly as he is supposed to use them. Competitors always seek out others who are slightly better than they are so that they can learn how to be better themselves. They are using the law of specific practice very concisely, namely if you want to play better, play better.

Minimize Interference

In the previous chapter forgetting due to interference was explained. Interference occurs when the wrong response is drawn out of long-term memory by mistake. One of the ways of minimizing interference is to tightly control the stimuli used to form that retrieval key. Another way of minimizing this interference is to use exactly the same responses during learning that you intend to use when you remember. When you do that, only the correct responses are stored in memory, so only the correct responses will be retrieved later on.

A classic example of this is learning to speak a foreign language. The pronunciations that you give to the words as you learn them are the ones you will use later when you speak. If you have not learned the correct pronunciation from the very first day, you have a great deal of difficulty correcting yourself later on. You have all those false pronunciations stored in your long-term memory and they are providing a lot of interference. Learn it right the first time.

I would estimate that there are several thousand experiments exploring the effects of specific practice. I will show you just one of these. In this experiment the person learns to associate a stimulus and a response. The stimulus is a nonsense syllable, the response the subject makes is a word, for example, "QFZ-writer." The person is shown a list that is made up of pairs like this example. He has to learn that when he sees QFZ he must respond "writer." QFZ is the stimulus and "writer" is the response. Figure 16-3 shows examples of such lists.

First List	Second List-Different	Second List-Same
BJH-Pickle	HNQ-cat	BJH-potato
HFK-mustard	XMG-trout	HFK-rice
JZH-relish	JSB-eagle	JZH-cornmeal
GXC-pepper	TJH-frog	GXC-oatmeal

Figure 16-3 Lists used in Interference Experiments

After the person has learned the original list, he is given a second list to learn. This second list can be constructed one of two ways: (1) both the stimuli and the responses of the second list are different than the first list, or (2) the stimuli of the second list are the same as the first list but the responses are different. Now this person has two sets of responses stored in memory.

As you would expect when the preson has two different responses stored to the *same set of stimuli* he has the most interference. More is forgotten in that situation than the situation where both the second list of stimuli and responses are different. Having two responses to the one stimulus causes more forgetting than when that person has just one.

For the language student, this would mean having *only* the correct pronunciation stored will make pronouncing the word easier, than if an incorrect pronunciation is also stored in there.

In this experiment the second list acts to interfere with the first list. As you might expect, first lists can interfere with second lists just as easily. The interfering effect of stored responses is well understood by behavioral scientists. The practical consequence of all of this basic research is the law of specific response, learn it as you'll use it. You'll remember it easier later on.

2,760 Words

CHAPTER 17 — REINFORCEMENT, REPETITION, AND ACTIVE LEARNING

Nothing succeeds like success.

Alexander Dumas, 1854

Reinforced behavior is learned (Law of Reinforcement)

Frequently used behavior is remembered best (Law of Repetition)

Activity increases learning (Law of Active Learning)

Summary

A reinforcement is a stimulus which when paired with a behavior increases the probability of that behavior occurring again. Positive reinforcers are stimuli that you like, such as affection, good music, success, or money. A reward is not always a reinforcer. Negative reinforcers are stimuli that you don't like such as pain, boredom, disgust or worry. A negative reinforcer does its work when it is turned off, whereas the same stimulus could be classified as a punishment when it is turned on. Both types of reinforcers can be used to learn new facts or habits, whereas punishment only suppresses habits that you already have. Success is the best reinforcer for students.

To be effective reinforcers must be delivered immediately, although it is not necessary to reinforce a behavior every time (partial reinforcement). Complex new behaviors can be shaped by successively reinforcing small parts of the final behavior.

Habits strengthen and knowledge increases the more often they are used (repetition), and the more actively you pursue this knowledge the faster you will learn it and the better you will remember it.

REINFORCEMENT

Introduction

Reinforcement is dynamite. The student who understands and uses reinforcements can blast away mountains of ignorance and build mighty structures of knowledge. The student who does not understand reinforcement labors at his learning to level that mountain with a pick and shovel. Just as the use of dynamite multiplies the power of the construction worker, the skillful use of reinforcement can multiply the effectiveness of a person's studying.

More than any other law of learning, the law of reinforcement has caused a revolution in psychological theory and practice in this century. The application of this law in the educational system has produced what is probably the first new invention in learning in the last five centuries, the teaching machine. Completely new and successful treatments for mentally ill and retarded people have been based largely on this law. Skilled professionals in many fields, the military, industry, health, and education are making use of the practical consequences of the law of reinforcement in their daily efforts to help or train people.

Reinforcement Defined

Susan Gilyard was puzzled over what she had just heard in my senior Perception and Sensation class. She had asked several questions during class, but still had not grasped the main point of the lecture. She stayed in her seat frowning over her notes. At the end of class, Bob Parnell, who had been making straight A's in this course, stopped at Susan's desk, borrowed her pen and worked out an example for her. This caught my eye because Bob was shy and I had not seen him speak to anyone in the class before. The example must have helped because Susan said, "Oh, I see that now. Thanks, Bob." She smiled at him and touched his hand as he returned her pen.

A psychologist would call the thanks, the smile, and the touch reinforcements, while the layman would probably call them rewards for helpful behavior. The psychologist has not merely invented a new piece of jargon for an old concept; he has discovered a new meaning and has given it a distinctive name. The student who understands reinforcement, and learns to use it properly in his day-to-day learning tasks will have grasped the most powerful learning tool discovered by behavioral scientists.

> **Definition:** A reinforcement is: (A) a *stimulus,* (B) which when *paired* with any behavior, (C) *increases the probability* of that behavior occurring again.

Let's consider this definition step by step. A reinforcement is a stimulus means that anything that can stimulate you can be a reinforcement. Any object or event that stimulates your senses, or your mind can be a reinforcer. For example, money, candy, affection, admiration, good music, or even the relief from a worry can all stimulate you and be reinforcers. Theoretically this means that anything in the whole world can be a reinforcer. The psychologist starts his definition in this broad manner to indicate that there is no special category of things or events that are reinforcers.

The next part of the definition, "which when paired with any behavior," narrows the concept to only those stimuli which occur in the same place and at the same time as the behavior. If Susan had thanked, touched and smiled at Bob an hour after he had helped her, these stimuli (stimuli is the plural of stimulus) would not satisfy this part of the definition. A layman would be perfectly willing to say that Bob was still being rewarded for helping Susan, but the psychologist would not agree that Bob's helpful behavior was being reinforced. The stimulus *must* be closely paired with a behavior in time and space. Since many stimuli are paired with any particular behavior a further restirction is needed to completely identify which stimulus is the reinforcer.

The key clause in the definition is the third one, which says that the stimulus paired with the behavior has the property of increasing the chance that the behavior will happen again. If Susan's smile was a reinforcer, in similar circumstances in the future Bob would be more likely to help her again. The same goes for the touch and the "Thanks, Bob." Whether a stimulus is a reinforcer is determined by its effect on behavior, namely that the stimulus increases the probability of the behavior occurring again.

The word probability in this definition bothers many students. Scientists are comfortable thinking in terms of probabilities and chances, but often ordinary people are not. They like the world to be more clear-cut. "Will Bob help Susan again or won't he?" We can't say for sure. If we knew all of the facts odds could be given, like those given on the chances of rolling sevens with dice. The behavioral scientist knows from experience in similar learning situations that the pairing of a reinforcer with a behavior does strengthen the behavior making its occurrence in the future more likely. Another way of saying this is that if Susan keeps reinforcing Bob's help with smiles and thanks, eventually she can depend on his help. If this works well she might believe that there was some magical property in smiles and thanks causes Bob to learn. She would be wrong if she believed this.

Money, Love, Power

A stimulus is a reinforcer only if it *increases* the chance of a behavior occurring again. Reinforcing stimuli are defined as such solely by their effect on behavior, not by any property of the stimulus itself. You might imagine that money, love, or granting power could always be used as reinforcers, but not so. For example, the welfare applicant would not welcome the ten extra dollars from a job it if would keep her from receiving a large welfare check. The twelve-year-old quarterback would not welcome his mother's gushing affections in front of his team on the practice field, nor would his dad, a badly overworked executive, welcome the boss's suggestion that he increase his responsibilities. There is nothing about money, love or power in themselves that makes them reinforcers. When they are paired with a behavior if they make that behavior more likely, then they would be reinforcers, but (I'll say it one more time) *only because they have this effect on the behavior.* This is the key to understanding reinforcement.

To sharpen your image of what a reinforcer is two examples of stimuli that are not reinforcers will be given. First, we will discuss those stimuli in any learning situation which are irrelevant, and then we will compare the concept of a reinforcer with the concept of a reward.

Bob had seen Susan sitting in that seat in my class for many weeks now, and had heard her asking questions. Yet the sight of Susan and her questions had not strengthened any helping behavior from him. On one occasion he had answered a question of Susan's, but she had not responded to his answer in any way. Neither the sight of Susan nor the sound of her voice by themselves are reinforcers. The "thanks" is not some magical word because Susan had said that word several times aloud as I handed out material during class. Bob had not leapt to her aid when she uttered it. Clearly the sight and sound of Susan and the words she utters by themselves are not reinforcers.

Most stimuli in learning situations are not reinforcers. It takes skill and cunning to discover what the reinforcers really are. This is not a simple task, but it is not terribly difficult either. A good use of common sense and a bit of knowledge can make any student a clever user of reinforcers.

Rewards

Would the student who was a clever user of rewards be as well off as the student who understands the usage of reinforcers? No, definitely not. The common meaning of a reward is something given as recompense for a good deed or merit. Only certain kinds of behavior are rewarded, and it is assumed that most behavior will not be rewarded. You would expect a reward for achieving the top grade in your anatomy class this year, but you would not expect to be rewarded for merely staying awake in that class's lectures. Reinforcers operate on *all* kinds of behavior, not just "good" behavior. Bad, indifferent, exciting, dull, stupid or ingenious behaviors can also be reinforced.

Rewards are usually defined as being rewarding by the giver or the receiver. In contrast, reinforcers are reinforcers because of what they do, not because of how they are perceived. A hunting Eskimo would say that warm, bloody liver, freshly cut from a seal is an excellent reward. A visiting white missionary might not think so at all. The billionaire John D. Rockefeller rewarded bellhops and taxi drivers with shiny new dimes. Most of the recipients of these coins thought the billionaire was miserly and felt cheated for their service.

The general definition of reinforcement should now be clear. It is any stimulus that strengthens our behavior when the behavior and stimulus occur together. Such reinforcing stimuli can be divided into two classes, positive and negative.

Positive Reinforcers

Positive reinforcers are things and events you like, or admire, or want, or would approach. Figure 17-1 lists items that students classify as positive reinforcers. Positive reinforcers give pleasure.

Positive reinforcers help you learn by strengthening behavior with their presence. When you succeed at a task you are pleased and will try it again.

When you use dog biscuits to train your puppy to come to you, or to heel, or sit you are using the food as a positive reinforcer. Saying "Good dog," is another positive reinforcer that works well with pups, and it is called a social reinforcer. A pat on the head is another social reinforcer. In the previous chapter I described how a pigeon could be trained to peck a key in a Skinner Box by using food as a positive reinforcer. This type of reinforcer is the best kind to use, because we feel good when we receive them.

Negative Reinforcers

Things and events that hurt you, make you withdraw and avoid them can also be reinforcing. Pain, boredom, fear, disgust, and worry would be negative reinforcers. You may be surprised that such stimuli can be used to strengthen behavior because you class them as punishments. They can also be punishments but it depends how they are used.

Strictly defined, a negative reinforcement strengthens behavior when it is withdrawn. Compare that to the positive reinforcement, which strengthens behavior when you receive it.

Using painful or upsetting stimuli to train somebody is an upsetting idea in itself. Painful events should not be used in training or any learning situation, because they cause people so much emotional disturbance. But sometimes negative reinforcers have to be used.

Imagine this grisly situation. A two-year-old child climbs up on a chair beside an electric stove. He sees the burner glowing, and is entranced by its bright red color. He reaches his finger out and touches the burner.

Compliments	Country music	Attention
Approval	Johnny Carson Show	Interest
Encouragement	Going to a party	Praise
Affection	Playing a game	Meeting new people
Jokes	Playing a guitar	Wine
Love	Playing a piano	Mail
Parents	Reading the Bible	Awards
Relatives	Helping others	Drawing
Friends	Helping a friend	Jaguars
A response	Taking a nap	Porsches
Popsicles	Talking on the phone	A movie
Visiting museums	Nice clothes	A play
Cycling	Fellowship	A dance
Skiing	Going to church	A show
Tennis	Making money	Ceramics
Baseball	Paychecks	Art
Basketball	Bonus wages	Watching TV
Football	Bowling	Studying (????)
Swimming	Coffee	Teaching (!!!!)
Beaches	Working with children	Tim
Lakes	Photography	Bob
Bikinis	A smile	Maureen
Traveling	A look	Marianne
Jewelry	A touch	A good date
Good food	Nods	Girls in general
Chewing gum	Waves	Boys in general
Relaxing	Elvis Presley movies	Shopping
Sleeping	A drive in the mountains	Sunshine flooding a room
Exercising	Walking in the woods	Visiting
Golf	A beautiful weekend	Horseback riding
Bird watching	Collecting records	Puppies
Cooking	Rock concerts	Being healthy
Eating	Speaking French	Dr. Pepper
Drinking	Writing poetry	Communication
Vacation	Good discussions	Good grades
Dancing	Messing around	Respect
Singing	Running with a dog	Chocolate

Figure 17-1 Positive Reinforcers

I don't even need to finish that, do I. The child would jerk his hand back as soon as it touched the hot burner. He would never touch a lit burner again. This frightening scene, which does happen, can be analyzed in terms of reinforcements. The child's reaching-to-touch behavior was punished by the initial stab of pain. The quick withdrawal of the hand was reinforced when the pain decreased as the finger left the burner. This is one instance where punishment and the use of negative reinforcement seem justified. From now on the child will be very cautious about approaching hot glowing objects, which is good.

Learning with negative reinforcers can be swift. Nature has evolved us that way to allow us to survive painful situations and avoid them in the future. Mildly negative reinforcers like boredom and dislike need many repetitions to work.

Negative reinforcers and punishments are not exactly the same thing.

Punishment

You have just learned that turning off an unpleasant stimulus is reinforcing. What happens if you turn it on? That's punishment.

Using punishment in learning is bad for two reasons. One, you cannot learn anything new using punishment; all you can do is suppress some behavior that you already have. Sometimes that is useful, for example, if you get a scare for running a stop sign you won't do that again. But the major purpose of education and learning is to give you new responses to new situations. Punishment cannot do that since its effect is to turn off existing behavior, not turn on new ones.

Second, we all get emotional about punishment, especially when it happens to us. A child cries when spanked, and we become resentful when friends snub us. Teachers sometimes assign extra school work to students as punishment for small crimes. The value of this work is usually lost because the student resents its imposition. All these emotions get in the way of our learning. We are paying attention to our hurt feelings, and not to the task to be learned. In the most severe cases of punishment people stop responding completely. It is too painful. If a person does not act, his behavior cannot be reinforced, and he won't learn.

Don't use punishment. Its effects are bad. Use it only in urgent situations-better to slap the child than have him burn his hand in the fire. For day-to-day learning use positive reinforcement.

The most useful positive reinforcer that you can use as a student is a very simple one built into your learning skills – success.

Success is Reinforcing

Success breeds success. If you are successful, you will want to do more learning; and if the following learning is successful you will want to do more, and more, and more!

Do not define success in learning as something stupendous and terrifically exciting. Define success in small, simple terms. Success is reading a paragraph, pausing, jotting down your notes from memory, and realizing that you have extracted the essence of the paragraph. This realization is your reinforcement, your success. Continue to Readrite for the rest of the chapter, pausing periodically to savor your successes.

Sometimes you will fail to remember the paragraph accurately. That's punishment. It is also knowledge. You have just discovered that your learning of that paragraph is faulty. Possibly your attention wavered, or you were distracted. Maybe a word confused you. NOW is the time to correct that flaw in your learning. Go back over the paragraph again and learn it. If the confusion still exists you may need to look elsewhere to clear up the difficulty. This is all work and effort, so that finally when you have your success, when you have mastered your paragraph and your notes, and recall proves it, your success will be that much larger. Great satisfaction is achieved through great effort.

The success discussed here is the minute by minute practical application of the law of Reinforcement. This application is easy to do because it flows naturally from the study situation, as you do it using the Readrite method.

Notice that in the Readrite method the successes, though small, are delivered immediately. As soon as you jot your notes you discover that you have learned that paragraph. Reinforcement is instantaneous.

Half a Second or Less

A half second delay between your behavior and its reinforcement can mean the difference between learning and not learning. That astounding fact was discovered by the scientist Ivan Pavlov early in this century. Food was the reinforcer used by Dr. Pavlov to train his laboratory dogs. If he delayed giving the dogs their food by as little as half a second, they would not learn the simple tasks he set for them.

The effect of delaying reinforcement has been exhaustively explored by behavioral scientists since Pavlov's pioneer discovery. They found that reinforcement is most effective if simultaneously paired with the behavior to be learned, and its effect rapidly plunges to zero if it is delayed. Some animals like dogs and rats cannot tolerate a reinforcement delay of more than a second, or at the most two. People can tolerate longer delays, because they have a language and can think.

When you test yourself after reading a section of your textbook you are still reinforced for correct answers even though you read the material several minutes before. You understand the connection between your answers and the material you read before. But, reinforcement is more effective if immediately paired with the behavior. That is why notetaking as you read and as you listen to lectures is so important. The instant success you achieve when you write notes is a powerful reinforcer.

Part-time Reinforcement

If you reinforce your learning every time, learning will be fast. If you reinforce your learning only part of the time, learning will be slower. Both kinds of reinforcement, *continuous* and *partial,* have their advantages and disadvantages.

When any behavior is not reinforced it *extinguishes,* it disappears. A girl I know extinguished on her music lessons. The teacher was not teaching her what she wanted to learn, jazz, so her interest in the lessons stopped, and soon she stopped practicing. The lessons were no longer reinforcing. The concept of extinction is introduced here because one of the disadvantages of continuous reinforcement is rapid extinction. Figure 17-2 shows that extinction after continuous reinforcement is rapid. Extinction after partial reinforcement is slow.

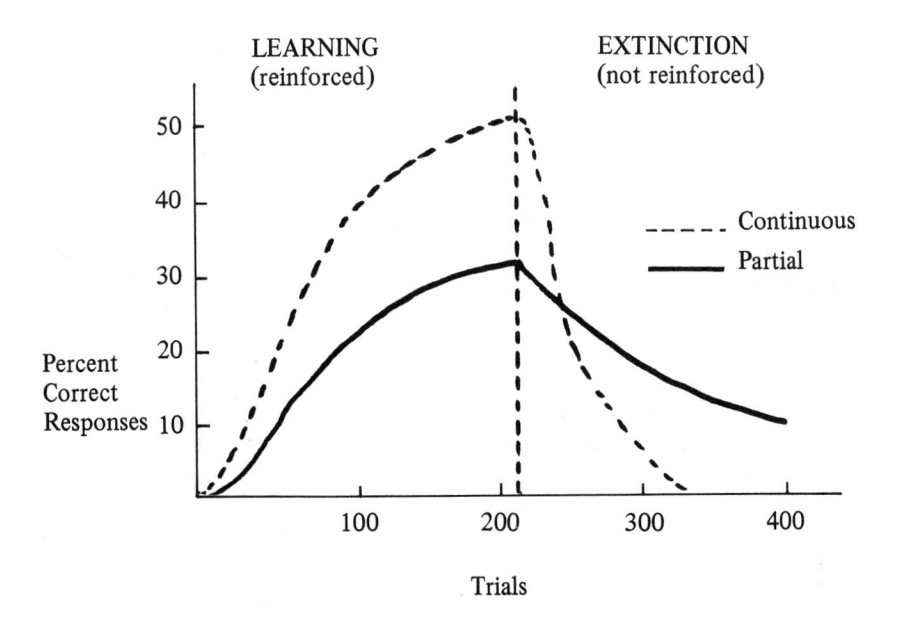

Figure 17-2 Learning and extinction under continuous and partial reinforcement.

You would like to learn quickly, but at the same time you would like to keep what you have learned. To learn quickly you need lots of reinforcement, but the danger is that if the reinforcement should stop you will lose your new behavior very quickly.

The advantage of partial reinforcement is that extinction is much slower. For example, when a mother is starting to train her baby to eat with a spoon she sits close by, guides the spoon into the mouth at first, and reinforces every mouthful, with a "Good baby!" Of course baby is also reinforced by successfully getting food into his mouth. After baby has got the hang of self-feeding, mother goes about her jobs in the kitchen, and only occasionally reinforces baby with a smile or an encouragement. Such partial reinforcement produces a strong habit. Very few 18-year olds have extinguished on feeding themselves, even though mother has not reinforced them for years for putting food in their mouths.

Start your new learning with lots of reinforcements, but once your habits get established, switch to the occasional reinforcement to stop extinction.

Since reinforcement is most effective when used steadily on small behaviors, you will have to build upwards towards larger, more complex behavior. This building of complex behaviors is called shaping.

Shaping

A sculptor does not expect to complete a marble statute in the first minute or the first hour. He knows that he will have to shape that rock by carefully chiseling and grinding away at it for days, possibly weeks.

The student cannot expect to learn everything instantly. He also must work patiently to shape his behavior towards his goals. You cannot learn the mathematics of calculus, or the history of the United States, or how to play championship class tennis overnight. But you can learn all of these tasks if you are patient, use your reinforcements and the technique of *successive approximations*.

Successive approximations means that in any complex learning you start small and simple. You only try to approximate the final behavior. You cannot go out and practice championship tennis, but you can break it down into its parts and practice them one at a time. Service, volley, ground shots, backhands, court position all can be practiced separately until perfected, then slowly combined until you master your game. Each skill is reinforced when you succeed in doing it. More and more your game approximates that of the championship tennis play.

Another example — you have decided to improve your learning skills, your craft as a student. Do you really expect that you will become a super student overnight by just reading the few pages of this book? I hope not. Yet you can become that super student if you are willing to shape your behavior towards that end. Practice each one of the skills taught in this book, one at a time, until it is mastered. Start small and succeed.

One more example, if you have not been in the habit of notetaking as you read, don't start to do this with all of your textbooks. Pick one book from an easy course and start with that (first approximation). After you are comfortable and happy with your notetaking with that textbook, start on another book in another course (second approximation), and slowly, slowly take notes more and more as you read until it becomes habitual.

Follow this rule — if you are not completely comfortable with your new learning step think smaller and simpler. Shape your behavior like the sculptor shapes his marble, lovingly and carefully. Something beautiful will be the result.

Summary

Understanding reinforcement can provide you a powerful tool. If you are having trouble learning a subject analyze your work in terms of reinforcers. Are you getting lots of reinforcers? Possibly negative reinforcers and punishments are defeating you. When you use reinforcers moment by moment in your study techniques you ensure automatic learning. Learning will not be instantaneous, but the steady application of reinforcement will work to strengthen your knowledge, habits and skills.

REPETITION

The law of repetition makes such strong common sense that I am only going to devote a few sentences to it. The more often you use your knowledge the easier it becomes to remember what you know. For example, frequently used words like *is, the, can, do,* or *ice cream* are on the very tip of your memory and easy to remember when you need them. Infrequently used words like *studiousness, imprint, graphite,* or *dentition* are not on the tip of our memory and have to be searched for.

Well-established habits like walking, eating with a knife and fork, or writing are easy to do. You use these habits every day. Habits like starting a motorboat, playing scrabble, or eating caviar are less frequently used and often require a moment's thought before they can be done correctly.

The principle is clear. The more you repeat any action the easier it is to do again. The more you use a piece of knowledge the easier it is to recall it in the future.

ACTIVE LEARNING

Since only your behavior can be reinforced the more active you are about your learning the more chances you will have of being reinforced.

The emphasis is on DOING. The quality of the actions counts as well as their simple repetition. Many different acts are better than the same action repeated. For example, if you wanted to memorize the French word for man, *l'homme,* you could silently say it to yourself a dozen times, or you could say it aloud, write it out, type it, use it in a sentence, use a dictionary to discover if it is combined like the English word into new words such as mankind or manhandle, say the word to every friend you meet before lunch, and so on. The latter tactics will produce better learning than the former. The more varied your actions in learning a word, the more clearly that word is defined, the more distinctly it stands out in your memory, the less likely it is to be confused with other words.

Here is an experience you probably have had that will show the difference between active and passive learning. A friend drives you to a new restaurant. Later you have to make the trip yourself, but you cannot remember the route so you look it up on a map. On another occasion you drive to another new restaurant the first time, and the second time you have no trouble driving there again.

What's the difference between these two situations? In the first situation you were the passenger. You passively sat in the car, chatting with the driver and idly watching the scenery go by. In the second case you were the driver. You had to pay attention to the proper turns and street signs to arrive at your destination. You were active so you learned the route.

You are not very active when you passively read a book, or sit in a class listening. When your mind and your hands become active, either thinking about the material, practicing your remembering, testing yourself, or notetaking you increase your chances of learning a thousandfold.

4,562 Words

SECTION VI.

APPENDIXES

A. Test Record
B. Study Problems List
C. Reading Tests

    1. Clouds - A Pilot's View
    2. Raising a Family - Zebra Finch Style
    3. When Memory is Super Good and Super Bad
    4. Tables - Reading Times, Scores and Indexes by Class Grades

D. Reading Power Drill - Calculation Form, Words Per Page
E. Reading Speed Record
F. Reading Speed Graph
G. Reading Speed Table
H. Action Plan
I. Chapter Tests
J. Answers for Chapter Tests
K. Learnometers
L. Time Sheets

TEST RECORD

Chapter	Score	Chapter	Score
2	____	10	____
3	____	11	____
4	____	12	____
5	____	13	____
6	____	14	____
7	____	15	____
8	____	16	____
9	____	17	____

First Reading Test   Score ____ WPM ____ Index ____ Rdg. Time ____

Second Reading Test Score ____ WPM ____ Index ____ Rdg. Time ____

Third Reading Test   Score ____ WPM ____ Index ____ Rdg. Time ____

PERSONAL STUDY PROBLEM LIST

In the left column list *all* your study and learning problems, and number them. In the column on the right, write all the solutions to your problems that you can think of now (if you cannot think of a solution to a problem leave it blank, but try for one). Be as thorough as you can with your problem list, If you think of more problems later on add them to the list. By the time you have finished this book this list will provide you an exhaustive record of your study skills difficulties.

Here are a few areas in which you may have problems. This list is not meant to be complete; you may have problems that do not fit into any of these categories. Use them as a guide to preparing your study problem list.

Self study	Notetaking in class	Time management
Classroom work	Assignments	Motivation
Reading	Concentration	Record keeping
Book learning	Study place	Taking tests

Problems	Solutions

> **Appendix C**
>
> Three reading tests and a table are included in this Appendix. The First Reading Test (*Appendix C-1*) is to be done on the first day of the fifteen day plan, before any of the chapters of the book are studied. The Second Reading Test is to be taken on the 7th day of the plan (*Appendix C-2*). The Third Reading Test is done on the 14th day of the plan (*Appendix C-3*). The table will allow you to compare your test results with other students who have taken these tests.

READING TEST – CLOUDS - A PILOT'S VIEW

INSTRUCTIONS

Read the following article as fast as you can *with good comprehension*. Before you begin, write the time you start reading to the nearest second in item 5b on the Scoring Sheet on the next page (SUGGESTION: start reading on the minute, for example, start at 9 hours, 12 minutes, 0 seconds). Read the article with the goal of learning the material in it, because you will take a test right after you have finished reading. When you have finished reading, but not before, note the time to the nearest second and write it down in item 5a on the Scoring Sheet.

Answer the questions in the test following the article without looking at the article again. Score the test using the Answer Key. Total your marks and write your test score in item 4 of the Scoring Sheet.

Calculate your reading time by subtracting your starting time from your finishing time on the Scoring Sheet. Round your reading time figure to the nearest minute. Subtract your reading time from your test score to find your efficiency index (see item 6 on the Scoring Sheet). Finally, find your reading speed on the table provided on the Scoring Sheet.

SUMMARY

1. Record the time you start reading
2. Read the article as fast as you can with good comprehension
3. Record the time you finish reading
4. Take and score test
5. Calculate a. your reading time
   b. your efficiency index
6. Find your reading speed from the table

Appendix C-1

SCORING SHEET

CLOUDS - A PILOT'S VIEW

1. Name _____ 2. Age _____

3. Class (circle one) *College* SR, JR, SO, FR;

   High School 12, 11, 10, 9, 8, 7

4. Test Score _____   Hr.   Min.   Sec.

5. **Reading Time**   a. Finished reading at _____   _____   _____

   _____ Minutes   b. Started reading at

   c. Reading Time

6. **Efficiency Index**

   To calculate this index subtract the reading time in minutes (to the nearest whole minute) from your test score:

   a. Test Score   _____

   b. Reading Time   _____

   c. Efficiency Index _____

7. **Reading Speed**

   Find your reading time in the table below. The number to the right of your time is your approximate reading speed for this article in words per minute. Draw a circle around your reading speed figure (WPM).

   READING SPEED TABLE

Min.	WPM	Min.	WPM	Min.	WPM	Min.	WPM	Min.	WPM	Min.	WPM
3	838	8	314	13	193	18	140	23	109	28	90
4	628	9	279	14	180	19	132	24	105	29	87
5	503	10	251	15	168	20	126	25	101	30	84
6	419	11	228	16	157	21	120	26	97	31	81
7	359	12	209	17	148	22	114	27	93	32	79

8. To find out how your test score, reading time, and efficiency index compare to those of other students who have taken this test see the table in *Appendix C-4*.

Clouds — A Pilot's View

A pilot must know how to predict the weather by looking at the clouds. By using this knowledge the pilot can determine whether a day is fit for flying, where he should fly for smooth comfortable flight, and cloud knowledge might even save his life someday.

You have been looking at clouds all of your life. As a child you stared up into the summer blue and imagined you could see castles, mushrooms, or your Uncle Ben's profile in the clouds drifting by. As an adult you have probably longed for the clouds to part after a miserable, wet winter week. The clouds are always up there and you can ignore them most of the time. As a pilot of your light Cessna 150 aircraft you are going to be "up there" with the clouds, and if they are ignored they might trap you in their damp tentacles someday and pull you down. You must stop looking at clouds as a ground dweller, and start to see them and think about them as a pilot.

There are two basic types of clouds, *horizontal clouds and vertical clouds*. The first type covers many square miles of the earth's surface and is not particularly thick. Vertical clouds are tall rather than broad, and are noted for the strong upward forces that create them.

Horizontal Clouds

Clouds cover the sky and hide the sun, right? WRONG! A most important lesson for you to learn as a new student pilot is that clouds cover the ground. Up where you are flying the sun is shining brilliantly, but it can be a black day if a cloud deck has slipped beneath you, hiding your airport as your fuel gauge reads EMPTY. Let's examine the types of horizontal clouds.

Horizontal clouds form layers, hence the use of the word stratus in their names. As your airplane climbs away from the airport the first of these layered clouds you will meet will be the *cumulo-stratus* clouds. They look a bit like the fluffy clouds you see early on a summer day, except they will be flatter and their edges may touch to form a continuous layer. They are usually the last clouds you have to struggle free from before you land your plane, and they will be found from ground level up to 6,000 feet.

As you continue your climb you will penetrate this first layer into the clear air about, only to be confronted with the next cloud layer, the *alto-stratus* clouds. These clouds can be found in the middle air between 6,000 and 18,000 feet. Because this air does not have as much vertical mixing as the first 6,000 feet the alto-stratus clouds have a smoother appearance. The sun shining on the earth heats the air from below like a stove under a pot of soup, causing the air to burble upwards. This unevenly rising air sculpts the lower clouds into puffy, irregular shapes. In the higher middle regions the air flows more smoothly and horizontally, and clouds are shaped to fit this flow.

By now you have levelled out and set course to where you are going. If

Appendix C-1 237

Figure 1 Horizontal Clouds — Location and Appearance

you look up you can see still another layer of cloud high above you. It is brilliant white without any of the somber greys of the cumulo-stratus or alto-stratus layers you have just flown through.

This high layer of cloud also appears to be quite thin; the sun is seen shining through it. These clouds are the cold, ice-crystals clouds called *cirro-stratus*. Often these clouds will form long swooping streamers, which old-time pilots call mare's-tails. Unless you become a military or airline jet pilot you are not likely to fly near the cirro-stratus layer because the air is thin up there. Your aircraft must be equipped with oxygen to fly above 12,000 feet.

Weather Reports

These horizontal cloud layers can cover vast areas of the earth's surface. Satellite photographs have shown as much as half of the North American continent blanketed by such clouds at one time. Remember, you are not yet trained to fly your light plane on instruments so you must be able to see the ground at all times. If any cloud layers slide beneath you so that you cannot see the ground you have a full-fledged emergency on your hands. You must plan every flight to avoid this possibility. The teletype weather report is as necessary to a pilot's safe flight planning as the air is to his breathing. Learning to read entire weather reports is too large a topic to deal with here, but the ways in which cloud cover is reported can be quickly grasped.

Appendix C-1

Table 1: Weather Report Cloud Cover Symbols

Symbol	Name	Ground Covered
◯	clear	0/10ths
⦶	scattered	1/10 - 5/10ths
⦷	broken	6/10 - 9/10ths
⊕	overcast	10/10ths

Table one shows the circular symbols used in a weather report to indicate the extent of the cloud cover. An open circle indicates that the sky is clear, zero tenths of the ground would be hidden from a pilot flying in that sky. A circle with a single vertical bar indicates scattered clouds, from one-tenth to five-tenths of the ground would be hidden from a pilot flying above such a cloud, and so on. In a weather report the height of each layer of cloud above the ground is reported, as well as how much that layer obscures the ground. For example:

$$\text{WS} \quad ⦶ \; 6 \quad ⦷ \; 60$$

The numbers before each symbol indicate that layer's height in hundreds of feet. This reads, "At Winston-Salem, North Carolina there is a scattered layer at 600 feet above the ground, another broken layer at 6000 feet." Note this important point, the ground obscuring property of each successive layer cumulates. Neither

Figure 2: Clouds Hiding Ground from Pilot

of the layers of cloud in this report need be solid overcast (see Figure 2), but the accumulated effect of the layers is to nearly hide the ground from a pilot flying above the top layer.

Reading Clouds

Even after the pilot has read these reports and is airborne he can fly more safely if he constantly "reads" the clouds in the sky. The flight described in this section will illustrate how a good airborne cloud reading can save a pilot's neck.

In the winter in the southeastern United States warm fronts are often accompanied by *freezing rain*, an extremely hazardous condition for lightplane pilots. Imagine that you are planning to fly from Winston-Salem, North Carolina to Atlanta, Georgia for Christmas. The weather reports show good flying weather, except that a warm front is moving northeastward across the southern states. The weather forecaster tells you that you should be able to reach Atlanta before the front does, so you decide to go. Unknown to the forecaster is the fact that the front picked up speed during the night. You take off.

At first flying conditions are beautiful — smooth, clear, cold air. After an hour's flying you notice some cirro-stratus and mare's tails high above you. This does not bother you, because by themselves these clouds can be fair-weather indicators, but another half hour's flying brings you into layers of alto-stratus. In a few more minutes you begin to see low cumulo-stratus and an alarm bell rings in your head. That particular sequence of clouds spells W-A-R-M F-R-O-N-T! Immediately you radio Atlanta for an up-to-the-minute weather report.

"Winston-Salem Cessna, " Atlanta calls back, "Our airport is closed. We have freezing rain here, and our runways are coated with ice."

Ice! Your little airplane flies like a rock with ice on its wings. You turn your aircraft around, locate a nearby airport that's open, land, and rest there until the warm front has gone past. You might even pat yourself on the back, because your skillful cloud reading had alerted you to the danger ahead.

Vertical Clouds

Vertical clouds hide the ground, but in addition to this property these clouds are noted for the strong air turbulence associated with them. On a pleasant summer morning the first of these vertical clouds that you will see is the *cumulus* cloud. It is a relatively small, cottony puff of a cloud usually spaced well apart. Cumulus clouds show the pilot that the atmosphere's pot is starting to burble. If you have any friends that get airsick these clouds are telling you to leave them at home today. Flying is going to be rough.

Towards noon on the same day these clouds change their appearance. They are larger across the base and much taller. The bases have flattened out. Your friend, the sailplane pilot, launched his long-winged craft an hour ago and can be seen soaring swiftly upward towards the base of one of these *mature*

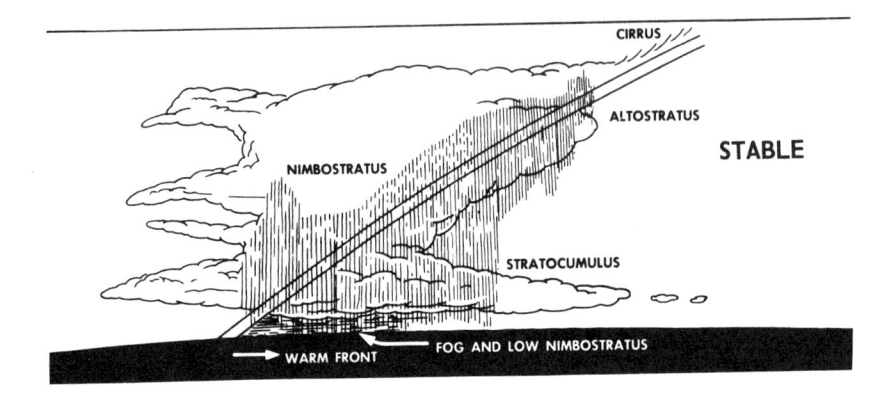

Figure 3: Cloud Sequence in a Warm Front (from Simonson, 1970).

cumulus clouds. Earlier roughness has now turned into strong upward thermals, vertical air movements capable of supporting a sailplane for hours.

The sun's heat engine can forge these mature cumulus clouds into larger and larger cells, until they become a full-fledged storm cloud, the *cumulonimbus, or thunderhead.* This cloud is dangerous to the pilot. The thermals of an earlier hour have developed into screaming vertical winds capable of tossing aircraft up or down of thousands of feet. Tornadoes develop from cumulo-nimbus clouds under certain conditions.

The thunderstorm, as the cumulo-nimbus is popularly called, can be seen for miles. In the southern plains states the tops of these storm centers often reach up to 60,000 feet. Two scientists in a stratospheric balloon reported one monster cloud that endangered their flight with a top estimated at 80,000 feet plus.

The vertical winds within a "*CB*", as thunderstorms are called by all pilots, can reach hurricane force. Shortly after World War II the United States Air Force studied these storms. They flew propellor and jet aircraft in and around and through many thunderstorms, and discovered many new facts. The dangerousness of these storm cells was amply confirmed. Several aircraft were destroyed, and one jet fighter limped back to base with its wings twisted like pretzels. Jet fighters are strong enough to withstand forces as much as five times

Figure 4: Vertical Cloud

the force of gravity, yet the buffeting this plane received in the cumulo-nimbus exceeded these forces!

What chance would a light plane have in such a storm?

Another dangerous feature of CB's is the precipitation they disgorge. All clouds have the potential for rain, or in colder air snow, but the cumulo-nimbus can produce *hail*. When driven by the internal gales of this storm cloud, hail can have the same effect on a light aircraft as a .50 caliber machine gun. Aluminum skin is dented, cloth covered control surfaces are ripped, and windshields are shattered. The pilot who feels safe because he is still flying in a smooth clear air alongside such a storm, but who is not really in it, may be in for a shock. Such storms can hurl hail out of their tops in long ballistic curves to pound an aircraft flying as much as five miles away from the visible edge of the cloud.

Often naive pilots will try to escape the turmoil of the thunderstorm by flying under it. From a distance the pilot believes that he can see a hole beneath the cloud which he then tries to fly through. As even the most confirmed non-flier knows thunderstorms don't give any warning before a shower. Visibility can drop to a few feet in heavy rain, and the pilot who is not yet trained to fly on instruments is in trouble. He can't see, the storm's turbulence is tossing his craft about, and he deliberately chose to fly near the ground to try to duck under the storm. Such misjudgment causes dozens of light-plane pilot deaths each year.

The rules for survival amongst vertical clouds are simple. Stay out of the mature cumulus, and stay away from the cumulo-nimbus, well away.

Storm Avoidance

Since the mature cumulus and the cumulo-nimbus are such huge and obviously visible clouds the pilot can easily avoid them most of the time. Occasionally thunderstorms cannot be seen because of other clouds or haze, and then the pilot needs help. A swiftly moving cold front lifts the warm moist air ahead of it forming a wall of thunderstorms hundreds of miles long. The pilot who has planned a cross country flight through such a line of storms should call for *radar advisory*. The heavy rain within each storm cell can be detected by radar, and the radar controller can direct an aircraft away from these cells. Passenger carrying jets carry their own radar for such storm avoidance.

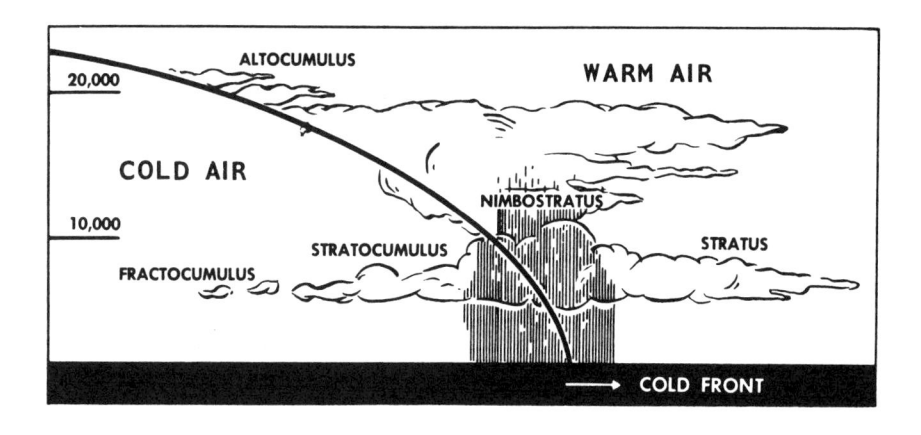

Figure 5: The Storm Front (from Simonson, 1970).

The radar controller cannot guarantee safe passage through a storm front. The pilot is still responsible for the safety of his aircraft. It is up to him to use all the means available to ensure a safe flight, and radar advisory is one means available to him.

Hybrid Clouds

All clouds do not neatly fit into the two categories of vertical or horizontal clouds. Some clouds would have to be placed in both categories, for example the *nimbo-stratus* and the *alto-stratus-castellanus* clouds.

The nimbo-stratus, as its name suggests, is a layered storm cloud. It has a large vertical development, often extending from near ground level up to 18,000 feet in one solid cloud mass, and horizontally it extends for hundreds, even thousands of square miles. This is the cloud that brings us that week of dreary winter rain. For the light plane pilot it usually means several days of "hangar flying," a good time to catch up on reading air regulations. Since the cloud touches the ground with its rain and fills the air up to where the pilot would need extra oxygen, he has nowhere to fly.

Figure 6: Alto-stratus castellanus

Alto-stratus castellanus is a layer of alto-stratus with thunderstorms imbedded in it. If a pilot tries to fly beneath such a cloud layer he cannot see the CB's and their violent turbulence. This cloud layer is spectacularily beautiful when viewed from above. The CB's look like mighty castles rising from a snowy plain.

Conclusion

Every flight that a pilot makes is at the whim of the weather. Only his intelligence and the speed and maneuverability of his aircraft allow the pilot some control over weather conditions. The clouds in the sky are a weather report written with a giant hand. Learn to read the clouds to survive.

Reference

Leroy Simonson, *Private Pilot Study Guide,* Simonson, Glendale, California, 1970.

Appendix C-1 245

READING TEST

Clouds - A Pilot's View

Marks   Answer the following questions in the spaces provided.

5   1. The two basic cloud types discussed in this article were

5   _____ and _____ clouds.

5   2. Smooth layers of cloud found between 6,000 and 18,000 feet above the ground are called _____ clouds.

5   3. Cirro-stratus clouds provide rough and dangerous flight conditions for the light plane pilot.   TRUE   FALSE

10   4. What causes the rough, irregular shapes of the cumulo-stratus layer of cloud? _____

5   5. What is the name given to the cloud cover described by this weather report symbol? _____

5   6. How much ground would be hidden from a pilot flying above this cloud cover? _____

5   7. A.   B.   C.
5

           alto-stratus   cumulo-stratus   cirrus

5   If you were flying toward a warm front you would see the clouds pictured above in a certain sequence. Using the letters next to each cloud typed order them as you would see them.

       1st _____ 2nd _____ 3rd _____

5   8. Rain falling from a winter warm front can produce _____ which is very dangerous for a light plane.

Marks

5   9. What kind of plane ride would you expect if the sky contained clouds like the one pictured here?
_____

5   10. Several hawks and a black vulture are seen soaring swiftly upwards the flat base of a large puffy cloud one summer afternoon. This cloud would be called a _____

5   11. The most turbulent and dangerous of all clouds is the _____

5   12. Pilots use the two letters __ __ to abbreviate the name of the cloud mentioned in question 11.

5   13. You are flying towards a cold front and you can see a line of storm clouds ahead. Where could you get help to steer your plane safely through this line? _____

5   14. What kind of flying is the light plane pilot without an instrument rating likely to do in nimbo-stratus clouds? _____

10   15. You can see that the base of the lowest solid cloud layer is about 1500 feet, with occasional heavy rain patches. You decide to fly cross country beneath the cloud. The weatherman calls this cloud alto-stratus castellanus. What is the danger here?

100

ANSWER KEY

Quiz: Clouds - A Pilot's View

If your answer is exactly correct, if you use the same words as this answer key, or words very close to them, give yourself full marks. Give yourself part marks if you are partly correct, and no marks for a clearly incorrect answer or no answer. Mark your paper as if you were a teacher trying to show a student how much he knew on this topic.

Answers	Marks (Allotted)	Yours
1. horizontal	(5)	____
vertical	(5)	____
2. alto-stratus	(5)	____
3. FALSE	(5)	____
4. Vertical air currents, or air rising unevenly, or turbulent air	(10)	____
5. broken	(5)	____
6. 10/10ths or all of the ground	(5)	____
7. 1st C	(5)	____
2nd A	(5)	____
3rd B	(5)	____
8. freezing rain or ice	(5)	____
9. rough or turbulence	(5)	____
10. mature cumulus (you must say mature)	(5)	____
11. Cumulo-nimbus or thunderstorm	(5)	____
12. CB	(5)	____
13. radar advisory	(5)	____
14. "hangar" flying or none at all	(5)	____
15. violent turbulence from the hidden cumulo-nimbus	(10)	____
Test Score	(100)	____

RAISING A FAMILY — ZEBRA FINCH STYLE

INSTRUCTIONS

Read the following article as fast as you can *with good comprehension.* Before you begin, write the time you start reading to the nearest second in item 5b on the Scoring Sheet on the next page (SUGGESTION: start reading on the minute, for example, start at 9 hours, 12 minutes, 0 seconds). Read the article with the goal of learning the material in it, because you will take a test right after you have finished reading. When you have finished reading, but not before, note the time to the nearest second and write it down in item 5a on the Scoring Sheet.

Answer the questions in the test following the article without looking at the article again. Score the test using the Answer Key, which follows it. Total up your marks and write your test score in item 4 of the Scoring Sheet.

Calculate your reading time by subtracting your starting time from your finishing time on the Scoring Sheet. Round your reading time figure to the nearest minute. Subtract your reading time from your test score to find your efficiency index (see item 6 on the Scoring Sheet). Finally, find your reading speed from the table provided on the Scoring Sheet.

SUMMARY

1. Record the time you start reading
2. Read the article as fast as you can with good comprehension
3. Record the time you finish reading
4. Take and score test
5. Calculate a. your reading time
            b. your efficiency index
6. Find your reading speed from the table

SCORING SHEET

RAISING A FAMILY – ZEBRA FINCH STYLE

1. Name _____ 2. Age _____

3. Class (circle one) *College* SR, JR, SO, FR

   High School 12, 11, 10, 9, 8, 7

4. **Test Score** _____   Hr.   Min.   Sec.

5. **Reading Time**   a. Finished reading at   ____   ____   ____

   _____ Minutes b. Started reading at   ____   ____   ____

   c. Reading Time   ____   ____   ____

6. **Efficiency Index**

   To calculate this index subtract the reading time in minutes (to the nearest whole minute) from your test score:

   a. Test Score   _____

   b. Reading Time   _____

   c. Efficiency Index _____

7. **Reading Speed**

   Find your reading time in the table below. The number to the right of your time is your approximate reading speed for this article in works per minute. Draw a circle around your reading speed figure (WPM).

   READING SPEED TABLE

Min.	WPM	Min.	WPM	Min.	WPM	Min.	WPM	Min.	WPM	Min.	WPM
3	1096	9	365	15	219	21	157	27	122	33	100
4	822	10	329	16	206	22	150	28	117	34	97
5	658	11	299	17	193	23	143	29	113	35	94
6	548	12	274	18	183	24	137	30	110	36	91
7	470	13	253	19	173	25	132	31	106	37	89
8	411	14	235	20	164	26	127	32	103	38	87

8. To find out how your test score, reading time, and efficiency index compare to those of other students who have taken this test, see the table in *Appendix C-4*.

RAISING A FAMILY – ZEBRA FINCH STYLE

"Chortle-dee! Chortle-dee! Chortle-dee! Tia - Tia - Tia!"

Red Bird was singing his love song to his sweetheart, Black Bar. Red Bird and Black Bar were a pair of Zebra Finches (see Figure 1) that I had bought in a distant city, Charlotte, North Carolina, and had recently placed in a large cage hoping that they would mate and raise young. So far, Red Bird had sung his song all day, but Black Bar just preened her wing-tips daintly, sipped some water, and hopped about quite indifferent to the male's passionate song. What if she refused him? All my plans would fail.

I had bought these birds so that my class in animal behavior could observe their reproductive cycle and general behavior. The Zebra Finch (scientific name – *Poephila guttata*) seemed ideal for this purpose. These birds were originally from Australia, but they had been domesticated as a cage bird for over 175 years. The bird is tiny, 10 centimeters long and about 12 grams in weight (about half the weight of the common House Sparrow), but very hardy. It raises young readily in cages, and under ideal conditions will produce a new family every six weeks. In Australia these finches live in highly social flocks of *25-100 birds*, and use a well developed set of songs and calls to communicate with each other. Even wild birds tolerate man well and they nest in the suburbs as well as in the vast semi-desert outback. They should be an ideal laboratory animal for student psychologists to study, that is if Black Bar would only show some interest in her suitor.

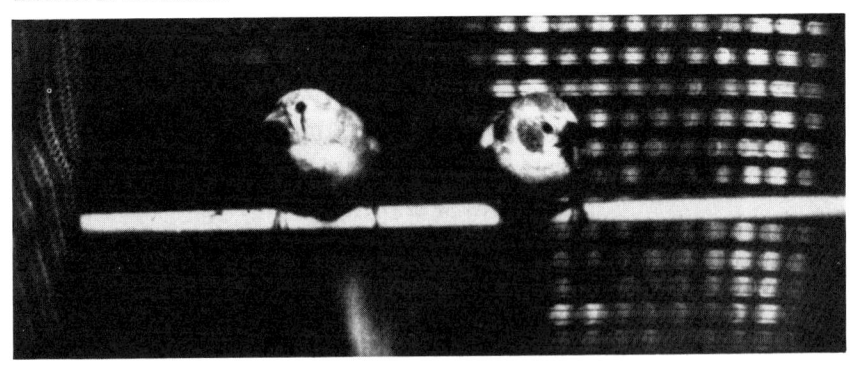

Figure 1: Black Bar, the female, perches on the left showing her black stripe and white facial patch. Red Bird the male turns his head to show his chestnut cheek patch.

COURTSHIP

Part of the problem was my own ignorance. Although I was reading everything I could find about these birds, I could not be sure that some small vital element was missing. I found out that the wild flock was composed of two parts, the mated adult pairs, and the swarm, chicks and juvenile birds not yet mated. Red Bird and Black Bar would have been part of that swarm, but here they were alone in their cage. I added a nest box and some grass, burlap threads, and cotton batting when I discovered that the female would not mate unless these items were present. They hopped all over the box, inside and out, and Red Bird sang harder and more lustily than ever. They began to court in earnest.

Both birds hopped back and forth between two perches, pointing their tails at each other. Red Bird strutted his male finery. The birds are an ash grey color with a black-barred tail, a black-streak running vertically on the face just behind the bright red beak with a white streak behind that. The feet and legs are pink. These are the characteristic marks of all adult Zebra-Finches. In addition, the males have chestnut brown cheek patches, white-spotted chestnut brown side feathers, and a handsome black and white striped necktie tucked into a black bib. The male, Red Bird, was a color variant and was missing his necktie and bib. The neck stripes give the bird its name. Red Bird, named for his deep crimson beak, began to do his *mating dance*. He stretched himself very tall, flattened his crest, and chortled his love song. At the same time he flared out his cheek and side feathers, putting all his male colors on display. While in full display, he "danced" down the perch towards Black Bar, pivoting from side to side showing off all his male finery. Black Bar crouched low on the perch as if she was going to fly away. Then it happened.

Black Bar fluttered her tail up and down.

She had accepted him! Just as clearly as a bride saying "I do," she had taken Red Bird as her mate. They mated at dawn for the next few days, and began to build a nest.

BUILDING A HOME

My worries were not finished. Neither bird seemed to know how to build a proper nest. Red Bird would select a long piece of grass which would snag on the cage side as he flew up making him drop it. When he delivered a piece to the nest box and fitted it in place, Black Bar would remove it and throw it out. Days went by in fruitless effort. What was wrong?

These two young birds had never seen a nest built, I was pretty sure of that. They were just four months old when I bought them and this was their first mating (these birds mate for life). I could not be sure that the cage or nest box or even the nest material was the same as they had been raised in. I hit the books once more.

Newly mated birds in the wild would carefully select a nest site in a brush or low tree. The male would choose a crotch and the female would inspect it. Usually she rejected it, and the male would try again. This selection could be repeated as much as a hundred times. When the male did find a homesite that suited her, the female would settle into it and coo gently, and he would join her. Using wild grasses that he would snip off with his beak, She could begin to build. The male collects and carries the nest material, while the female helps construct.

The nest has a *domed top* with a hole in one side for an entrance. It is lined with feathers and soft grasses. Zebra finches are avid nest builders. They build a new nest to raise each clutch of chicks, sometimes as many as half-a-dozen clutches a year, and they build extra nests for the parents to sleep in when they are without chicks.

About the fifth day of their struggle, Red Bird and Black Bar began to get the hang of it. Nest building is an inherited behavior in all birds, and the genes need some time to start sending out the right messages the first time the bird builds. They do get more expert at it and learn better techniques. Red Bird discovered that burlap threads were easier to carry if he used his beak and foot to fold the threads into compact loops before flying with them in his beak. Both he and Black Bar developed the special head shake needed to vibrate staws into place in the rapidly forming nest. The dome was raised by Black Bar butting it into shape with her head as she crouched in the egg cup she has formed in the nest's floor with her body. The inside was lined with burlap and cotton.

All this building took *14 days.* Later they would build a nest in a week to ten days, and another pair of finches once built a nest in four days. The home was ready, now the family.

EGGS

The first egg looked like a pearl. It was pure white, a centimeter and a half long and a centimeter wide, about the size of the tip of your little finger. I felt like an uncle seeing his newborn nephew or niece for the first time. Mom and Dad ignored the egg, and sat out on a branch preening themselves. What's the matter with these two? Couldn't they do anything right? Eggs must be incubated if they are to hatch! My books once again set my mind at ease. The parents knew what they were doing.

Females will lay an average of four or five eggs, one per day. They will not start to incubate them until the last egg is laid, and even then it will take a couple of days for the birds to settle down to their jobs. By starting the incubation of all the eggs at the same time, the parents ensure that the chicks will all hatch within a few hours. This gives all of the chicks an equal chance of surviving. If incubation began with the first egg, that chick would be five days old by the time the fifth egg hatched. The younger birds would have a poor time of it competing with these much larger older brothers and sisters for food and space.

Both birds share the "baby sitting" chores, relieving each other every hour or so. They place their bare breasts directly on the eggs, raising their temperatures to about 38.6 degrees C. The parents do not *incubate* continuously, since they leave the nest several times a day to join the flock to feed, bathe, or preen. In Northern Australia where daytime temperatures regularly exceed 37 degrees C, the parents will let the sun incubate for them much of each day.

The hormone *prolactin* controls incubation, and once it starts flowing the birds are determined incubators. Ordinarily, if I approached the cage Red Bird and Black Bar would fly up to the highest perch for safety. They were not afraid of me, just cautious. After all, I weighed 70,000 grams to their 12 grams. I would probably be just as cautious if I was in a room with an African elephant, no matter how gentle or friendly I thought he was. Once these finches start incubating, this new drive overcomes their safety flight reflex. I could stand with my nose on the cage wire, six inches from Red Bird's beak and he would stay put. He would even scrunch down more firmly on the eggs. By staying firmly on the eggs they were kept warm, and by not flying away as I approached Red Bird did not give away the nest's location. In the predator infested wilds this freezing on the nest has great survival potential for both the parents and the new generation.

Chicks

Fourteen days after incubation started, I found the first chick *hatched* in the nest. The chicks were no longer than my little fingernail, and ugly! Naked, scrawny, covered with a straggly down, and blind, this little fellow looked as delicate as could be. The eggshells were gone and I assume that the parents had eaten them (later I saw them do this). Black Bar hopped back into the nest, plunked herself down on this frail-looking baby, and continued her incubation of the remaining eggs. All four eggs hatched over the next 36 hours, and all the chicks were alive.

For the next three days I watched the birds almost continuously. I had a photographer take their pictures just as any proud parent would. As closely as I sat watching, I still did not see the parents feed the chicks. I set a banquet for them to eat. Special finch food can be brought ready mixed. It contains red, white and yellow millet seeds, oats, wheat and a small amount of canary seed. The mixture I stocked their feed dishes with was extra clean. Each day fresh lettuce, spinach or some other green was chopped and fed to these new parents. To provide the extra protein that the young would need to grow I fed the parents freshly chopped hard-boiled eggs daily. Their drinking water was changed each day, and a few drops of vitamins were added to it to make sure the diet was perfect.

In the wild, parent birds would *feed* their young ripe and half-ripe grass seeds, plus insects that they would pick off of the ground or catch on the wing.

Despite all my lavish preparations I could not be sure that the young birds were being fed. The entrance to the nest was too small and the nest interior too dark to allow me to see what was happening inside it. My books were discouraging, since they informed me that first-time parents often abandoned the young. I telephoned long-distance to a breeder of Zebra Finches and asked him if there was anything I could do.

"Sure," he said. "Look at the *crops* on either side of the neck (see Figure 2). They are not yet covered with feathers, and are transparent. If the chicks are fed you can see the seeds in the crops."

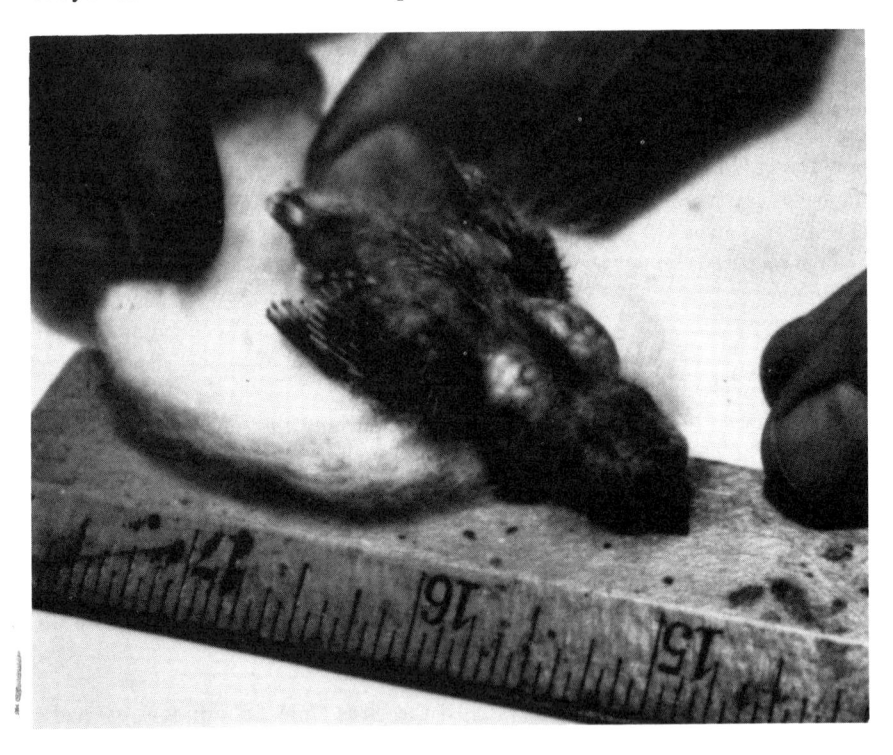

Figure 2: This four-day-old chick's full crops can be seen bulging on either side of its neck.

I dashed back to my laboratory, took my flashlight and peered into the nest. All four chicks were sleeping cozily in the nest's warm cotton-lining. On either side of each scrawny neck was a pea size bulge, full crops. I could even count the individual seeds and see green pieces of lettuce and yellow egg yolk through the crops' thin walls. The chicks looked like children with bellies bulging, snoozing after a birthday feast.

Red Bird and Black Bar sat on a far perch watching my inspection alertly, but calmly. They were cool. Many small birds become so upset when their nests are disturbed that they abandon them. Not Zebra Finches. The emotional stability of these tough little birds partly accounts for their continent-wide distribution in Australia, and their happy co-existence with man. No other Australian finch lives in so many different habitats.

Gape Marks

I looked back into the nest and tapped it gently with my finger. Four little beaks opened wide at what they thought was a parent landing on the nest to feed them. I got my first look at the babies' *gape marks*. Many perching (Passerine) birds have distinctive markings inside their mouths when they are chicks. Each species has its own distinctive set. The Zebra Finches' are small black spots in specific places on the roof and floor of the mouth and on the tongue. As each little bird gaped up at me it gently wagged its tongue back and forth, moving one pair of gape marks to attract the parents' attention. Scientists know that these marks stimulate the parent to regurgitate food and stuff it down into the chick's crop. The corners of each chick's mouth were a bright white color, the *pearls*, to help guide the parents' feeding in the dark nest interior.

Since I could not feed these eager mouths, I backed quickly away to let the parents do their duty, which they soon did. This time I was able to watch them feed by using the flashlight to light the inside of the nest. I had opened up the entrance a bit for my inspection. I could see Black Bar look at her gaping children, see the choking action as she regurgitated, brought up a mouthful of food from her own crop, and the bobbing head movement as she crammed her beak deep down the throat of each chick. As each chick was fed, it closed its beak and settled back to sleep.

I was so used to seeing my adult birds with a full coat of warm feathers that the nakedness of the babies disturbed me. The ideal temperature for raising Zebra Finch chicks in the laboratory is 30 degrees C, and my lab was only 27.5 degrees C. Although birds are warm blooded animals (38.9 degrees C for these finches), the young take several days before their body temperature stabilizes. Until then their temperatures act like those of a cold-blooded reptile, going up or down with the outside air temperature. Red Bird and Black Bar helped their babies keep warm. They took turns for the first few days *brooding* their young, keeping the chicks well tucked under their warm feathers as they sat in the nest.

Red Bird and Black Bar were now doing a fine job.

Growing Up

I will have to wait about twenty years to see my three children grow to adulthood. These Zebra Finch chicks will be fully grown and capable of having families of their own in four months. This will allow my students to observe a full growth cycle from courtship to adulthood, in one semester.

Like most babies, the chicks sleep most of the time during the first few days, only waking to be fed. They grow at a furious rate. Four days after hatching their first feathers appear, the wing primaries. By the sixth day all the *feather tracts* are well on their way (birds do not grow feathers all over their bodies like a mammal's fur; feathers grow in strips call tracts). A week after birth their eyes open and they start to preen their feathers. They are moving around in the nest a lot more.

By their second week of life the chicks now look like real birds, instead of some semi-naked, semi-reptile. They have a full coat of soft grey feathers and two shiny black eyes peer curiously from the nest at the big world in the aviary. Their beaks have turned black and their faces have the Zebra Finch characteristics, black stripe and white patch. The sexes look alike now, but eventually I will learn that these babies are three sisters and a brother.

Day sixteen is filled with excitement. I have opened a hole in the back of the nest so that I can see the chicks better and on this day when I peek in - whoosh! All four chicks leave the nest at once. They're flying! At first they crash a lot, but their supple young bodies absorb these shocks without harm.

Figure 3: This chick has just flown for the first time a few minutes before this picture was taken. At this age, it is very tame.

Red Bird and Black Bar are crowing their excitement, and busily luring each youngster up to a perch off of the aviary floor where he landed. By evening the chicks have developed enough skill to fly from the perch to their nest for the night (see Figure 3 for a first day flying chick).

Each day is now filled with new lessons. They find their voices. Now when they gape for food they cry like hungry babies. They develop their first true social behavior by grooming each other. Adults preen each other's heads, but it takes the chicks awhile to decide which end is up, so they groom both heads and tails. At the beginning of the fourth week, they join their parents at the seed feeders and begin to feed themselves. In another couple of weeks they will be fully weaned.

In the sixth week, after hatching I discover which chick is the brother. All the chicks still look alike, although they have started their first moult which will soon give them their adult feathers. The male chick gave himself away by his behavior. As Red Bird flew around the aviary singing, he was followed closely by this one chick who rasped and squealed a crude *imitation* of his dad's song. He sounded just like a teenage boy trying out his new "manly" voice. Soon his sisters would find their voices and learn the dozen or so calls that make up the Zebra Finch language.

Ten weeks after Red Bird and Black Bar first mated, their first clutch of chicks had grown their adult plummage. The parents were so enthusiastic over their success, they started raising a second family even before the first one had grown up. The chicks grew stronger every day, developing their flying skills in games of tag, follow the leader, and races.

My Zebra Finch flock was well established and before the year was out would number over forty birds, who would fascinate and teach many classes of students of animal behavior.

References

1. Cyril H. Rogers, *Zebra Finches*, K & R Books Ltd., 1979.

2. Klaus Immelman, *Australian Finches in Bush and Aviary*, Angus and Robertson, London, 1965.

Appendix C-2

READING TEST

Raising a Family - Zebra Finch Style

MARKS   Answer the following questions in the spaces provided.

5   1. The female bird takes part in the nest building.   TRUE   FALSE

5   2. On the average the female Zebra Finch lays _____ eggs.

      a. two   b. four   c. six   d. eight

10   3. Name two ways in which the male Zebra Finch's feathers are colored differently than the females.

      a. _____

      b. _____

5   4. When the bird has a high level of the hormone prolactin in its body it has a strong tendency to

      a. build a nest

      b. lay eggs

      c. freeze on the nest when disturbed

      d. loop burlap into coils to carry it

10   5. What do wild Zebra Finches feed their young?

      a. _____   b. _____

10   6. What is the function of the chick's gape marks?

      a. _____

      b. _____

10   7. a. What is brooding?   b. Why must it be done?

      a. _____

      b. _____

Appendix C-2

MARKS

5   8. In the wild this bird lives in flocks of 25 to 100 birds.

           TRUE   FALSE

5   9. How did the female, Black Bar, show her acceptance of her mate, Red Bird, when he courted her? _____

           _____

5   10. This finch's nest is built differently from the cup shaped nest of most birds; it has a _____

5   11. When a bird raises its eggs' temperature by placing its bare breast on them it is said to be _____ the eggs.

5   12. The eggs must be warmed for _____ days before they hatch.

           a. five   b. seven   c. fourteen   d. twenty-one

5   13. Food is stored in the chick's _____ before it is digested.

5   14. Male chicks learn their song

           a. on their own

           b. by imitating their father

           c. by listening to other males in the aviary

10   15. How do feathers grow over a bird's body? _____

           _____

100

ANSWER KEY

Quiz: Raising a Family - Zebra Finch Style

If your answer is exactly correct, if you use the same words as this answer key, or words very close to them, give yourself full marks. Give yourself part marks if you are partly correct, and no marks for a clearly incorrect answer or no answer. Mark your paper as if you were a teacher trying to show a student how much he knew on this topic.

Answers	Marks (allotted)	Yours
1. TRUE	(5)	____
2. b. four	(5)	____
3. (any two of) chestnut brown cheek patches, white spotted chestnut brown side	(5)	____
feathers, chest stripes and bib	(5)	____
4. c. freeze on the nest when disturbed	(5)	____
5. (any two of) ripe grass seeds, half-ripe seeds, or insects	(5)	____
	(5)	____
6. a. to attract attention	(5)	____
b. stimulate the parent to regurgitate food	(5)	____
7. a. to keep the chicks warm	(5)	____
b. the chicks are not yet warm-blooded	(5)	____
8. TRUE	(5)	____
9. fluttering her tail	(5)	____
10. domed top	(5)	____
11. incubating	(5)	____
12. c. fourteen	(5)	____
13. crops	(5)	____
14. b. by imitating their father	(5)	____
15. in strips called tracts	(10)	____
Test Score	(100)	____

Appendix C-3 **261**

WHEN MEMORY IS SUPER GOOD OR SUPER BAD

INSTRUCTIONS

Read the following article as fast as you can with good comprehension. Before you begin, write the time you start reading to the nearest second in item 5b on the Scoring Sheet on the next page (SUGGESTION: start reading on the minute, for example, start at 9 hours, 12 minutes, 0 seconds). Read the article with the goal of learning the material in it, because you will take a test right after you have finished reading. When you have finished reading, but not before, note the time to the nearest second and write it down in item 5a on the Scoring Sheet.

Answer the questions in the test following the article without looking at the article again. Score the test using the Answer Key. Total your marks and write your test score in item 4 of the Scoring Sheet.

Calculate your reading time by subtracting your starting time from your finishing time on the Scoring Sheet. Round your reading time figure to the nearest minute. Subtract your reading time from your test score to find your efficiency index (see item 6 on the Scoring Sheet). Finally, find your reading speed on the table provided on the Scoring Sheet.

SUMMARY

1. Record the time you start reading
2. Read the article as fast as you can with good comprehension
3. Record the time you finish reading
4. Take and score test
5. Calculate a. your reading time
              b. your efficiency index
6. Find your reading speed from the table

SCORING SHEET

When Memory is Super Good or Super Bad

1. Name _____ 2. Age _____

3. Class (circle one)
   College SR, JR, SO, FR; *High School* 12, 11, 10, 9, 8, 7.

4. **Test Score** _____   Hr.   Min.   Sec.

5. **Reading Time**   a. Finished reading at   ____   ____   ____

   _____ Minutes   b. Started reading at   ____   ____   ____

                             c. Reading Time   ____   ____   ____

6. **Efficiency Index**
   To calculate this index subtract the reading time in minutes (to the nearest whole minute) from your test score.

   a. Test Score   _____

   b. Reading Time   _____

   c. Efficiency Index _____

7. **Reading Speed**
   Find your reading time in the table below. The number to the right of your time is your approximate reading speed for this article in words per minute. Draw a circle around your reading speed figure (WPM).

READING SPEED TABLE

Min.	WPM	Min.	WPM	Min.	WPM	Min.	WPM	Min.	WPM	Min.	WPM
3	1170	9	390	15	234	21	167	27	130	33	106
4	878	10	351	16	219	22	160	28	125	34	103
5	702	11	319	17	207	23	153	29	121	35	100
6	585	12	293	18	195	24	146	30	117	36	98
7	502	13	270	19	185	25	140	31	113	37	95
8	439	14	251	20	176	26	135	32	110	38	92

8. To find out how your test score, reading time, and efficiency index compare to those of other students who have taken this test, see the table in *Appendix C-4*.

WHEN MEMORY IS SUPER GOOD OR SUPER BAD

Studies of the Abnormal

Real insight can be gained into human behavior by studying abnormal behavior. What is a healthy mind? Our definition of mental health has been shaped and reformed by studying what goes on in the unhealthy mind; the psychotic, the neurotic, the psychopath. Similarly, understanding human memory has been advanced by studying cases of unusually perfect memories, and highly forgetful people.

Four instances of abnormal memory function are described in this article. The first instance is the case of photographic memory, followed by the history of a man whose memory was so powerful he had to devise special techniques to help him forget. Forgetfulness is explored through the tragedies of people whose brains have become damaged, and who have lost their ability to learn. They can only remember what happened long ago, or what happened just now.

We all forget, yet occasionally events will impress themselves so strongly on our brains that they are remembered for years as if they occurred only a moment ago. Why is this so? The study of abnormal memory function has given us a few answers.

Eidetic Imagery

The prime minister of South Africa during the Second World War, Jan Smuts, had a *photographic memory*. Supposedly, he could look at the page of a book and in some mysterious way capture an image of that page so that he could "read" it later on from memory. Stories about such memories abound. A French scientist was able to project vivid mental images of his microscope slides on nearby walls. Once when he was at a dinner party and bored by the company, he was casually inspecting his mental file of slide images by projecting them on a nearby wall. Suddenly he "saw" something on one image that he had been searching for for months. Hurriedly he excused himself, rushed back to his laboratory, and pulled out that slide to confirm his finding. His photographic memory was correct!

Such vivid mental images are called *eidetic images*. The possessors of this imagery have been investigated in the research laboratory to confirm their powers, and explore this wonderful ability.

Five hundred children were tested for eidetic imagery by University of Rochester psychologist Ralph Haber. Twenty of these children were found to have this ability. Professor Haber's tests were simple yet very convincing. He sat each child before a three-foot-square gray screen. A colored picture would be laid on the screen and the child told to inspect it. He would be told, "Move your

Figure 1: Alice looking at Cheshire Cat (Adapted from Haber, 1969.)

eyes around so that you can be sure to see all the details." Each child inspected the picture for 30 seconds, the picture was then removed, and the child asked if he could see anything on the blank gray screen. Most children could not, but occasionally a child would begin to describe what he "saw" in detail. One of the pictures used in this test showed Alice in Wonderland talking to the Cheshire cat who was reclining on the lower limb of a large tree. One 10-year-old boy could "see" his eidetic image so clearly that he could describe the flowers, tell of the positions of the tree's roots and leaves, note the colors of Alice's dress and the background sky, and even give an accurate count of the number of stripes on the cat's tail.

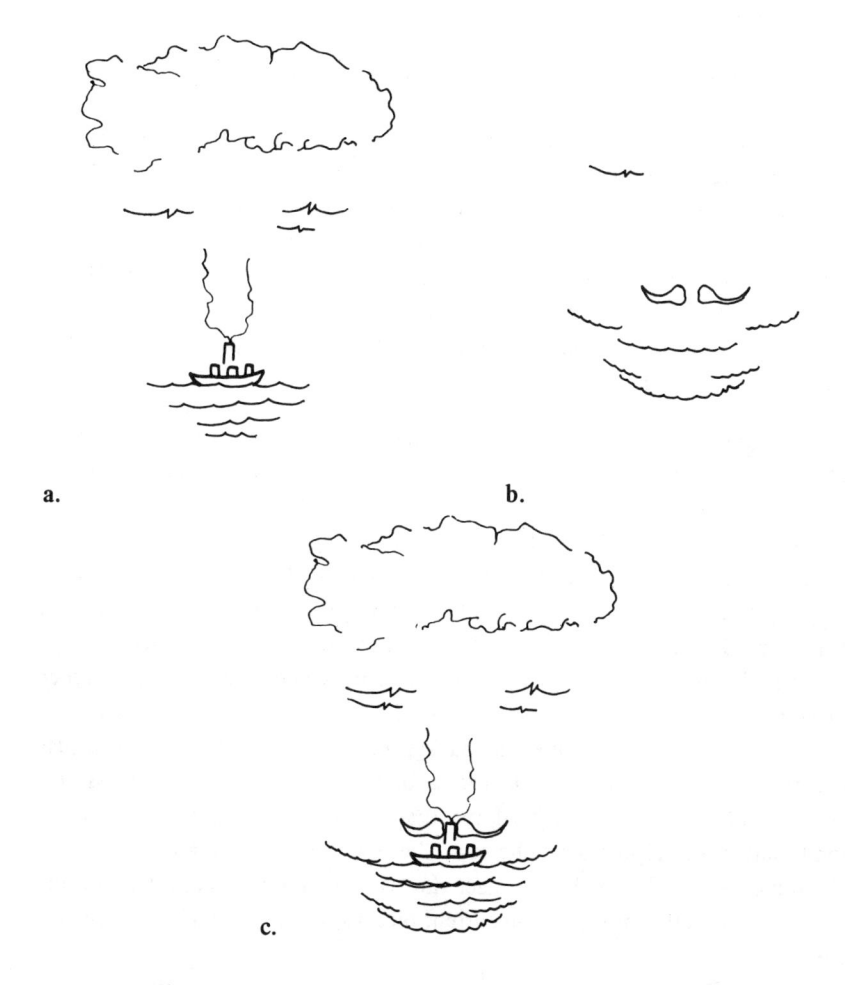

Figure 2: The eidetic children placed their image of a. on top of b. to see the composite picture c., a human face. None of the children saw a face in picture a. (adapted from Haber, 69).

Professor Haber could rule out such explanations as afterimages and verbal memorizing. A visual *afterimage*, such as you get when you look at a bright light then look away, requires that a person stare fixedly at one spot. The children were not allowed to do this at all, yet their eidetic images persisted for as long as long as ten minutes. If the eidetic children were made to describe out loud what they saw in the pictures, they could not form their images. Using *verbal memory* destroyed the eidetic image, and for this reason the eidetic imagery did not work very well for words or numbers, which the children would automatically say to themselves. These experimental controls showed what the children were not doing, but could a test be devised to prove that the children really were seeing clear mental pictures?

The *overlap test* does just this. An eidetic child was shown a line drawing of what appeared to be a ship under a cloudy sky (see Figure 2a). When this picture was removed another was placed on the screen, which by itself seemed meaningless. The child was asked to place his eidetic image of the first picture on top of the second picture and report what he saw. If the child really had a vivid mental picture of the ship scene, when he projected it on top of the second picture, the two pictures would overlap in such a way to form a new picture, a human face (see Figure 2c). Four of the children saw this face, and one child exclaimed that the experimenter was pretty "tricky" to have fooled him that way.

Two Harvard scientists used the overlap test to provide one of the most dramatic demonstrations of the power and clarity of eidetic imagery. These researchers had found an artist who claimed to have this power so strongly that she could paint portraits from her images days after forming them. To see if she really could do this the scientists tested her with stereo pictures. Normally such pictures are viewed together in a stereo viewer (remember the View Masters you played with as a child?), but the artist was shown each picture separately a day apart. The pictures were random dot patterns which when viewed together in a stereo viewer would combine to show part of the picture, a square, a number, or letter, floating above the background. Alone, each picture was just a meaningless jumble of dots. On the second day of the test, the artist was asked to superimpose her image of the first day's picture right on top of the second picture and report what she saw. She saw the square floating above the background! To do this she had to place the 10,000 random dots of the previous day's picture exactly on top of the current picture, an astoundingly vivid eidetic image!

Appendix C-3 267

a.

b.

c.

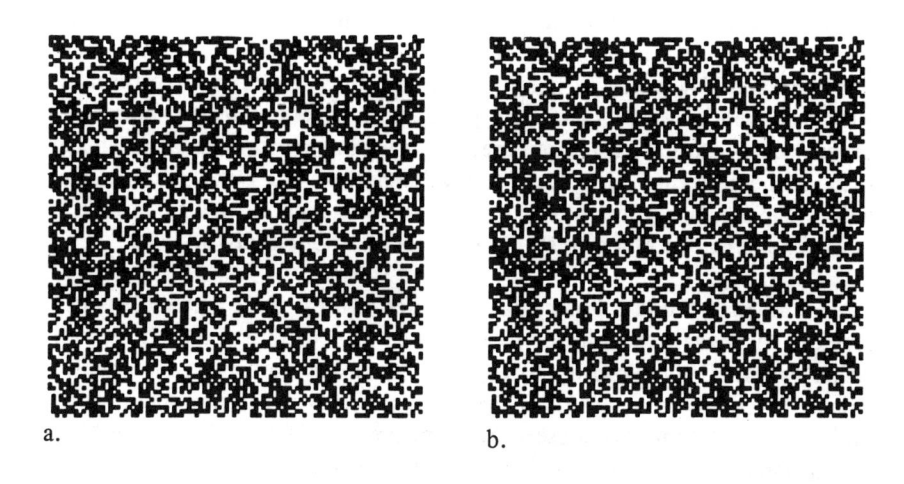

Figure 3: The artist viewed picture a. on the first day, then superimposed her image of it on b. the second day. She "saw" a small central square floating off the surface as illustrated in c. (Simulation of artist's task)

The Mnemonist

In every field of human endeavor there are the super performers. In muscular skills and power there are the Olympic athletes, in music there are the gifted prodigies like the violinist Menuhin or the composer Mozart, and in science there are the brilliant thinkers who make astounding contributions, the Einsteins, and Newtons. The field of human memory has its super performers as well. You may have seen the former professional basketball player, Jerry Lucas, or his collaborator, Harry Lorrayne, on television performing their amazing feats of memorization. The Russian psychologist, A. R. Luria, studied a man with a super memory for nearly thirty years and reported his findings in his book, *The Mind of a Mnemonist – A Little Book About a Vast Memory*.

This man, Luria calls him S., could perform the most incredible feats of memory. If he was read a list of 70 words once, he could reproduce it perfectly, either forwards or backwards. When Luria chose one word from the middle of the list, S. could easily remember the words on either side of it. Table 1 shows a table of numbers that Luria asked S. to memorize in May of 1939. After studying the table for three minutes, S. was able to give a faultless reproduction of the table column by column, or row by row, or backwards, or he could give the four number diagonals that zigzag through the table or he could convert the digits into one huge number to be read off all at once. The most astounding fact about

Table 1 S. memorized these numbers perfectly in 3 minutes

Table 1

6	6	8	0
5	4	3	2
1	6	8	4
7	9	3	5
4	2	3	7
3	8	9	1
1	0	0	2
3	4	5	1
2	7	6	8
1	9	2	6
2	9	6	7
5	5	2	0
x	0	1	x

this performance is that S. could do it just as well several months later without any review. He did not forget! Luria once tested S. on a list that he had learned sixteen years before without being told at that time that he was going to have to remember it for so long a time period. After a few moments of orientation and recollection, "Yes, yes ...you were sitting at the table and I in the rocking chair ...You were wearing a grey suit and you looked at me like this...Now, then, I can see you saying..." S. would remember the list perfectly.

Was S's remarkable power of memorization and retention an inherited gift or was it the result of intense practice? We cannot be sure but the evidence suggests that his ability was genetic. Unlike most of us, S. could remember events from the earliest years of his childhood, even as early as three-years-old (S. was 30 when Luria first discovered him), and when the scientist first informed him of his unusual power, S. was amazed because he thought that everyone remembered like he did.

S. was able to memorize easily because he had a talent for *synesthesia*. Unlike the eidetic children he did not rely on visual images alone, but could create vivid images that blended the experiences of all of his senses together. This is the technique of synesthesia, and it is often taught in books designed to help people improve their memories. For example, if you met a man named Julian Blackburn you could help yourself remember his name by imagining him wearing a toga (like Julius Caesar) and standing in a forest that had been burned black. You would be converting the sounds of his name into visual images. S. did this image construction quite unconsciously and used all of his sensory systems, not just vision. Let S. describe his synesthesia; "To this day I can't escape from seeing colors when I hear sounds. What first strikes me is the color of someone's voice. Then it fades off . . .for it does not interfere." "The late S. M. Einsenstein had just such a voice: listening to him, it was as though a flame with fibers protruding from it was advancing right toward me." "For me 2, 4, 6, 5 are not just numbers. They have forms. 1 is a pointed number — which has nothing to do with the way it's written. It's because it's somehow firm and complete. 2 is flatter, rectangular, whitish in color sometimes almost gray." We know that if people with ordinary memories use synesthesia deliberately their memory for facts will improve. S. did this all of the time quite unconsciously, and it had a lot to do with his tremendous ability to memorize.

Eventually S. put his talent to practical use and became a stage performer, a *mnemonist*. This gave him new and special problems. Since a large part of his performance consisted of remembering very long lists he had the problem of *forgetting* the list from one performance so that it would not interfere with the next act. Because his retention was very strong this posed a real difficulty for him and gave him many anxious moments. He solved this by writing down the lists after each performance. Once the list was written he knew he did not need to hold it in memory any more so he forgot it. In other words, he wrote things down TO FORGET THEM!

By now you are probably wishing that you had a memory like S's, so that you could remember all that stuff you have to learn for quizzes and examinations in school. Wouldn't that be great? No it would not. S. paid a heavy price for his super memory. His memory was concrete and factual, not general and creative. Our ability to forget blends ideas together and helps us to form generalities and be creative. S. could not do this because he remembered everything exactly as he had heard it or had seen it without any change at all. If we all had memories like that there would be no invention or artistry. Because S. used synesthesia to the extremes he could not control it. He was forced to stop reading poetry because his own vivid imagery would interfere with the imagery the poet was trying to get across. S. was like a modern electronic computer with its perfect memory and high-speed recall; he could remember but not create.

Amnesia-Total Forgetting

The people described so far have had truly superb memories, far better than the average man's. At the other end of the normal memory range are people with terrible memories, men and women who cannot remember at all, the amnesics. To show you what it is like to be an amnesic we shall report a hypothetical interview between a doctor and his patient.

The patient, a thin, balding, middle-age man, has been sitting in the doctor's waiting room for an hour with three other people, all amnesics. They have not spoken to each other, and have not even read the magazines. The patient is ushered into the doctor's office.

"Good morning Sergeant MacLeod, I'm Doctor Logue."

"Good morning Doctor Logue," the patient replies.

The doctor asks, "Why are you here in the hospital, Sergeant, and how long have you been here?"

"I seem to have a stomach ache, Doctor. I came in here last week to get it fixed up," Sergeant MacLeod cheerfully replies.

"Stomach trouble, eh? What did you eat for breakfast this morning?" asks the doctor.

The patient looks a bit vague and frowns with the effort to remember. "I had the usual, bacon and eggs and coffee."

The doctor is called from the office for five minutes. Upon his return he introduces himself again, only this time he calls himself Dr. Yasinski, and asks the patient if they have ever met before.

"No, Doctor, I don't believe so. I've not seen you before."

"Have you had any visits from your family lately?" asks the doctor.

"No, my wife can't bring my little girls up here, but they write me letters," the sergeant replies.

The doctor has confirmed once again that Sergeant MacLeod's amnesia is just as bad as ever. Sergeant MacLeod exhibits the symptoms of *Korsakoff's syndrome*, an incurable mental disease. A few facts about Sergeant MacLeod will illustrate the nature and severity of his amnesia.

Fact 1 — He has been in this hospital for 15 years, not just a week. He was admitted as a chronic alcoholic and Korsakoff's syndrome patient.

Fact 2 — He had porridge and tea for breakfast.

Fact 3 — His wife divorced him shortly after he was admitted to the hospital, and both his daughters are now married. They will have nothing to do with their father.

Notice the peculiar nature of the memory defect that the sergeant has. He can remember events from his distant past. He remembers how to speak, read, and write, He remembers his wife and children, but only as they were many years ago. He remembers enough of what is going on around him at the moment to carry on a conversation, but he cannot remember what he had for breakfast that morning, or even the doctor's face if it has been out of his sight for more than a minute or so. He is disoriented in time, not knowing how long he has been in the hospital. He will have to be led back to his ward by an orderly, because he will not remember how to get there, even though he has walked the route many times.

Both Sergeant MacLeod's *short-term memory* and *long-term memory* seem to function by themselves, so why is he amnesic? A high continuous intake of alcohol damages the brain. His brain has been permanently injured in such a way that he cannot move information from his short-term memory into his long-term memory storage. He can retrieve information from his long-term storage that was put there before the brain damage occurred, but he cannot put anything new into long-term storage.

The past 15 years are an enormous blank for the sergeant. He has very little understanding of what is wrong with him. He realizes that he should remember what he had for breakfast, so he makes up a story. For the sergeant, out of sight is literally out of mind, because once people, places and events have passed from the present into the past they are lost for him. He totally forgets.

The Hippocampus

When Korsakoff patients' brains are examined after they die, they show a particular pattern of damage. Broken blood vessels have caused small strokes in certain parts of the brain that are necessary for normal memory function. One of these parts is called the *hippocampus*, and it is located deep within the center of the brain (See Figure 4). Time and again autopsies on these amnesic persons have shown severe damage in the hippocampus, thousands and thousands of dead cells. This leads the scientist to suspect that this part of the brain is important, even necessary, for moving information in and out of long-term memory.

When a brain researcher wants to know whether a certain part of the brain is necessary for a particular behavior, he experiments. Usually the experiments are done on animals, and these experiments can then be compared to our knowledge of human brain function. For example, if the scientist wanted to know if a small collection of cells in the brain were needed to make a rat eat he could remove these cells by careful surgery to find out if the animal stopped eating. These *lesion experiments* have been widely used in brain research to discover what parts of the brain control what behavior. This kind of research is not done on people because once the brain has been damaged it cannot be repaired.

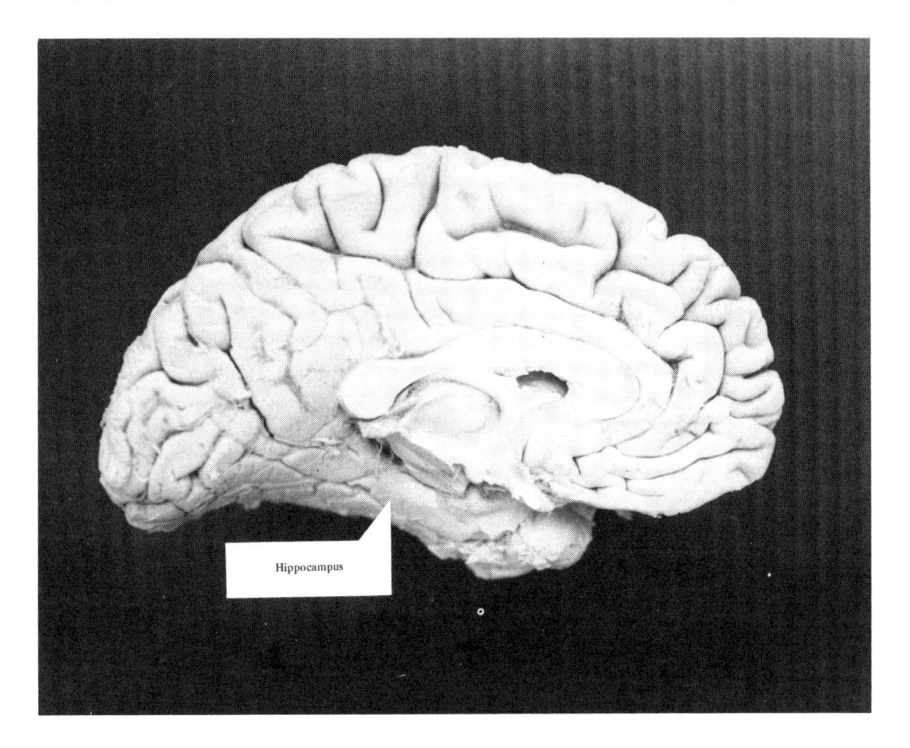

Figure 4: A middle view of the right half of a human brain showing the location of the hippocampus.

Dr. Brenda Milner of McGill University in Montreal, Canada reported on an operation that produced an amnesia almost exactly like that found in Korsakoff's syndrome. The patient, who is referred to as H. M., was slowly dying of epilepsy. Epilepsy is a brain disease that causes convulsions. H. M. first showed the symptoms of epilepsy at the age of eight. The disease had become progressively worse, and he had not responded to the many kinds of treatment that had been tried. H. M.'s doctor decided that an operation on the brain was the only possible way to save the patient. In this operation the surgeon removed the hippocampus on both sides of the brain. The operation was successful in reducing the epileptic seizures almost to zero.

After the operation H. M. had amnesia. He had not lost his intellectual powers, on the contrary his IQ showed an increase from 104 to 117, probably because his seizures had stopped. Like the Korsakoff patient, H. M. had lost the ability to store new information in his long-term memory. He could not find his way around the hospital when he was there. Ten months after his operation his family moved to a new house, and H. M. never could learn his new address. He did remember his past, and would tell long stories about events from his childhood, indicating that these long past events were all that he had to occupy his mind. He would work on the same jigsaw puzzle over and over again as if it was a new puzzle each time. Unlike the Korsakoff patient, H. M. did realize that he had something wrong with his memory.

Although H. M.'s operation was not intended to be a lesion experiment, it turned out that way. We now know that the hippocampus is an important area in the brain involved in moving information between short-term and long-term memories. Other patients with similar operations have been examined and confirm the finding that if the hippocampus is damaged by surgery, a memory deficit occurs.

Summary

The eidetic children and the mnemonist S. show us what it can be like to have extraordinarily perfect memories. They also show us that having such a super memory can be a mixed blessing. If you remember the facts too well you may not be able to blend them together to create new concepts. Facts remain facts. If you can visualize past events clearly and with great strength these visions may hamper your perception of reality.

The amnesics have taught us more about the nature of memory. Their illness shows that short-term memory and long-term memory can operate independently, and that there is a connection between the two. If this connection is damaged information cannot be put into long-term storage, but information already stored there can be retrieved. The hippocampus appears to be the place in the brain where this connection is located.

References

1. Ralph Norman Haber, *Eidetic Images*, Scientific American, April 1969

2. Brenda Milner, *Amnesia Following Operation on the Temporal Lobes*, in *Amnesia*, by Whitty and Zangwill (see below).

3. C. W. M. Whitty and O. L. Zangwill, *Amnesia*, Butterworth, London, 1966.

READING TEST

When Memory is Super Good or Super Bad

MARKS		Answer the following Questions in the spaces provided.
5	1.	The study of abnormal behavior can never help our understanding of normal behavior. TRUE FALSE
5	2.	Of the 500 children tested for eidetic imagery _____ were found to have it. a. all b. 70 c. 20 d. 3
5	3.	Another name for eidetic imagery is _____
10	4.	Why were the eidetic children not able to use their imagery for words or numbers? _____
5	5.	What is the name of the test used to prove that persons who claim to have eidetic imagery really *see* an actual image?
5	6.	A person who performs memory tricks on a stage is called a _____
5	7.	The man S., who had such a remarkable memory, could remember long meaningless lists for years. TRUE FALSE
5	8.	When asked to memorize a table of numbers, S. could reproduce the numbers accurately a. in rows c. in diagonals b. in columns d. all of these

Appendix C-3

10   9. Give an example of the use of synesthesia to help memorization. _____

10   10. What technique did S. use to help him forget lists? _____

5   11. A person who has any disease which causes him to forget almost all he learns is said to have _____

5   12. A person with Korsakoff's syndrome has a faulty

         a. short-term memory

         b. long-term memory

         c. connection between a. and b.

         d. stomach

10   13. The part of the brain which causes memory loss when it is damaged is called the _____

5   14. If a scientist wants to find out if a particular part of the brain is necessary for a *certain* behavior he can perform a _____ experiment.

10   15. H. M.'s memory loss was just like a Korsakoff Patient's except that _____

100

ANSWER KEY

Quiz: When Memory is Super Good or Super Bad

If your answer is exactly correct, if you use the same words as this answer key, or words very close to them, give yourself full marks. Give yourself part marks if you are partly correct, and no marks for a clearly incorrect answer or no answer. Mark your paper as if you were a teacher trying to show a student how much he knew on this topic.

Answers		Marks (allotted)	Yours
1.	FALSE	(5)	___
2.	c. 20	(5)	___
3.	photographic memory	(5)	___
4.	verbalizing or saying the words or numbers destroyed the image	(10)	___
5.	overlap test	(5)	___
6.	mnemonist	(5)	___
7.	TRUE	(5)	___
8.	d. all of these	(5)	___
9.	think of Julius Caesar standing in a burned forest to help remember the name Julian Blackburn	(10)	___
10.	he wrote things down	(10)	___
11.	amnesia or amnesic	(5)	___
12.	c. connection between a. and b.	(5)	___
13.	hippocampus	(10)	___
14.	lesion	(5)	___
15.	he understood that his memory was faulty	(10)	___
	Total Score	(100)	___

Appendix C-4 277

Reading Test Results

Grade 9 Students

Columns: Percentiles**, Test Scores (out of 100), Reading Times (in minutes), Efficiency Indexes

Test	Percentile	Test Score	Reading Time	Efficiency Index
Clouds n=48	90	89	10	79
	80	81	12	69
	70	75	13	62
	60	70	14	56
	50	66	15	51
	40	61	15	46
	30	56	16	40
	20	51	17	34
	10	43	19	24
Zebra Finches n=47	90	96	14	82
	80	90	17	73
	70	85	19	66
	60	81	21	60
	50	78	22	56
	40	74	24	50
	30	70	25	45
	20	66	27	39
	10	59	30	29
Memory n=45	90	99	11	88
	80	93	13	80
	70	88	14	74
	60	84	15	69
	50	81	17	64
	40	77	18	59
	30	73	19	54
	20	69	20	49
	10	63	22	41

Grade 10 Students

Test	Percentile	Test Score	Reading Time	Efficiency Index
Clouds n=99	90	90	10	85
	80	83	12	75
	70	78	13	67
	60	74	14	61
	50	70	15	55
	40	66	16	49
	30	61	17	41
	20	56	17	34
	10	49	19	23
Zebra Finches n=99	90	98	16	82
	80	92	18	74
	70	88	20	68
	60	84	22	62
	50	80	23	57
	40	77	24	53
	30	73	26	47
	20	69	28	41
	10	63	30	33
Memory n=98	90	98	11	87
	80	93	13	80
	70	90	15	75
	60	86	16	70
	50	84	17	67
	40	81	18	63
	30	78	19	59
	20	74	21	53
	10	69	23	46

n=the number of students in each Test Table

** Percentile means - the percent of students who have a particular score, or reading time, or efficiency index, or a better one (for example, 50% of the grade 10 students had a test score of 70 or better in the Clouds Test). See where your results fit.

Reading Test Results

Grade 11 Students

Test	Percentiles**	Test Scores (out of 100)	Reading Times (in minutes)	Efficiency Indexes
Clouds n=102	90	86	11	75
	80	81	12	69
	70	76	13	63
	60	73	14	59
	50	70	15	55
	40	66	16	50
	30	63	16	47
	20	59	17	42
	10	43	19	34
Zebra Finches n=102	90	95	16	79
	80	90	18	72
	70	87	20	67
	60	84	22	62
	50	81	23	58
	40	78	25	53
	30	75	26	49
	20	72	28	44
	10	67	30	37
Memory n=95	90	95	12	83
	80	92	14	78
	70	89	15	74
	60	86	17	69
	50	84	18	66
	40	82	19	63
	30	79	20	59
	20	77	21	56
	10	73	23	50

Grade 12 Students

Test	Percentiles**	Test Scores (out of 100)	Reading Times (in minutes)	Efficiency Indexes
Clouds n=63	90	85	10	75
	80	79	12	67
	70	74	13	61
	60	71	14	57
	50	67	14	53
	40	64	15	49
	30	60	16	44
	20	55	17	38
	10	49	19	30
Zebra Finches n=63	90	94	15	79
	80	90	17	73
	70	87	19	68
	60	85	21	64
	50	83	23	60
	40	81	24	57
	30	79	26	53
	20	76	28	48
	10	72	31	41
Memory n=60	90	98	12	86
	80	94	13	81
	70	91	15	76
	60	88	16	72
	50	86	17	69
	40	84	18	66
	30	81	19	62
	20	78	20	58
	10	74	22	52

n=the number of students in each Test Table

** Percentile means - the percent of students who have a particular score, or reading time, or efficiency index, or a better one (for example, 50% of the grade 10 students had a test score of 70 or better in the Clouds Test). See where your results fit.

Reading Test Results

Adults

Test	Percentiles**	Test Scores (out of 100)	Reading Times (in minutes)	Efficiency Indexes
Clouds n=60	90	84	11	73
	80	78	12	66
	70	73	13	60
	60	69	14	55
	50	65	15	50
	40	62	16	46
	30	58	16	42
	20	53	17	36
	10	47	19	28
Zebra Finches n=59	90	96	16	80
	80	91	18	73
	70	87	20	67
	60	84	22	62
	50	81	24	57
	40	78	25	53
	30	75	27	48
	20	71	29	42
	10	66	31	35
Memory n=58	90	100	11	89
	80	95	13	82
	70	91	15	76
	60	87	17	70
	50	84	18	66
	40	81	19	62
	30	78	21	57
	20	74	23	51
	10	69	25	44

n=the number of students in each Test Table

** Percentile means - the percent of students who have a particular score, or reading time, or efficiency index, or a better one (for example, 50% of the grade 10 students had a test score of 70 or better in the Clouds Test). See where your results fit.

Appendix D

READING POWER DRILL

CALCULATIONS FORM FOR WORDS PER PAGE

You need to know the number of words per page for your book.

Follow these simple steps:

1. Count the number of words in five full lines _____ .

2. Divide this number of words by five to get the average words per line (WPL). Round this latter figure to eliminate decimals.

$$5 \overline{\big)\underline{}} = WPL$$

3. Count the number of lines on a full page, lines per page (LPP) _____ .

4. Multiply the number of words per line by the numbers of lines per page to find the total number of words per page (WPP).

   (WPL) _____ x (LPP) _____ = _____ (WPP)

   Now that you have the number of words per page in the book you are reading, write this figure on the inside front cover of the book so that you will be able to find it easily each time you do a drill.

5. Finally, estimate as closely as you can the number of pages you read for each of the three blocks, 0-1, 0-4, and 4-5 (estimate to the nearest 1/2, 1/3, or 1/4 page).

   0-1 _____   0-4 _____   4-5 _____

6. Use these figures, the words per page and the page estimates, to find your reading speeds for each of the three blocks from the Table in *Appendix G*.

7. Enter your three reading speeds in your Reading Speed Record *(Appendix E)*.

READING SPEED RECORD

1. Introduction of the textbook — (words # minutes it took to read it)
   _____ WPM*

2. A. Reading test Number One — Clouds   _____ WPM

   B. Reading Test Number Two — Zebra Finches   _____ WPM

   C. Reading Test Number Three — Memory   _____ WPM

3. Spot checks of *study speed* in text book

Chapter	Date Read	Total words read	time in minutes	= Working Rate
A. ___	_____	_____	_____	_____WPM
B. ___	_____	_____	_____	_____WPM
C. ___	_____	_____	_____	_____WPM

4. **Reading Speed Drills**

	First 2 minutes (0-1)	Maximum Overload (0-4)	Last Two Minutes (4-5)
A.	_____ WPM	_____ WPM	_____ WPM
B.	_____ WPM	_____ WPM	_____ WPM
C.	_____ WPM	_____ WPM	_____ WPM
D.	_____ WPM	_____ WPM	_____ WPM
E.	_____ WPM	_____ WPM	_____ WPM
F.	_____ WPM	_____ WPM	_____ WPM
G.	_____ WPM	_____ WPM	_____ WPM
H.	_____ WPM	_____ WPM	_____ WPM
I.	_____ WPM	_____ WPM	_____ WPM
J.	_____ WPM	_____ WPM	_____ WPM
K.	_____ WPM	_____ WPM	_____ WPM
L.	_____ WPM	_____ WPM	_____ WPM
M.	_____ WPM	_____ WPM	_____ WPM
N.	_____ WPM	_____ WPM	_____ WPM

GRAPH — WPM for the Last Two Minutes (4 - 5).

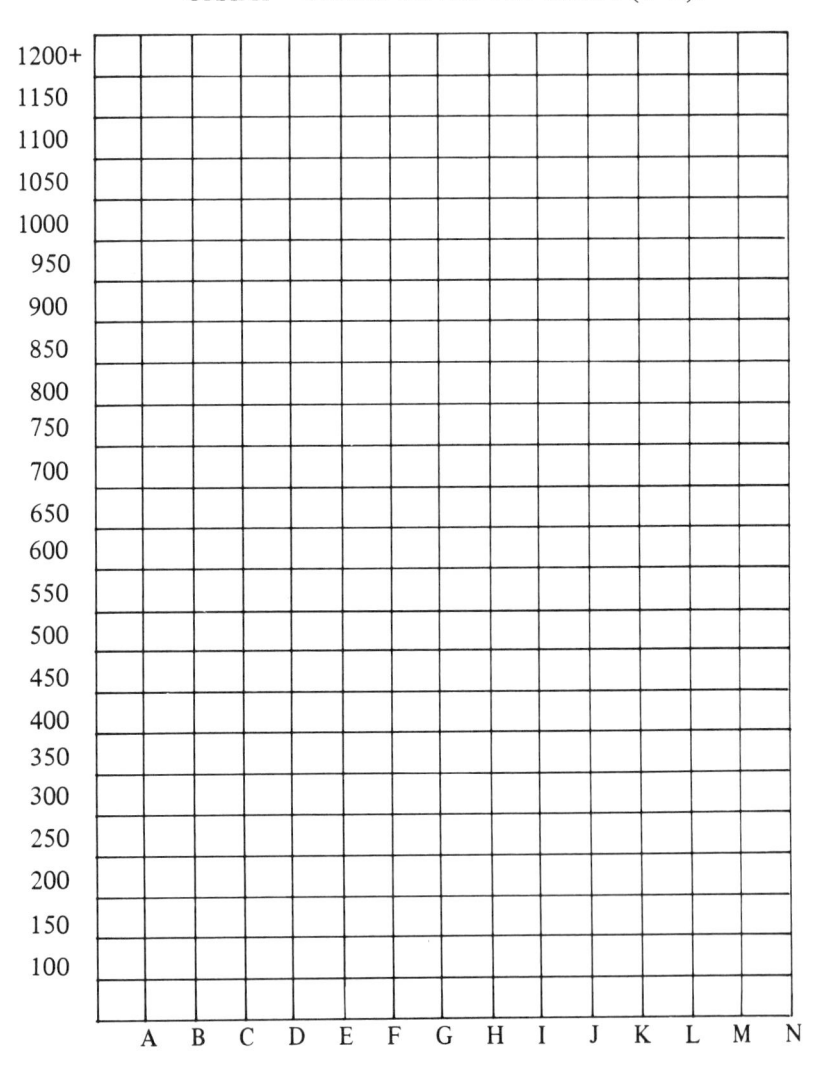

READING SPEED TABLE — WORDS PER MINUTE

The table on the next three pages will allow you to look up your reading speed without doing calculations. All you need to use it is the number of words on a page of your book, and the estimate of the number of pages you read in two minutes.

INSTRUCTIONS

1. In the left column locate the number closest to the words per page (WPP) you calculated for your book.

2. On the top row of the numbers locate the number closest to your estimate of the number of pages you read in two minutes.

3. Where this column and row come together in the body of the table is your reading speed in words per minute (WPM).

4. Example: If words per page equals 240, and the pages read equals 2/3, then your reading speed would be 80 words per minute (See Table).

   Footnote 1: Extra words per page. If your book has more than 600 words per page this table can still be used as follows:
   a. Divide the number of words per page in your book by two, then,
   b. Use this number to find the row you need in the table.
   c. Match this row with the correct Pages Read column to find WPM.
   d. Double the WPM from the table to give you your correct reading speed.

   Footnote 2: Extra Pages. If you should read more than 9 pages in your drill you can extend the usefulness of this table, as follows:
   a. Divide the number of pages read by two, then,
   b. Use this page to find the column you need in the table.
   c. Match the column up with the correct row.
   d. Take the reading speed (WPM) you obtain and double it to give you your correct speed.

   Footnote 3: Formula. If you wish to calculate your reading speed instead of using the table, use the formula: [words per page] x [pages read] ÷ 2 = words per minute.

Appendix G

Pages Read in 2 Minutes

Words per page	1/4	1/3	1/2	2/3	3/4	1	1 1/4	1 1/3	1 1/2	1 2/3	1 3/4	2	2 1/4	2 1/3	2 1/2	2 2/3	2 3/4	3
200	25	33	50	67	75	100	125	133	150	167	175	200	225	233	250	267	275	300
220	28	37	55	73	83	110	138	147	165	183	193	220	248	257	275	293	303	330
240	30	40	60	80	90	120	150	160	180	200	210	240	270	280	300	320	330	360
260	33	43	65	87	98	130	163	173	195	217	228	260	293	303	325	347	358	390
280	35	47	70	93	105	140	175	187	210	233	245	280	315	327	350	373	385	420
300	38	50	75	100	113	150	188	200	225	250	263	300	338	350	375	400	413	450
320	40	53	80	107	120	160	200	213	240	267	280	320	360	373	400	427	440	480
340	43	57	85	113	128	170	213	227	255	283	298	340	383	397	425	453	468	510
360	45	60	90	120	135	180	225	240	270	300	315	360	405	420	450	480	495	540
380	48	63	95	127	143	190	238	253	285	317	333	380	428	443	475	507	523	570
400	50	67	100	133	150	200	250	267	300	333	350	400	450	467	500	533	550	600
420	53	70	105	140	158	210	263	280	315	350	368	420	473	490	525	560	578	630
440	55	73	110	147	165	220	275	293	330	367	385	440	495	513	550	587	605	660
460	58	77	115	153	173	230	288	307	345	383	403	460	518	537	575	613	633	690
480	60	80	120	160	180	240	300	320	360	400	420	480	540	560	600	640	660	720
500	63	83	125	167	188	250	313	333	375	417	438	500	563	583	625	667	688	750
520	65	87	130	173	195	260	325	347	390	433	455	520	585	607	650	693	715	780
540	68	90	135	180	203	270	338	360	405	450	473	540	608	630	675	720	743	810
560	70	93	140	187	210	280	350	373	420	467	490	560	630	653	700	747	770	840
580	73	97	145	193	218	290	363	387	435	483	508	580	653	677	725	773	798	870
600	75	100	150	200	225	300	375	400	450	500	525	600	675	700	750	800	825	900

Appendix G

Pages Read in 2 Minutes

Words per page	3 1/4	3 1/3	3 1/2	3 2/3	3 3/4	4	4 1/4	4 1/3	4 1/2	4 2/3	4 3/4	5	5 1/4	5 1/3	5 1/2	5 2/3	5 3/4	6
200	325	333	350	367	375	400	425	433	450	467	475	500	525	533	550	567	575	600
220	358	367	385	403	413	440	468	477	495	513	523	550	578	587	605	623	633	660
240	390	400	420	440	450	480	510	520	540	560	570	600	630	640	660	680	690	720
260	423	433	455	477	488	520	553	563	585	607	618	650	683	693	715	737	748	780
280	455	467	490	513	525	560	595	607	630	653	665	700	735	747	770	793	805	840
300	488	500	525	550	563	600	638	650	675	700	713	750	788	800	825	850	863	900
320	520	533	560	587	600	640	680	693	720	747	760	800	840	853	880	907	920	960
340	553	567	595	623	638	680	723	737	765	793	808	850	893	907	935	963	978	1020
360	585	600	630	660	675	720	765	780	810	840	855	900	945	960	990	1020	1035	1080
380	618	633	665	697	713	760	808	823	855	887	903	950	998	1013	1045	1077	1093	1140
400	650	667	700	733	750	800	850	867	900	933	950	1000	1050	1067	1100	1133	1150	1200
420	683	700	735	770	788	840	893	910	945	980	998	1050	1103	1120	1155	1190	1208	1260
440	715	733	770	807	825	880	935	953	990	1027	1045	1100	1155	1173	1210	1247	1265	1320
460	748	767	805	843	863	920	978	997	1035	1073	1093	1150	1208	1227	1265	1303	1323	1380
480	780	800	840	880	900	960	1020	1040	1080	1120	1140	1200	1260	1280	1320	1360	1380	1440
500	813	833	875	917	938	1000	1063	1083	1125	1167	1188	1250	1313	1333	1375	1417	1438	1500
520	845	867	910	953	975	1040	1105	1127	1170	1213	1235	1300	1365	1387	1430	1473	1495	1560
540	878	900	945	990	1013	1080	1148	1170	1215	1260	1283	1350	1418	1440	1485	1530	1553	1620
560	910	933	980	1027	1050	1120	1190	1213	1260	1307	1330	1400	1470	1493	1540	1587	1610	1680
580	943	967	1015	1063	1088	1160	1235	1257	1305	1353	1378	1450	1523	1547	1595	1643	1668	1740
600	975	1000	1050	1100	1125	1200	1275	1300	1350	1400	1425	1500	1575	1600	1650	1700	1725	1800

Pages Read in 2 Minutes

Words per page	6 1/4	6 1/3	6 1/2	6 2/3	6 3/4	7	7 1/4	7 1/3	7 1/2	7 2/3	7 3/4	8	8 1/4	8 1/3	8 1/2	8 2/3	8 3/4	9
200	625	633	650	667	675	700	725	733	750	767	775	800	825	833	850	867	875	900
220	688	697	715	733	743	770	798	807	825	843	853	880	908	917	935	953	963	990
240	750	760	780	800	810	840	870	880	900	920	930	960	990	1000	1020	1040	1050	1080
260	813	823	845	867	878	910	943	953	975	997	1008	1040	1073	1083	1105	1127	1138	1170
280	875	887	910	933	945	980	1015	1027	1050	1073	1085	1120	1155	1167	1190	1213	1225	1260
300	938	950	975	1000	1013	1050	1088	1100	1125	1150	1163	1200	1238	1250	1275	1300	1313	1350
320	1000	1013	1040	1067	1080	1120	1160	1173	1200	1227	1240	1280	1320	1333	1360	1387	1400	1440
340	1063	1077	1105	1133	1148	1190	1233	1247	1275	1303	1318	1360	1403	1417	1445	1473	1488	1530
360	1125	1140	1170	1200	1215	1260	1305	1320	1350	1380	1395	1440	1485	1500	1530	1560	1575	1620
380	1188	1203	1235	1267	1283	1330	1378	1393	1425	1457	1473	1520	1568	1583	1615	1647	1663	1710
400	1250	1267	1300	1333	1350	1400	1450	1466	1500	1534	1550	1600	1650	1667	1700	1733	1750	1800
420	1313	1330	1365	1400	1418	1470	1523	1540	1575	1610	1628	1680	1733	1750	1785	1820	1838	1890
440	1375	1393	1430	1467	1485	1540	1595	1613	1650	1687	1705	1760	1815	1833	1870	1907	1925	1980
460	1438	1457	1494	1533	1553	1610	1668	1687	1725	1763	1783	1840	1898	1917	1955	1993	2013	2070
480	1500	1520	1560	1600	1620	1680	1740	1760	1800	1840	1860	1920	1980	2000	2040	2080	2100	2160
500	1563	1583	1625	1667	1688	1750	1813	1833	1875	1917	1938	2000	2063	2083	2125	2167	2188	2250
520	1625	1647	1690	1733	1755	1820	1885	1907	1950	1993	2015	2080	2145	2167	2210	2253	2275	2340
540	1688	1710	1755	1800	1823	1890	1958	1980	2025	2070	2093	2160	2228	2250	2295	2340	2363	2430
560	1750	1773	1820	1867	1890	1960	2030	2053	2100	2147	2170	2240	2310	2333	2380	2427	2450	2520
580	1813	1837	1885	1933	1958	2030	2103	2127	2175	2223	2248	2320	2393	2417	2465	2513	2538	2610
600	1875	1900	1950	2000	2025	2100	2175	2200	2250	2300	2325	2400	2475	2500	2550	2600	2625	2700

ACTION PLAN

Introduction

You have read the book, and completed all the exercises. Now you want to use these skills, and apply your new knowledge. You need a plan of action. This appendix will help you make this plan.

First of all, any plan that you make will be in the form of a series of *suggestions* to yourself to follow. It will not be a blueprint to which you feel you must slavishly adhere. Any plan is better than none at all, and a good one is better yet. Make this plan as thorough as you can, realizing that you may have to change some parts of it later. Long experience has shown that it is easier for a student to make changes in an existing plan, than it is to try to muddle through without any plan at all.

Secondly, for this plan to be effective it has to be real. That means it is to be written with real times, places people, and events.

Finally, these last two suggestions will help you work with this plan.

1. Don't try to do too much at once. If you attempt to put all of the skills from this book into action at once, you'll blow a fuse. You will end up saying to yourself, "I can't handle this, it's too much." As you will see from the plan outline below, I suggest that you start small and build slowly. Only add another skill, or another subject to work on when you feel comfortable with what you are already doing. Do it this way and you will be sure to succeed.

2. Use Learnometers for a few weeks, say for the first semester.

Adapt the plan outline to your circumstances. If it doesn't fit you precisely, twist it until it does.

Plan Outline

1. List all of the courses you will have this coming semester and the times and days you will have classes and laboratories. For example: English II, MTuWThF 9 a.m., Writing lab Fri. 3 p.m.

Appendix H

Class	Weekday and Time
a.	
b.	
c.	
d.	
e.	
f.	
g.	
h.	

2. Estimate how much time you spent studying in an average week last semester. Do not count classroom hours.
TIME SPENT STUDYING =

3. Use the form on page 291 of the Action Plan to record your activities during the second full week of classes at the beginning of the semester. Don't do it the first week, because that week is usually confused and erratic.

4. Use the form on page 293 of the Action Plan to make a mini-max schedule for the third week of the semester. Reconsider it at the end of the third week, and again at the end of the fourth week, and so on until you have your routines clearly established.

5. Write the name of the course on which you want to start using your learning skills. If you feel confident about using these skills, choose a tough course so that you can get the maximum benefit. If you do not feel confident, choose an easy course, one that you can handle well at the same time you are beginning your skills.

FIRST COURSE –

Once you are successfully using your learning skills on that first course, start using them on a second course.

SECOND COURSE –

Appendix H 289

After you are using learning skills in two courses, add a third, a fourth, and so on. List them below.

    THIRD COURSE –

    FOURTH COURSE –

    FIFTH COURSE –

6. List the study skills in the order you want to work on:

    Self study   1.

                      2.

                      3.

    Classroom   1.

                      2.

                      3.

    Study habit   1.

                      2.

                      3.

Try for a successful mixture of courses and skills. You could work on classroom skills for one course and self study skills in another. Use your best judgement here. Be prepared to experiment a bit.

7. Turn to page 233 and re-read your list of study problems. List your major problems below, and beside each problem write the study skill(s) that will help you solve this problem.

                Problem   **Skill**

1.

2.

3.

4.

5.

8. List the names of people you could co-teach with. Make your list as long as you are able. If you can, select a person for each course. List people even though you are not sure whether they will co-teach with you. The list can be changed later.

               Course   **Co-teacher**

1.

2.

3.

4.

5.

6.

9. Buy a calendar on which you can keep a record of events for the next semester; for exaple, exams, papers due, parties, football games, field trips, concerts, and so on. Fill in as much of this calendar as you can *now*, and keep it up to date.

10. Now you have a plan to develop your STUDY POWER. Follow it, amend it, go beyond it, just don't ignore it. **Good luck!**

Second Week - Activity Record

	Monday	Tuesday	Wednesday	Thursday	Friday	Saturday	Sunday
7:00							
8:00							
9:00							
10:00							
11:00							
Noon							
1:00							
2:00							
3:00							

Second Week - Activity Record

	Monday	Tuesday	Wednesday	Thursday	Friday	Saturday	Sunday
4:00							
5:00							
6:00							
7:00							
8:00							
9:00							
10:00							
11:00							
12:00							

Third Week - Mini-Max Schedule

	Monday	Tuesday	Wednesday	Thursday	Friday	Saturday	Sunday
7:00							
8:00							
9:00							
10:00							
11:00							
Noon							
1:00							
2:00							
3:00							

Third Week - Mini-Max Schedule

	Monday	Tuesday	Wednesday	Thursday	Friday	Saturday	Sunday
4:00							
5:00							
6:00							
7:00							
8:00							
9:00							
10:00							
11:00							
12:00							

Fourth Week - Revised Mini-Max Schedule

	Monday	Tuesday	Wednesday	Thursday	Friday	Saturday	Sunday
7:00							
8:00							
9:00							
10:00							
11:00							
Noon							
1:00							
2:00							
3:00							

Fourth Week - Revised Mini-Max Schedule

	Monday	Tuesday	Wednesday	Thursday	Friday	Saturday	Sunday
4:00							
5:00							
6:00							
7:00							
8:00							
9:00							
10:00							
11:00							
12:00							

Appendix I   **297**

CHAPTER TESTS

Introduction

These chapter tests will show you how well you have learned the material. Answers are in Appendix J, page 321 following. Each chapter test is scored out of 100 so that you can compare your scores, chapter by chapter. Record your scores in Appendix A, page 232 onwards. If your answer is not exactly the same as the one given, use your judgment to decide if the meaning is the same. If your answer is partly correct give yourself part marks. Good luck.

Chapter 2 - Readrite

1. Name the three steps in the Readrite system.

    a.   b.   c.

2. List eight items you could look at before you read a chapter.

    a.   e.
    b.   f.
    c.   g.
    d.   h.

3. How much material should you read in a textbook before you stop to take notes? _____

4. When is the best time to test yourself on a chapter? _____
   _____

5. How much time should you take to look over a chapter? _____

6. Give three good reasons to look over a chapter before you read it.

    a.   b.   c.

7. When you learn to swim you practice by swimming. Give two ways you could practice your history lessons.

    a.   b.

8. You are rewarded for learning as you read your textbook and take notes from it by (*mark the correct answer*)

a. the neatness of your notes.
b. successfully remembering what you read.
c. correctly copying the facts from your notebook.

9. Underlining is a useful substitute for notetaking as you read.

   TRUE   FALSE

10. Reading your textbook is the final step in learning the material.

    TRUE   FALSE

11. When you store facts in your memory you need to tag each fact with a retrieval cue so that you can find it later. Which one of the Readrite steps does this? _____

12. Professor Gates' research showed that immediate self testing _____ learning.

    a. does not improve   b. slightly improves   c. doubles

ANSWERS ON PAGE 319

Chapter 3 - Co-teaching

1. Define Co-teaching.

2. What are the four steps of co-teaching?

   a.

   b.

   c.

   d.

3. Suggest a way that you could use co-teaching and be the teacher all the time. _____

Appendix I 299

4. Give two reasons why co-teaching can make you learn better.
   a.

   b.

5. What is the job of the co-teaching teacher?

6. How can the co-teaching student help make the sessions more useful and enjoyable?
   a.

   b.

7. Discussions are best when they are spontaneous.

   TRUE   FALSE

8. The best way to find out what you don't know so that you can study it

   is a _____ with a friend several days before a test.

9. How could you discover if you know your French vocabulary, history dates, grammar rules or part in a school play?

10. a. The best way to co-teach is to prepare you co-teaching lesson first, then set up an appointment to teach it.   TRUE   FALSE

    b. A classroom is necessary for co-teaching.   TRUE   FALSE

    c. Having one particular place for co-teaching is good stimulus control.   TRUE   FALSE

    d. One person should teach in each co-teacing session.   TRUE   FALSE

    e. A shy person can co-teach because sessions are private, with a friend.   TRUE   FALSE

    f. A good co-teaching lesson plan should be several pages long.   TRUE   FALSE

    g. After teaching a chapter, you would be bored listening to your friend teach the same chapter   TRUE   FALSE

    ANSWERS ON PAGE 319

Chapter 4 - Reading Speed

1. What are two advantages of reading faster?

    a.   b.

2. How is the overload technique applied to reading speed?

3. The success of the Reading Power Drill lies in two simple facts, which are:

    a.

    b.

4. Reading is as purely an intellectual skill as can be found.

    TRUE   FALSE

5. _____ must be sacrificed a bit during high speed reading drills.

    a. calculations   b. regressions   c. comprehension

6. What equipment and materials would you need to do a Reading Power Drill?

    a.   b.   c.

7. What does AFAYCWGC mean?

8. The reading Power Drill has five two-minute steps. Name them.

    a.   b.   c.

    d.   e.

9. Calculating your reading speed at the end of a drill gives you a
   _____

a. reinforcement   b. pain in the neck   c. saccad

10. Match the following terms with their correct definitions.

   a. Saccadic movement ___   1. When your eyes are moving you cannot see.
   b. Regression ___
                                 2. Backwards eye movement
   c. Movement blindness ___
                                 3. Where eyes stop on a line of print
   d. Fixation ___
                                 4. Stop-and-go eye movement

                                 5. Record of your reading speed

11. A fast reader does not move his eyes faster than a slow reader, but he has fewer eye fixations per page.

   TRUE   FALSE

12. Two reasons for keeping records of your daily reading rates are

   a.   b.

13. The standard measure of reading rate is _____.

ANSWERS ON PAGE 319

Chapter 5 - In Class

1. You will spend over _____ hours sitting in classrooms during high school and college.

   a. 400   b. 5,000   c. 12,000

2. You should _____ a physical distraction that occurs only once or twice.

3. What is one way of avoiding people distractions in the classroom?

4. List three reasons students have for choosing a seat in class?

   a.   b.   c.

5. How can you use stimulus intensity dynamism to help you learn better in class?

6. Which is the best side of the room to sit if you have a right-handed teacher? _____

7. Time _____ the small effects in our lives.

8. List three ways you can be ready before a day's class begins.

    a.

    b.

    c.

9. How can you use questions if your teacher won't let you ask them during class.

    a.   b.

10. Can you be active during a lecture? If so, how?

11. What is the best way of being sure you have learned a class's material?
    _____

12. When is the best time to do your question 11. answer?

ANSWERS ON PAGE 320

Chapter 6 - Notetaking

1. List six reasons for taking notes (*in any order*).

    a.   d.

    b.   e.

    c.   f.

Appendix I 303

2. What is the best type of notebook?

3. State the big advantage of this type of notebook.

4. How can you save yourself a lot of "thumbing through" your notes?

5. What is the best (a) pen, and (b) colors of ink for day-to-day use?

    a.   b.

6. What size of notepaper has the widest choice of forms? _____

7. Name the best style of notetaking. _____

8. This style of notetaking forces you to _____ your material.

9. Name three other styles of notetaking.

    a.   b.   c.

10. What is meant by page formats?

11. If you were a brief notetaker you could use a _____ page format.

12. You could organize a list of animals alphabetically or by the animal's biological categories. The second organization is an example of

    (a) _____ organization, and has the advantage

    of (b) _____ .

13. Why should you number your note pages?

14. List three ways of putting emphasis into your notes.

    a.   b.   c.

15. List three common faults in notetaking.

    a.   b.   c.

ANSWERS ON PAGE 320

Chapter 7 - Examinations

1. Essay exams have few questions so you read (a)_____,

   and write (b)_____ .

2. Give three examples of objective exams.

   a.   b.   c.

3. Objective exams require you to recognize answers, but essay exams go further. How?

4. Why is it important to read all the questions on an essay exam before answering any of them?

5. Which exam would most likely get you the most marks, one in which you

   a. recognize answers?

   b. recall answers?

6. What are the six steps to correctly answering an essay exam (*in any order*)?

   a.

   b.

   c.

   d.

e.

f.

7. What are the five steps to correctly answering an objective exam (*in any order*)?

   a.

   b.

   c.

   d.

   e.

8. State the three rules for pacing yourself during an exam.

   a.

   b.

   c.

9. What is a good way to rehearse for an essay exam?

10. The disadvantages of fear and anxiety about a test is that your behavior becomes _____ .

11. The advantage of excitement and enthusiasm about a test is that they will

    _____ .

ANSWERS ON PAGE 321

Chapter 8 - Student-Teacher Relations

1. The best kind of teaching must be actively pursued.

   TRUE   FALSE

2. An example of a professional relationship would be

   a. a lawyer loving his wife

   b. a policeman helping a woman across the street

   c. a gardener and a stone mason designing a garden

3. What is the hidden contract between student and teacher?

4. State the common meeting ground all students have with their teachers.

5. What risk do you take if you don't ask teacher questions?

6. List the three steps you would use in seeking extra work.

   a.

   b.

   c.

7. Give one way you could reinforce teacher for helping you.

8. What are a couple of advantages of not being an anonymous student?

   a.   b.

9. Rotten teaching prohibits a useful student-teacher relationship.

   TRUE   FALSE

10. List four good ways of actively seeking a teacher's help.

    a.

    b.

c.

d.

ANSWERS ON PAGE 321

Chapter 9 - A Place and a Time

1. A study place must be used for study only.

   TRUE   FALSE

2. What is meant by place conditioning?

3. What's wrong with your bedroom as a study place?

4. Describe three physical qualities a good study place should have.

   a.

   b.

   c.

5. An imposing work place that you use solely for study will be treated with _____ by your family.

   a. hilarity   b. contempt   c. respect

6. The ideal study place is always isolated from people.

   TRUE   FALSE

7. What is the ideal secret of developing a powerful study habit?

8. Give three reasons this ideal cannot be met?

   a.   b.   c.

9. Describe one life situation that would allow you to easily change a habit "cold turkey."

10. The gradual method of habit formation has two rules, which are:

    a.   b.

11. Three little tricks that will help you when you start to backslide in your habits are:

    a.

    b.

    c.

ANSWERS ON PAGE 322

Chapter 10 - Using Time

1. Time is one of three important resources in human affairs. Can you remember the other two?

    a.   b.

2. What are the three steps to wise time budgeting?

    a.

    b.

    c.

3. List the six "must" items in a week's time budget (*hint-sleep is one of them*).

    a.   b.   e.

    d.   e.   f.

4. Studying is a "must" item in the week's time budget.

    TRUE   FALSE

Appendix I

5. How many hours a week did you put down for total "must" items?_____

6. Use your time sheet from yesterday and figure out how much time you spend (a) eating, (b) studying, and (c) in class.

   a.   b.   c.

7. The key to successful time planning is _____ .

8. List the five steps in successful time planning. _____

   a.

   b.

   c.

   d.

   e.

9. Give an example of your Mini-Max planning.

10. How do you determine if a Mini-Max plan is successful?

11. Give two examples of scraps of time you could use.

    a.   b.

12. What type of work can be done best using time scraps?

13.
    a. Leave lots of open times in the evenings to fit in study during the week.   TRUE   FALSE

    b. Plan a definite end to each work day.   TRUE   FALSE

    c. A desk calendar keeps track of long range items like tests, papers, and beach weekends.   TRUE   FALSE

    d. A little black book helps you remember assignments until they can be transferred to your calendar.   TRUE   FALSE

e. Recreation does not need to be planned. TRUE   FALSE

14. How could you repair a time plan that was not working well?

ANSWERS ON PAGE 322

Chapter 11 - Concentration

1. The concentration drill has five steps starting with (a) "Work until your attention wanders." What are the remaining steps?

    b.

    c.

    d.

    e.

2. What property does the "extra work" step have in the above drill that makes it possible to do?

3. Give examples of two kinds of breaks you can take in the above drill.

4. To be effective the Concentration Drill should be used on *all* the subjects you study.
    TRUE   FALSE

5. The Concentration Drill can help your work motivation in a couple of ways. What are they?

    a.

    b.

6. How can you improve your concentration on a long, long dull task?

7. You can tighten your concentration by speeding up your work.
    TRUE   FALSE

Appendix I **311**

8. The secret of setting deadlines to finish your work is to

9. What alternative method could you use to improve your concentration if sitting still does not work?

10. What is the real danger of taking a break as soon as your mind wanders?

ANSWERS ON PAGE 323

Chapter 12 - Record Keeping

1. What is the purpose of keeping track of work on the Learnometer?

2. Why bother keeping track of how much time it takes to do your work?

3. Why do students not keep study skills records when they do keep track of clothing sizes, their height and weight, and how much they earn at their jobs?

4. The singing teacher asked three questions to find out the work that her student had done. What were they?

    a.

    b.

    c.

5. What are two reasons for keeping records of your day-to-day learning skills performance?

    a.

b.

ANSWER ON PAGE 324

Chapter 13 - Fight Boredom with Variety

1. "Variety is the spice of life."

    TRUE   FALSE

2. Define boredom.

3. _____ are a major symptom of boredom.

4. Nerve cells that detect pressure on the skin's surface send electrical messages to the brain

    a. when the probe is pressed deeper into the skin

    b. when the probe is being released

    c. when the probe is held steady

    d. both a. and b.

5. When you looked at the blurred grey circle in the book it disappeared after about 15 seconds. Because the circle did not present the brain enough varied information the brain effectively said

    "_____."

6. Describe three experiences people had when they were severely deprived of sensory stimulation.

    a.

    b.

    c.

7. What is a daydream?

Appendix I 313

8. State four ways of coping with boredom.

   a.

   b.

   c.

   d.

ANSWERS ON PAGE 324

Chapter 14 - Motivation to Study

1. What are the three parts of the motivation cycle? Give an example of each one.

   a.

   b.

   c.

2. Which one of these parts energize and direct your behavior?

3. The best way to discover if you truly have a need for something is to

   _____ .

4. Give one explanation why a lot of American students have low to moderate motivation for their schooling.

5. Define incentives.

6. Give examples of:

   a. extrinsic incentive —

   b. intrinsic incentive —

7. If your goals are to be useful motivation they must be _____ and _____ .

8. What does Balance Theory say?

9. Give an example of Balance Theory at work.

10. The rule for making the "As If" technique work is

11. Motivation affects your performance not your learning.

    TRUE   FALSE

12. More learning is a *direct* result of more work.

    TRUE   FALSE

13. Motivation can improve your learning by making you work more, and also by making you _____ .

ANSWER ON PAGE 324

Chapter 15 - Gradualness

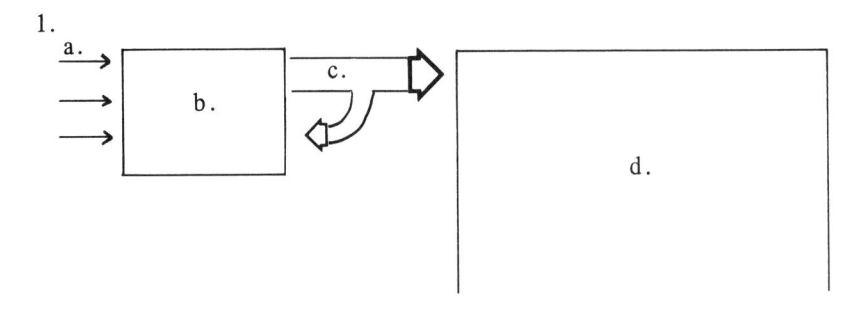

1.

   Identify the components of the memory system in the above diagram.

   a.   c.

   b.   d.

2. How long is information stored in your short-term memory?

3. What kind of information is moved from short-term memory to long-term memory?

4. How do you transfer information from short-term memory to long-term memory?

5. How long is information stored in long-term memory?

6. What is the size of long-term memory?

7. Short-term memory is like

   a. electricity flowing through the wires of a radio

   b. a photograph

   c. a printed page

8. Forgetting from short-term memory is caused by

9. How can you minimize forgetting due to interference?

10. Learning slowly is always more efficient than trying to learn too fast.

    TRUE   FALSE

11. A day's rest will improve your recall from memory without any further work on your part. What does this indicate about your performance at the end of the previous day.

12. State the Law of Gradualness.

ANSWERS ON PAGE 325

316   *Appendix I*

Chapter 16 - Stimulus Control and Specific Practice

1. Research scientists control the sights and sounds an animal receives during training by placing it in _____ .

2. This careful control of sights and sounds is called

3. A bird trained to peck a key when it was green would peck it _____ when it was yellow or blue.   MORE   LESS

4. The bird will peck at stimuli similar to the one he has been trained to peck even though they are not exactly like it.

    Responding to such similar stimuli is called _____ .

5. Give an example of changing contexts between learning and remembering.

6. State the Law of Stimulus Control.

7. The best way to train for a five mile running race would be to

    a. bike five miles a day

    b. walk long distances

    c. run long distances

8. The best way to study for a written vocabulary test in French would be to _____ .

9. Which of the following stimulus-response pair sets would provide the most interference forgetting?

    a. PLQ-rabbit, NTF-owl

b. BRF-fish, BRF-trout

   c. MZL-rose, MZL-mother

10. State the Law of Specific Practice.

ANSWERS ON PAGE 325

Chapter 17 - Reinforcement, Repetition, and Active Learning

1. A reinforcement is: a.

   b.

   c.

2. Money, love, and power are always reinforcers.

   TRUE   FALSE

3. Give six examples of positive reinforcers.

   a.   b.   c.

   d.   e.   f.

4. When does a negative reinforcer do its work?

5. What is the difference between a negative reinforcer and a punishment?

6. Give two reasons not to use punishment in learning.

   a.

   b.

7. Success is a positive reinforcer for students.

   TRUE   FALSE

8. Reinforcers are most effective

   a. when they are delayed an hour

   b. when they are received on the same day

   c. when they are received immediately

9. Use _____ reinforcement for fast learning.

10. Use _____ reinforcement for slow extinction.

11. The technique of reinforcing simple behaviors first then gradually approaching your final behavior by successive approximations is called

12. State the Law of Repetition.

13. State the Law of Active Learning.

ANSWERS ON PAGE 325

ANSWERS TO CHAPTER TESTS

Chapter 2 - Readrite

Marks

Marks		
9	1.	a. Look-it-Over
		b. Notes
		c. Test yourself
8	2.	a. Titles
		b. Subtitles
		c. Italicized words
		d. Pictures and captions
		e. Tables and graphs
		f. Boldface print
		g. Chapter summary
		h. Chapter outline
9	3.	As much as you can remember
9	4.	Immediately
8	5.	2-3 minutes *or* SHORT
9	6.	a. Maps
		b. helps evaluation
		c. improves your confidence
8	7.	a. remembering what you read
		b. writing notes
8	8.	b. successfully remembering what you read
8	9.	FALSE
8	10.	FALSE
8	11.	Test yourself
8	12.	c. doubles
$\overline{100}$		

Marks

Marks		
16	2.	a. Set a time and a place to co-teach
		b. Study material
		c. Make a brief outline (one 3x5 card) to use as a teaching aid
		d. Meet a friend and teach lesson
8	3.	Be a tutor
10	4.	*Any two of* - better preparation, helps motivation, improves organization, beats loneliness, discovers weaknesses, or reinforces learning.
7	5.	Present the facts clearly and see that the student learns them.
10	6.	a. asks questions
		b. seeks explanations
4	7.	TRUE
7	8.	Quizzing session
7	9.	Recite them to a friend
21	10.	a. FALSE
		b. FALSE
		c. TRUE
		d. TRUE
		e. TRUE
		f. FALSE
		g. FALSE
$\overline{100}$		

Chapter 3 - Co-teaching

Marks

Marks		
10	1.	Learning better through teaching another student (*or words to that effect*).

Chapter 4 - Reading Speed

Marks

Marks		
10	1.	*Any two of* - read more in less time, improved confidence, improved comprehension

ANSWERS TO CHAPTER TESTS

Marks

10	2. You force yourself to read very fast and your normal speed increases
10	3. a. You can read at high speed for brief spurts
	b. You can read faster the second time through the material
5	4. FALSE
5	5. c. comprehension
6	6. a. practice book
	b. pen
	c. clock
5	7. As Fast As You Can With Good Comprehension
10	8. a. Pretest
	b. 1st overload
	c. 2nd overload
	d. 3rd overload
	e. Post-test
7	9. a. reinforcement
12	10. a. 4 b. 2 c. 1 d. 3
5	11. TRUE
10	12. a. for reinforcement
	b. To see your progress
5	13. Words per minute (WPM)

$\overline{100}$

Chapter 5 - In Class

Marks

8	1. b. 5,000
8	2. ignore
8	3. sit near the front of the classroom
9	4. *Any three of* - friends, habits, teacher, eyesight, recreation
8	5. sit near the front *or* in some way make the class bigger, brighter, clearer, more intense
8	6. right side
8	7. multiplies
8	8. a. have assignments done and with you
	b. be on time
	c. preview
9	9. a. write them in your notes
	b. ask them after class
9	10. Yes. Write brief, numbered, outlined notes
8	11. Test yourself
8	12. Immediately

$\overline{100}$

Chapter 6 - Notetaking

Marks

12	1. a. record information
	b. improve understanding
	c. focus attention
	d. organize material
	e. for test review
	f. to LEARN
6	2. Three-ring, looseleaf
6	3. flexibility of use
6	4. use index tabs
6	5. a. ballpoint
	b. black or dark blue
6	6. 8 1/2 x 11 inches
8	7. numbered outline
6	8. organize
6	9. a. paragraph
	b. indent
	c. primitive messy

ANSWERS TO CHAPTER TESTS

Marks		Marks	
6	10. the way a page is divided for use	18	6. *In any order* - read all questions (jotting notes), answer questions from easy to hard, re-read and analyze each question carefully, make an outline, write your essay, check your answer
6	11. two-column		
8	12. a. related b. meaning *or* making sense		
6	13. for cross referencing *or* keeping track of your notes		
6	14. *Any three of* - underline boxes, color, arrows, N.B.		
6	15. *Any three of* - copying, taking dictation, illegible handwriting, no organization, wordiness, no pagination, using shorthand, doodling, using pencil, or no notes at all.	15	7. *In any order* - see how marks are allotted, allot time accordingly, leave toughies to the last, guess, check your answers
$\overline{100}$		9	8. a. be on time b. allot time according to marks and questions difficulty c. keep track of time

Chapter 7 - Examinations

Marks			
		7	9. Write outlines to a few likely exam questions
8	1. a. **a little** b. **a lot**	7	10. any one of - inhibited, simpler, stereotyped, more primitive
9	2. *Any three of* - multiple choice, true-false, fill-in-the-blanks, matching tests	7	11. will carry you over rough spots in the exam
7	3. *Any one of* - recall the answers, select the material, organize the material	$\overline{100}$	

Chapter 8 - Student-Teacher Relations

Marks		
7	4. to tap subconscious memory	
6	5. a. recognize answers	7	1. TRUE
		8	2. c. a gardener and a stone mason designing a garden

ANSWERS TO CHAPTER TESTS

Marks		Marks	
8	3. they agree on manipulating each other so that the student learns.	10	3. You are conditioned to sleep there
8	4. The subject matter being taught.	12	4. a. good lighting b. straight backed chair c. a large enough desk
8	5. You might get lost.	5	5. c. respect
15	6. a. have a specific problem b. show that you have already worked on it c. show a willingness to do more work	5	6. FALSE
		10	7. Study at your study place at your regular time, and never make an exception.
8	7. *Any one of* - show how teacher's help has worked, thank you's, a smile or nod when receiving help	12	8. a. conflicts b. distractions c. old habit interference
		10	9. When you have a large change in your life, such as going away to a new school
10	8. *Any two of* - get extra help, improve your motivation, being known when papers are graded, having your questions answered in class	10	10. a. start small b. reinforce your new habit
		12	11. a. never quit completely b. go through the motions c. trick yourself into doing it
8	9. FALSE		
20	10. a. focus on subject matter being taught b. be an agressive questioner c. ask for extra work d. reinforce good teaching		

$\overline{100}$ $\overline{100}$

Chapter 9 - A Place and a Time

Chapter 10 - Using Time

Marks		Marks	
4	1. TRUE	6	1. a. materials b. people
10	2. Some behavior automatically occurs in that place, for example, shooting baskets in a basketball court.	9	2. a. discover how you spend your time b. prepare a flexible time plan c. follow your plan intelligently

ANSWERS TO CHAPTER TESTS

Marks			
10	3.	a.	sleep
		b.	classes
		c.	personal
		d.	eating
		e.	travel
		f.	exercise
5	4.	FALSE	
5	5.	See Figure 10-1 on page , Totals.	
9	6.	a. b. c. — check your own time sheets	
5	7.	flexibility	
15	8.	a.	Make your plan in advance
		b.	Write your plan
		c.	Write in hours, then activities
		d.	Write in study times for each course (Mini-Max).
		e.	Leave lots of empty slots
6	9.	example, (*Yours should resemble this*) English maximum hours planned = 5, minimum acceptable = 3	
5	10.	You have met your minimums	
6	11.	a bus ride, or time between classes, or similar scraps of your own	
6	12.	Routine, repetitive work like vocabulary learning, spelling, math problems	
8	13.	a.	FALSE
		b.	TRUE
		c.	TRUE
		d.	TRUE
		e.	FALSE

Marks			
5	14.	Look it over after the week is finished and adjust it.	
100			

Chapter 11 - Concentration

Marks			
16	1.	b.	Promise yourself a break
		c.	work intensively for a short period of time
		d.	take your break
		e.	return to work
10	2.	it is brief	
10	3.	a.	switch to another kind of work
		b.	take a real break, a coke, a walk, phone a friend
10	4.	FALSE	
7	5.	a.	You develop a positive mental attitude towards improving your concentration
		b.	You are permissive with yourself
10	6.	break it up, keep work periods short	
7	7.	TRUE	
10	8.	involve other people	
10	9.	physical activity, (e.g., take notes, recite out loud)	
10	10.	you reinforce quitting and reinforce laziness	
100			

Appendix J 323

ANSWERS TO CHAPTER TESTS

Marks

Chapter 12 - Record Keeping

Marks

Marks		
20	1.	to give you feedback on how you are doing
20	2.	to discover how long you take at your studies so you can improve
20	3.	they do not value study skills
20	4.	a. how much...? b. how often...? c. what...?
20	5.	a. so that you can perceive your improvements clearly b. so that you reinforce your skills
100		

Chapter 13 - Fight Boredom with Variety

Marks

6	1.	FALSE
12	2.	Boredom is the feeling you have when the world appears dull, uninteresting, and monotonous.
12	3.	daydreams
8	4.	d. both a. and b.
12	5.	"there is nothing there."
18	6.	a. tactile hallucinations like insects crawling on their skin b. auditory hallucinations like voices

Marks

		c. visual hallucinations like geometrical shapes or animals.
12	7.	a daydream is the brain's way of filling a dull spot in the day
20	8.	a. Vary what you are working on b. Vary your actions c. keep work sessions short d. work fast
100		

Chapter 14 - Motivation to Study

Marks

12	1.	a. needs - food b. actions - open the refrigerator c. goals and incentives - ice cream
7	2.	needs
7	3.	deprive yourself of that thing
7	4.	they have never been deprived of schooling *or* they are satiated with schooling
7	5.	rewards you strive for
8	6.	a. money or food or affection b. success or perfection or a job well done
8	7.	immediate and concrete
7	8.	You cannot believe one thing and do another thing for very long

Appendix J

ANSWERS TO CHAPTER TESTS

Marks		
8	9.	believing a Rabbit is a good car yet rejecting it for a Honda *or* working hard at a course you dislike and continuing to dislike it
8	10.	to improve your motivation act "As If" you were well motivated
7	11.	TRUE
7	12.	TRUE
7	13.	pay better attention
100		

Chapter 15 - Gradualness

Marks		
16	1.	a. information b. short-term memory c. "use it" d. long-term memory
8	2.	20 seconds to an hour
8	3.	useful information
8	4.	by using it
8	5.	permanently - for your lifetime
8	6.	infinitely large *or* it never fills up
6	7.	a. electricity flowing through wires of a radio
8	8.	a real loss of information
8	9.	make each fact learned distinctive *or* compare facts and develop relations between them
6	10.	FALSE
8	11.	it was inhibited

Marks		
8	12.	Learn at the right speed, not too fast or too slowly
100		

Chapter 16 - Stimulus Control and Specific Practice

Marks		
10	1.	an apparatus
10	2.	stimulus control
5	3.	LESS
10	4.	stimulus generalization
10	5.	one example, learning your history in a dingy attic, then taking the test in a bright classroom
15	6.	The more learning stimuli resemble remembering stimuli the better you will remember
5	7.	run long distances
10	8.	*write* French vocabulary
10	9.	BRF-fish, BRF-trout
15	10.	Learn it as you'll use it
100		

Chapter 17 - Reinforcement Repetition, and Active Learning

Marks		
12	1.	a. a stimulus b. which when paired with a behavior

326   *Appendix J*

ANSWERS TO CHAPTER TESTS

Marks

		c. increases the probability of that behavior occuring again
5	2.	FALSE
6	3.	*see page 224*
7	4.	when it is turned off
7	5.	both are painful, but punishment does its work when it is turned on, negative reinforcement when it is turned off
8	6.	a. you cannot learn anything new with it b. the emotional behavior it generates interferes with learning
5	7.	TRUE
6	8.	c. immediately
7	9.	continuous
7	10.	partial
6	11.	shaping
12	12.	frequently used knowledge is remembered best
12	13.	activity increases learning

100

LEARNOMETERS

Keep a daily record to show your progress in using study skills. The Learnometer will show your day-to-day improvements in clear, numerical form. Slight gains will become visible right away. Keep one Learnometer in your notebook each day and mark it throughout the day as you use the skills. The numbered items below match each of the skills listed on the reverse side of this form, and explain each skill briefly.

INSTRUCTIONS

DAILY SUMMARY
A. Print your name.
B. Print the date — day, month, year.
C. Write the total number of minutes you worked at your studies today.
D. Write the total number of new textbook pages you studied today.
E. Count the total number of checks below and write that here.
F. Write your reading speed if you take a speed test or do a speed drill.
G. Compute your study speed and write it here.
H. The initials of a parent, a friend, a teacher, or yourself certifies your day's learning skills.

CHECKLIST
1. You worked at your special study place.
2. You started to work promptly at the scheduled study time.
3. Check once for each activity on your MINI-MAX schedule you did today.
4. Concentration drills will increase your stick-to-it power; do daily.
5. Vary the material you study each hour to avoid boredom.
6. Teach a subject to a friend. It helps you learn it better.
7. Before you quit today, plan tomorrow's work.
8. Work that is reinforced will become easy to do, a habit.
9. Slowly increase the number of study skills you employ.
10. Ease into your work to make it more enjoyable.
11. Prepare a mental map of your reading material before you read it.
12. Read with the intention of learning the material.
13. Stop reading frequently to jot notes from memory on what you have read.
14. Test yourself on what you have read. Have you learned it well?
15. Read spontaneously. Don't be a drudge, follow your interests.
16. A daily speed reading drill will improve and maintain your speed.
17. Use warmup to get your mind on the class before it starts.
18. Over the years, good seating in class will aid your learning a lot.
19. Students who participate in class learn more — ask questions.

20. Write questions in your notes. They will aid exam preparation.
21. If you cannot ask questions during class, ask them afterwards.
22. Take notes; they are tangible proof of your learning.
23. Class lessons are best learned immediately, not later on.
24. Read all the essay questions before answering any of them.
25. Write from an outline. You will present your ideas more clearly.
26. Look for silly mistakes before you turn in your exam.
27. Don't ponder tough questions. Return to them at the end of the exam.
28. Let your subconscious improve grades, guess at questions you don't know.
29. Let the distribution of marks and your ability determine your time plan.

ACTIVITIES — write down what material you worked on, texts, tests, labs, etc.
TIMES — note the time you start and finish each activity. Total for the day.

Learnometer

DAILY SUMMARY

Name_____ Date_____
Total work time _____ minutes
Total pages studied _____ pages
Total number of checks _____ checks
Reading speed _____ words per minute
Study speed _____ words per minute
Initials _____

Times
start = s
finish = f

f	Total
s	Time=
f	
s	
f	
s	
f	
s	
f	
s	
f	
s	
f	
s	
f	
s	

Description of Activities

Copyright by
Greencrest Press Inc.
Box 7745
Winston-Salem, N.C.

STUDY HABITS	1.	Work at my study place
	2.	Work at my study time
	3.	Follow a MINI-MAX schedule
	4.	Do a concentration drill
	5.	Vary study
	6.	Co-teach
	7.	Sew seeds of future work
	8.	Reinforce my work (write how)
	9.	Add a new study skill today
SELF-STUDY	10.	Warm up
	11.	Look it over
	12.	READRITE – read to learn
	13.	– write notes from memory
	14.	SELF-TEST – use the material I learn
	15.	Follow your nose
	16.	Speed Reading Drill
CLASSROOM	17.	Pre-class warm up
	18.	Sit in the best seat
	19.	Ask questions in class
	20.	Write questions in notes
	21.	Ask teacher questions after class
	22.	Write brief, numbered, outline notes
	23.	Self test before leaving classroom
TESTS	24.	Essay – read all questions
	25.	– rough outline
	26.	– look back
	27.	Objective – bypass tough questions
	28.	– guess
	29.	Time yourself

Learnometer

DAILY SUMMARY

Name _____ Date _____
Total work time _____ minutes
Total pages studied _____ pages
Total number of checks _____ checks
Reading speed _____ words per minute
Study speed _____ words per minute

Initials _____

Times
start = s
finish = f

Total Time =

| f | s | f | s | f | s | f | s | f | s | f | s | f | s | f | s |

Description of Activities

Copyright by
Greencrest Press Inc.
Box 7745
Winston-Salem, N.C.

STUDY HABITS	1. Work at my study place
	2. Work at my study time
	3. Follow a MINI-MAX schedule
	4. Do a concentration drill
	5. Vary study
	6. Co-teach
	7. Sew seeds of future work
	8. Reinforce my work (write how)
	9. Add a new study skill today
SELF-STUDY	10. Warm up
	11. Look it over
	12. READRITE — read to learn
	13. — write notes from memory
	14. SELF-TEST — use the material I learn
	15. Follow your nose
	16. Speed Reading Drill
CLASSROOM	17. Pre-class warm up
	18. Sit in the best seat
	19. Ask questions in class
	20. Write questions in notes
	21. Ask teacher questions after class
	22. Write brief, numbered, outline notes
	23. Self test before leaving classroom
TESTS	24. Essay — read all questions
	25. — rough outline
	26. — look back
	27. Objective — bypass tough questions
	28. — guess
	29. Time yourself

Learnometer

DAILY SUMMARY

Name _____ Date _____
Total work time _____ minutes
Total pages studied _____ pages
Total number of checks _____ checks
Reading speed _____ words per minute
Study speed _____ words per minute
Initials _____

Times
start = s
finish = f

f	s	f	s	f	s	f	s	f	s	f	s	f	s	Total Time=

Description of Activities

Copyright by
Greencrest Press Inc.
Box 7745
Winston-Salem, N.C.

STUDY HABITS	1. Work at my study place
	2. Work at my study time
	3. Follow a MINI-MAX schedule
	4. Do a concentration drill
	5. Vary study
	6. Co-teach
	7. Sew seeds of future work
	8. Reinforce my work (write how)
	9. Add a new study skill today
SELF-STUDY	10. Warm up
	11. Look it over
	12. READRITE – read to learn
	13. – write notes from memory
	14. SELF-TEST – use the material I learn
	15. Follow your nose
	16. Speed Reading Drill
CLASSROOM	17. Pre-class warm up
	18. Sit in the best seat
	19. Ask questions in class
	20. Write questions in notes
	21. Ask teacher questions after class
	22. Write brief, numbered, outline notes
	23. Self test before leaving classroom
TESTS	24. Essay – read all questions
	25. – rough outline
	26. – look back
	27. Objective – bypass tough questions
	28. – guess
	29. Time yourself

Learnometer

DAILY SUMMARY

Name _____ Date _____
Total work time _____ minutes
Total pages studied _____ pages
Total number of checks _____ checks
Reading speed _____ words per minute
Study speed _____ words per minute

Initials _____

Times
start = s
finish = f

Total Time=

| f | s | f | s | f | s | f | s | f | s | f | s | f | s |

Description of Activtities

Copyright by
Greencrest Press Inc.
Box 7745
Winston-Salem, N.C.

STUDY HABITS	1.	Work at my study place
	2.	Work at my study time
	3.	Follow a MINI-MAX schedule
	4.	Do a concentration drill
	5.	Vary study
	6.	Co-teach
	7.	Sew seeds of future work
	8.	Reinforce my work (write how)
	9.	Add a new study skill today
SELF-STUDY	10.	Warm up
	11.	Look it over
	12.	READRITE — read to learn
	13.	— write notes from memory
	14.	SELF-TEST — use the material I learn
	15.	Follow your nose
	16.	Speed Reading Drill
CLASSROOM	17.	Pre-class warm up
	18.	Sit in the best seat
	19.	Ask questions in class
	20.	Write questions in notes
	21.	Ask teacher questions after class
	22.	Write brief, numbered, outline notes
	23.	Self test before leaving classroom
TESTS	24.	Essay — read all questions
	25.	— rough outline
	26.	— look back
	27.	Objective — bypass tough questions
	28.	— guess
	29.	Time yourself

Learnometer

DAILY SUMMARY

Name_____ Date_____
Total work time _____ minutes
Total pages studied _____ pages
Total number of checks _____ checks
Reading speed _____ words per minute
Study speed _____ words per minute
Initials _____

Times
start = s
finish = f

| f | s | f | s | f | s | f | s | f | s | f | s | f | s | Total Time= |

Description of Activitities

Copyright by
Greencrest Press Inc.
Box 7745
Winston-Salem, N.C.

STUDY HABITS	1.	Work at my study place
	2.	Work at my study time
	3.	Follow a MINI-MAX schedule
	4.	Do a concentration drill
	5.	Vary study
	6.	Co-teach
	7.	Sew seeds of future work
	8.	Reinforce my work (write how)
	9.	Add a new study skill today
SELF-STUDY	10.	Warm up
	11.	Look it over
	12.	READRITE – read to learn
	13.	– write notes from memory
	14.	SELF-TEST – use the material I learn
	15.	Follow your nose
	16.	Speed Reading Drill
CLASSROOM	17.	Pre-class warm up
	18.	Sit in the best seat
	19.	Ask questions in class
	20.	Write questions in notes
	21.	Ask teacher questions after class
	22.	Write brief, numbered, outline notes
	23.	Self test before leaving classroom
TESTS	24.	Essay – read all questions
	25.	– rough outline
	26.	– look back
	27.	Objective – bypass tough questions
	28.	– guess
	29.	Time yourself

Learnometer

DAILY SUMMARY

Name _____
Total work time _____ minutes
Total pages studied _____ pages
Total number of checks _____ checks
Reading speed _____ words per minute
Study speed _____ words per minute

Initials _____

Times start = s finish= f	Total Time=
	J
	S
	J
	S
	J
	S
	J
	S
	J
	S
	J
	S
	J
	S

Description of Activities

Copyright by
Greencrest Press Inc.
Box 7745
Winston-Salem, N.C.

STUDY HABITS	1.	Work at my study place
	2.	Work at my study time
	3.	Follow a MINI-MAX schedule
	4.	Do a concentration drill
	5.	Vary study
	6.	Co-teach
	7.	Sew seeds of future work
	8.	Reinforce my work (write how)
	9.	Add a new study skill today
SELF-STUDY	10.	Warm up
	11.	Look it over
	12.	READRITE – read to learn
	13.	– write notes from memory
	14.	SELF-TEST – use the material I learn
	15.	Follow your nose
	16.	Speed Reading Drill
CLASSROOM	17.	Pre-class warm up
	18.	Sit in the best seat
	19.	Ask questions in class
	20.	Write questions in notes
	21.	Ask teacher questions after class
	22.	Write brief, numbered, outline notes
	23.	Self test before leaving classroom
TESTS	24.	Essay – read all questions
	25.	– rough outline
	26.	– look back
	27.	Objective – bypass tough questions
	28.	– guess
	29.	Time yourself

Learnometer

DAILY SUMMARY

Name _____ Date _____
Total work time _____ minutes
Total pages studied _____ pages
Total number of checks _____ checks
Reading speed _____ words per minute
Study speed _____ words per minute

Initials _____

Times
start = s
finish = f

Total Time =

| f | s | f | s | f | s | f | s | f | s | f | s | f | s | f | s |

Description of Activities

Copyright by
Greencrest Press Inc.
Box 7745
Winston-Salem, N.C.

STUDY HABITS	1. Work at my study place																						
	2. Work at my study time																						
	3. Follow a MINI-MAX schedule																						
	4. Do a concentration drill																						
	5. Vary study																						
	6. Co-teach																						
	7. Sew seeds of future work																						
	8. Reinforce my work (write how)																						
	9. Add a new study skill today																						
SELF-STUDY	10. Warm up																						
	11. Look it over																						
	12. READRITE – read to learn																						
	13. – write notes from memory																						
	14. SELF-TEST – use the material I learn																						
	15. Follow your nose																						
	16. Speed Reading Drill																						
CLASSROOM	17. Pre-class warm up																						
	18. Sit in the best seat																						
	19. Ask questions in class																						
	20. Write questions in notes																						
	21. Ask teacher questions after class																						
	22. Write brief, numbered, outline notes																						
	23. Self test before leaving classroom																						
TESTS	24. Essay – read all questions																						
	25. – rough outline																						
	26. – look back																						
	27. Objective – bypass tough questions																						
	28. – guess																						
	29. Time yourself																						

Learnometer

DAILY SUMMARY

Name_____ Date_____
Total work time _____ minutes
Total pages studied _____ pages
Total number of checks _____ checks
Reading speed _____ words per minute
Study speed _____ words per minute

Initials _____

Times
start = s
finish= f

	Total Time=
f	
s	
f	
s	
f	
s	
f	
s	
f	
s	
f	
s	
f	
s	
f	
s	

Description of Activtities

Copyright by
Greencrest Press Inc.
Box 7745
Winston-Salem, N.C.

STUDY HABITS	1. Work at my study place
	2. Work at my study time
	3. Follow a MINI-MAX schedule
	4. Do a concentration drill
	5. Vary study
	6. Co-teach
	7. Sew seeds of future work
	8. Reinforce my work (write how)
	9. Add a new study skill today
SELF-STUDY	10. Warm up
	11. Look it over
	12. READRITE – read to learn
	13. – write notes from memory
	14. SELF-TEST – use the material I learn
	15. Follow your nose
	16. Speed Reading Drill
CLASSROOM	17. Pre-class warm up
	18. Sit in the best seat
	19. Ask questions in class
	20. Write questions in notes
	21. Ask teacher questions after class
	22. Write brief, numbered, outline notes
	23. Self test before leaving classroom
TESTS	24. Essay – read all questions
	25. – rough outline
	26. – look back
	27. Objective – bypass tough questions
	28. – guess
	29. Time yourself

Learnometer

DAILY SUMMARY

Name _____ Date _____
Total work time _____ minutes
Total pages studied _____ pages
Total number of checks _____ checks
Reading speed _____ words per minute
Study speed _____ words per minute
Initials _____

Times
start = s
finish = f

| f | s | f | s | f | s | f | s | f | s | f | s | f | s | Total Time= |

Description of Activitities

Copyright by
Greencrest Press Inc.
Box 7745
Winston-Salem, N.C.

STUDY HABITS	1. Work at my study place
	2. Work at my study time
	3. Follow a MINI-MAX schedule
	4. Do a concentration drill
	5. Vary study
	6. Co-teach
	7. Sew seeds of future work
	8. Reinforce my work (write how)
	9. Add a new study skill today
SELF-STUDY	10. Warm up
	11. Look it over
	12. READRITE – read to learn
	13. – write notes from memory
	14. SELF-TEST – use the material I learn
	15. Follow your nose
	16. Speed Reading Drill
CLASSROOM	17. Pre-class warm up
	18. Sit in the best seat
	19. Ask questions in class
	20. Write questions in notes
	21. Ask teacher questions after class
	22. Write brief, numbered, outline notes
	23. Self test before leaving classroom
TESTS	24. Essay – read all questions
	25. – rough outline
	26. – look back
	27. Objective – bypass tough questions
	28. – guess
	29. Time yourself

Learnometer

DAILY SUMMARY

Name _____ Date _____
Total work time _____ minutes
Total pages studied _____ pages
Total number of checks _____ checks
Reading speed _____ words per minute
Study speed _____ words per minute

Initials _____

Times
start = s
finish = f

	Total Time=
f	
s	
f	
s	
f	
s	
f	
s	
f	
s	
f	
s	
f	
s	
f	
s	

Description of Activtities

Copyright by
Greencrest Press Inc.
Box 7745
Winston-Salem, N.C.

STUDY HABITS
1. Work at my study place
2. Work at my study time
3. Follow a MINI-MAX schedule
4. Do a concentration drill
5. Vary study
6. Co-teach
7. Sew seeds of future work
8. Reinforce my work (write how)
9. Add a new study skill today

SELF-STUDY
10. Warm up
11. Look it over
12. READRITE – read to learn
13. – write notes from memory
14. SELF-TEST – use the material I learn
15. Follow your nose
16. Speed Reading Drill

CLASSROOM
17. Pre-class warm up
18. Sit in the best seat
19. Ask questions in class
20. Write questions in notes
21. Ask teacher questions after class
22. Write brief, numbered, outline notes
23. Self test before leaving classroom

TESTS
24. Essay – read all questions
25. – rough outline
26. – look back
27. Objective – bypass tough questions
28. – guess
29. Time yourself

Learnometer

DAILY SUMMARY

Name_____ Date_____
Total work time _____ minutes
Total pages studied _____ pages
Total number of checks _____ checks
Reading speed _____ words per minute
Study speed _____ words per minute
Initials _____

Times
start = s
finish= f

	Total Time=
f	
s	
f	
s	
f	
s	
f	
s	
f	
s	
f	
s	
f	
s	
f	
s	

Description of Activtities

Copyright by
Greencrest Press Inc.
Box 7745
Winston-Salem, N.C.

STUDY HABITS	1.	Work at my study place
	2.	Work at my study time
	3.	Follow a MINI-MAX schedule
	4.	Do a concentration drill
	5.	Vary study
	6.	Co-teach
	7.	Sew seeds of future work
	8.	Reinforce my work (write how)
	9.	Add a new study skill today
SELF-STUDY	10.	Warm up
	11.	Look it over
	12.	READRITE – read to learn
	13.	– write notes from memory
	14.	SELF-TEST – use the material I learn
	15.	Follow your nose
	16.	Speed Reading Drill
CLASSROOM	17.	Pre-class warm up
	18.	Sit in the best seat
	19.	Ask questions in class
	20.	Write questions in notes
	21.	Ask teacher questions after class
	22.	Write brief, numbered, outline notes
	23.	Self test before leaving classroom
TESTS	24.	Essay – read all questions
	25.	– rough outline
	26.	– look back
	27.	Objective – bypass tough questions
	28.	– guess
	29.	Time yourself

Learnometer

DAILY SUMMARY

Name _____ Date _____
Total work time _____ minutes
Total pages studied _____ pages
Total number of checks _____ checks
Reading speed _____ words per minute
Study speed _____ words per minute
Initials _____

Times
start = s
finish = f

| s | f | s | f | s | f | s | f | s | f | s | f | s | f | Total Time= |

Description of Activities

Copyright by
Greencrest Press Inc.
Box 7745
Winston-Salem, N.C.

STUDY HABITS	1. Work at my study place
	2. Work at my study time
	3. Follow a MINI-MAX schedule
	4. Do a concentration drill
	5. Vary study
	6. Co-teach
	7. Sew seeds of future work
	8. Reinforce my work (write how)
	9. Add a new study skill today
SELF-STUDY	10. Warm up
	11. Look it over
	12. READRITE – read to learn
	13. – write notes from memory
	14. SELF-TEST – use the material I learn
	15. Follow your nose
	16. Speed Reading Drill
CLASSROOM	17. Pre-class warm up
	18. Sit in the best seat
	19. Ask questions in class
	20. Write questions in notes
	21. Ask teacher questions after class
	22. Write brief, numbered, outline notes
	23. Self test before leaving classroom
TESTS	24. Essay – read all questions
	25. – rough outline
	26. – look back
	27. Objective – bypass tough questions
	28. – guess
	29. Time yourself

Learnometer

DAILY SUMMARY

Name _____ Date _____
Total work time _____ minutes
Total pages studied _____ pages
Total number of checks _____ checks
Reading speed _____ words per minute
Study speed _____ words per minute

Initials _____

Times
start = s
finish = f

											Total Time=
f	f	f	f	f	f	f	f	f	f	f	
s	s	s	s	s	s	s	s	s	s	s	

Description of Activities

Copyright by
Greencrest Press Inc.
Box 7745
Winston-Salem, N.C.

STUDY HABITS	1. Work at my study place
	2. Work at my study time
	3. Follow a MINI-MAX schedule
	4. Do a concentration drill
	5. Vary study
	6. Co-teach
	7. Sew seeds of future work
	8. Reinforce my work (write how)
	9. Add a new study skill today
SELF-STUDY	10. Warm up
	11. Look it over
	12. READRITE – read to learn
	13. – write notes from memory
	14. SELF-TEST – use the material I learn
	15. Follow your nose
	16. Speed Reading Drill
CLASSROOM	17. Pre-class warm up
	18. Sit in the best seat
	19. Ask questions in class
	20. Write questions in notes
	21. Ask teacher questions after class
	22. Write brief, numbered, outline notes
	23. Self test before leaving classroom
TESTS	24. Essay – read all questions
	25. – rough outline
	26. – look back
	27. Objective – bypass tough questions
	28. – guess
	29. Time yourself

Learnometer

DAILY SUMMARY

Name _____ Date _____
Total work time _____ minutes
Total pages studied _____ pages
Total number of checks _____ checks
Reading speed _____ words per minute
Study speed _____ words per minute

Initials _____

Times
start = s
finish = f

	Total Time=
f	
s	
f	
s	
f	
s	
f	
s	
f	
s	
f	
s	
f	
s	
f	
s	

Description of Activities

Copyright by
Greencrest Press Inc.
Box 7745
Winston-Salem, N.C.

STUDY HABITS	1. Work at my study place
	2. Work at my study time
	3. Follow a MINI-MAX schedule
	4. Do a concentration drill
	5. Vary study
	6. Co-teach
	7. Sew seeds of future work
	8. Reinforce my work (write how)
	9. Add a new study skill today
SELF-STUDY	10. Warm up
	11. Look it over
	12. READRITE – read to learn
	13. – write notes from memory
	14. SELF-TEST – use the material I learn
	15. Follow your nose
	16. Speed Reading Drill
CLASSROOM	17. Pre-class warm up
	18. Sit in the best seat
	19. Ask questions in class
	20. Write questions in notes
	21. Ask teacher questions after class
	22. Write brief, numbered, outline notes
	23. Self test before leaving classroom
TESTS	24. Essay – read all questions
	25. – rough outline
	26. – look back
	27. Objective – bypass tough questions
	28. – guess
	29. Time yourself

Learnometer

DAILY SUMMARY

Name _____ Date _____
Total work time _____ minutes
Total pages studied _____ pages
Total number of checks _____ checks
Reading speed _____ words per minute
Study speed _____ words per minute

Initials _____

Times
start = s
finish = f

| s | f | s | f | s | f | s | f | s | f | s | f | s | f | Total Time= |

Description of Activities

Copyright by
Greencrest Press Inc.
Box 7745
Winston-Salem, N.C.

358

STUDY HABITS	1. Work at my study place
	2. Work at my study time
	3. Follow a MINI-MAX schedule
	4. Do a concentration drill
	5. Vary study
	6. Co-teach
	7. Sew seeds of future work
	8. Reinforce my work (write how)
	9. Add a new study skill today
SELF-STUDY	10. Warm up
	11. Look it over
	12. READRITE – read to learn
	13. – write notes from memory
	14. SELF-TEST – use the material I learn
	15. Follow your nose
	16. Speed Reading Drill
CLASSROOM	17. Pre-class warm up
	18. Sit in the best seat
	19. Ask questions in class
	20. Write questions in notes
	21. Ask teacher questions after class
	22. Write brief, numbered, outline notes
	23. Self test before leaving classroom
TESTS	24. Essay – read all questions
	25. – rough outline
	26. – look back
	27. Objective – bypass tough questions
	28. – guess
	29. Time yourself

Learnometer

DAILY SUMMARY

Name _____ Date _____
Total work time _____ minutes
Total pages studied _____ pages
Total number of checks _____ checks
Reading speed _____ words per minute
Study speed _____ words per minute

Initials _____

Times
start = s
finish = f

| s | f | s | f | s | f | s | f | s | f | s | f | s | f | s | f | Total Time= |

Description of Activities

Copyright by
Greencrest Press Inc.
Box 7745
Winston-Salem, N.C.

STUDY HABITS	1.	Work at my study place
	2.	Work at my study time
	3.	Follow a MINI-MAX schedule
	4.	Do a concentration drill
	5.	Vary study
	6.	Co-teach
	7.	Sew seeds of future work
	8.	Reinforce my work (write how)
	9.	Add a new study skill today
SELF-STUDY	10.	Warm up
	11.	Look it over
	12.	READRITE – read to learn
	13.	– write notes from memory
	14.	SELF-TEST – use the material I learn
	15.	Follow your nose
	16.	Speed Reading Drill
CLASSROOM	17.	Pre-class warm up
	18.	Sit in the best seat
	19.	Ask questions in class
	20.	Write questions in notes
	21.	Ask teacher questions after class
	22.	Write brief, numbered, outline notes
	23.	Self test before leaving classroom
TESTS	24.	Essay – read all questions
	25.	– rough outline
	26.	– look back
	27.	Objective – bypass tough questions
	28.	– guess
	29.	Time yourself

Learnometer

DAILY SUMMARY

Name_____ Date_____
Total work time _____ minutes
Total pages studied _____ pages
Total number of checks _____ checks
Reading speed _____ words per minute
Study speed _____ words per minute
Initials _____

Times
start = s
finish = f

f	f	f	f	f	f	f	f	f	Total
s	s	s	s	s	s	s	s	s	Time=

Description of Activities

Copyright by
Greencrest Press Inc.
Box 7745
Winston-Salem, N.C.

STUDY HABITS	1. Work at my study place
	2. Work at my study time
	3. Follow a MINI-MAX schedule
	4. Do a concentration drill
	5. Vary study
	6. Co-teach
	7. Sew seeds of future work
	8. Reinforce my work (write how)
	9. Add a new study skill today
SELF-STUDY	10. Warm up
	11. Look it over
	12. READRITE – read to learn
	13. – write notes from memory
	14. SELF-TEST – use the material I learn
	15. Follow your nose
	16. Speed Reading Drill
CLASSROOM	17. Pre-class warm up
	18. Sit in the best seat
	19. Ask questions in class
	20. Write questions in notes
	21. Ask teacher questions after class
	22. Write brief, numbered, outline notes
	23. Self test before leaving classroom
TESTS	24. Essay – read all questions
	25. – rough outline
	26. – look back
	27. Objective – bypass tough questions
	28. – guess
	29. Time yourself

TIME SHEET

Time	Activity	Time	Activity

TIME SHEET

Time	Activity	Time	Activity

TIME SHEET

Time	Activity	Time	Activity

TIME SHEET

Time	Activity	Time	Activity

TIME SHEET

Time	Activity	Time	Activity

TIME SHEET

Time	Activity	Time	Activity

REFERENCES

1. Atkinson, R. C. & Schiffrin, R. M. Human memory: A proposed system and its control processes. In K. W. Spence & J. T. Spence (Eds.) *The psychology of learning and motivation: Advances in research and theory*, Vol. 2, New York: Academic Press, 1968, 89-195.
2. Beck, R. C. *Motivation: Theories and principles.* Prentice-Hall, 1978.
3. Bettger, Frank. *How I raised myself from failure to success in selling.* Cornerstone, 1975.
4. Brown, Roger, W. & McNeil, David. The "tip-of-the-tongue" phenomenon, *Journal of Verbal Learning and Verbal Behavior*, 1966, *5*, 325-337.
5. Cornsweet, Tom N. *Visual perception*, New York: Academic Press, 1970.
6. Drucker, Peter F. *The Effective Executive*, New York: Harper and Row, 1966.
7. Duchastel, Philippe. Effect of testing on the retention of prose. *Psychological Reports*, 1980, *46*, 182.
8. English, H. B., Welborn, E. L., & Killian, C. D. Studies in substance memorization. *Journal of General Psychology*, 1934, *11*, 233-299.
9. Falkenberg, P. R. Recall improves in short-term memory the more recall context resembles learning context. *Journal of Experimental Psychology*, 1972, *95*, 39-47.
10. Flexner, L. B., Flexner, J. R., de La Haba, G. & Roberts, R. B. Loss of memory as related to inhibition of cerebral protein synthesis. *Journal of Neurochemistry*, 1965, *12*, 535-541.
11. Gates, A. I. Recitation as a factor in memorizing. *Archives of Psychology*, New York, No. 40.
12. Guttman, Norman & Kalish, Harry I. Experiments in discrimination. *Scientific American*, Jan., 1958.
13. Hart, Joseph T. Second-try recall, recognition, and the memory monitoring process. *Journal of Educational Psychology*, 1967, *58(4)*, 193-197.
14. Heron, Woodburn. The pathology of boredom. *Scientific American*, Jan., 1957.
15. Hilgard, Ernest R. & Bower, Gordon H. *Theories of Learning*, New York: Prentice Hall, 1975.
16. Kimble, G. A. & Shatel, R. B. The relationship between two kinds of inhibition and the amount of practice. *Journal of Experimental Psychology*, 1952, *44*, 355-59.
17. Klatzky, Roberta L. *Human memory: Structures and processes.* W. H. Freeman, 1980.
18. Miller, Merle. *Plain speaking: An oral biography of Harry S. Truman.* Berkley, 1973.
19. Morgan, Clifford T. & Deese, James. *How to study.* (2nd edition) McGraw-Hill, 1969.
20. Nafe, J. P. & Kenshalo, D. R. Stimulation and neural response. *American Journal of Psychology*, 1958, *71*, 199-208.

21. Parkinson, C. Northcote. *Parkinson's Law.* Houghton-Miffliin, 1957.
22. Peterson, Lloyd R. & Peterson, Margaret Jean. Short-term retention of individual verbal items. *Journal of Experimental Psychology,* 1959, *58*, 193-8.
23. Russel, Bertrand. Portraits from memory: I: Alfred North Whitehead, *Harpers Magazine,* Dec. 1952, 50-52.
24. Smith, N. B. *Read faster and get more from your reading,* Prentice-Hall, 1958.

INDEX

A

Academic subject, practice of, 33
Active learning
  defined, 42, 52
  law of, 230
Actions, motivate, 187
Action motivation, defined, 191
Advanced techniques, after basics, 34
AFAYCWGC, defined, 59
Aid to review, notes as, 36
Alarm timer, in reading power drill, 58
Alternation, reading and note writing, 30
Anxiety, exam's, 118
"As if", technique, 192-193
Assignments, in preparation for class, 78
Astronauts, power defined, 7
"The A-to-D student", an example, 7
Attention
  focused by notetaking, 85
  paying, 73
Attitude, on exams, 118
Automatic cues, needed, 39

B

Backsliding, tricks to overcome, 141
Balance theory, defined, 192
Ball point pens, use of, 88-89
Basic drill, power reading, 56-57
Basics, come first, 34-35
Behavior, some beyond measurement, 174
Behavior records, value of recording, 175
Boredom
  demonstration, 181
  what is it, 178-179
"Brain", well coached, 9
Burton, Richard, as example, 149

C

Calendars, use of, 151
Categories, finding best, 40
Chapter tests, purpose of, 169
Classroom
  distraction, 72-73
  for co-teaching, 45-46
Classroom time, preparation for using, 77-78
Class seat
  and friends, 73
  hours spent, 77
  importance of, 71
  people distractions, 73
  perfect, 75
  physical distractions, 72
  reason for choosing, 71-72
  which side of room, 76
Class time, using, 77
Classmates, compete for attention, 73
College student, reading speed, 55
Comprehension, importance of, 57
Concentration
  and motivation 157
  break, 156
  deadlines, 159-160
  extra work, 155-156
  brevity, 156
  perfect, 162
  physical activity improves, 160-161
  reinforce extra work, 155-157
  speed tightens it, 158-159
  training yourself, 154-155
Concentration drill
  permissiveness, 158
  positive mental attitude, 157
  5-steps, 154
Conditioning, defined, 132
Confidence, importance of, 33
Context, influences recall, 215
Co-teaching
  in classroom, 45-46

instructions, 16-17
learning through, 44
steps, 45
success of, 45
the student, 50
the teacher, 49
"turning on" to, 48
value of, 44
Contract, hidden, 122
Craft, students improve, 10
Cues, for remembering, 42
Cumulative records, importance of, 63

D

Daydream, defined, 183
Days off, important/needed, 19
Deadlines, involve other people, 160
Demonstration
 boredom, 181
 movement "blindness", 66
 saccadic movements, 64
Discussion
 importance of joining, 79
 organized, 50
 spontaneous, 50
Distractions, in the classroom, 72-73
Dull work
 boredom, 184
 break it up, keep it short, 158

E

Electronic computers, memories, 203
Enthusiasm, during exam, 118
Equipment, for study skills, 14
Essay exam
 taking, 103-104
 reading questions, 103
 rehearsal, 117
 subconscious memory, 103
Evaluate, while reading, 32-33

Exam
 anxiety, 118
 attitude towards, 118
 enthusiasm, 118
 essay, 102
 fear, 118
 inhibition, 118
 objective, 102, 109-112
 packing yourself, 112-115
 payday, 101-102
 preparation, 115-116
 rehearsal, 116-117
 review for, 90-92
 studying for, 102
 teacher's style, 116
 types, 102
Extinction, no reinforcement, 227
Extra work, how to seek it, 125
Eye contact, importance of, 75-76
Eye Fixations, examples, 65
Eye movements, in reading speed, 63-64

F

Facts, labeling of, 41
Fast reader, key to being, 67
Fear, during exam, 118
Feedback, reinforcement, 36
Files, memory, 208
Filing, categories important, 39-40
Filing systems, lost facts, 39-40
Forgetting
 explanation of, 207-208
 loss of information, 207
 minimize, 217-218
 short term memory, 207
Formats, notetaking, 94
Friends, class seat, 73-74

G

Gates, experiement, 41-42
Goals and incentives
 motivate, 187

INDEX

why needed, 189-191
Goals
  concrete, 190
  immediate, 190
  sub goals, 191
Good grades, positive reinforcer, 35
Gradualness, defined, 42
Guessing, correction for, 110-111

H

Habit formation
  backsliding, 141-142
  change in lifestyle, 139
  cold-turkey, 139
  gradual, 140-141
  how to, 138-141
  ideal, 138
  large change, 139
  methods of, 139-141
  reality, 138
  start abruptly, 139
Hallucinations, stimulus deprivation, 182
Help, teacher's, 127-128
High School student, reading speed, 57
Horsepower, power illustrated, 7

I

Incentive
  extrinsic, 190
  intrinsic, 190
Index tabs, use of, 16, 87-88
Inhibition, during exam, 118
Interference
  language student, 218
  minimized, 217-218
Interviews with students, 3
Intimidation, of students, 77

J

Javal, observations of, 63-64

K

Key points, underlining of, 36
Knowledge, defined, 6

L

Labeling, of facts, 41
Lateness, hazards of, 78
Law of specific practice
  defined, 40
  importance of, 34
Laws
  co-teaching, 52
  of learning, 42
Learned laziness, defined, 161-162
Learning and memory, more practical knowledge, 200
Learning and performance, a distinction, 194-195
Learning inhibition, explanation of, 208-209
Learning, publications on, 3
Learning skills
  defined, 8
  lack of, 8
Learning speed, explanation of, 209-210
Learning through teaching, co-teaching, 44
Learnometer
  how to use, 167-168
  purpose of, 165-166
Learn-to-Learn Course
  created, 3
  who needs it, 9-10
  work plan, 12, 14 ff
Lesson outline, use of, 45
Lesson plans, brief, 47-48
Little black books, use of, 151
Long term memory
  chilled hamster experiment, 205-206
  interference forgetting, 207
  like photographic prints, 205-206

permanent storage, 205
proteins, 206
vast, 205
Look-it-over, list of items, 28

M

Major section topics, in testing yourself, 29
Map, as example, 32
McGill University, deprivation experiments, 182
Memorize, not enough, 40
Memory
   distinctive, 208
   electronic computers, 203
   files, 205
   long term, 205-207
   poor for time passage, 145
   publications on, 3
   temporary, 203
Memory structure, explanation of, 200-201
Method, learning skill, 8
Michelangelo, training of, 7
Mini-max schedule, 148
Minimize, forgetting, 217-218
Motivation
   awareness and action, 193-194
   and deprivation, 188-189
   deprived of schooling, 189
   diagram of cycle, 187
   for school, 189
   indirect results, 195-196
   interrupted schooling, 189
   performance and attention, 195-197
   produces better attention, 196
   produces more work, 196
   teenage materialism, 188
   value of, 45
Movement "blindness", defined, 65

N

Needs
   energize and direct, 187-188
   motivate, 186
Negative reinforcers, defined, 223-225
Neuron adaptation, 179
Notebook
   flexibility of use, 86
   learning skill, 8
   lending, 87
   three-ring, 85-86
Notes
   aid to review, 36
   boiled down, 30-31
   dates in, 98
   during class, 79
   from memory, 29
   how to begin, 29
   in readrite technique, 18
   reason for, 84-85
Notetaking
   common errors, 99
   cross reference, 98
   diagrams, 97
   emphasis, 98
   exam review, 90-92
   formats, 94
   immediate review, 98-99
   importance of, 84
   indent style, 92
   key phrases, 97
   materials, 85
   numbered outline form, 89-90
   opinions, 98
   organization, 95-97
   outline, 22
   pagination, 98
   paragraph style, 92
   primitive messy, 92
   questions, 97-98
   related organization, 97
   sentence style, 92
   small column format, 94
   styles, 89-92
   tips, 97-98
   two column format, 94
   unrelated organization, 97
   wide left margin format, 94
Numbered outline, notes, 89-90

INDEX

O

Objective exam
   correction for guessing, 111-112
   guessing, 110-112
   steps to answering, 109-112
Organization
   important, 48
   in notes, 95-97
   of book, 10
Outline notetaking, use of, 22
Overload, defined, 55-56

P

Pacing, during exam, 112-115
Paperback novel, for reading speed drill, 21
Paperbacks, practice READRITE with, 15
Paper
   choosing margins, 88
   color, 88
   graph, 88
   most practical size, 88
Parkinson, C. Northcote, law of, 159
   Partial reinforcement, 227-228
Part-time reinforcement, advantage of, 228
Passive reader, "the A-to-D student", 7
Pavlov's dogs, an example, 212
Paying attention, made easier, 75
Payoff, in reading, 38
Pens
   ball-point, 88-89
   color choice, 89
   learning skill, 8
Perfect, class seat, 75-76
Personal records, importance of, 171
Physical distractions, defined, 136
Place conditioning, defined, 132

Positive reinforcer
   defined, 223-224
   praise as, 35
Power, defined, 6
Power drill, steps of, 57-59
Power, two meanings, 6-7
Practice books, choice of, 57
Practice (Specific), defined, 42, 52
Practice
   of academic subject, 33
   remembering and writing, 34
Praise, positive reinforcer, 35
Preparation
   effectiveness of, 53
   for teaching, 44-45
Preview, importance of, 78
Procedure, learning skill, 8
Professionalism, student, 121
Professional, relationship, 121
Psychoanalysis, subconscious memory, 106
Punishment
   cf negative reinforcers, 225
   bad for two reasons, 225

Q

Questioning, aggressive, 124-125
Questions
   at end of class, 80
   dumb, 124-125
   in class, 79
   what to ask, 124-125
   writing of, 79
Quiz, each other, 50-51
Quizzing, self testing, 42
Quizzing sessions, time, 51

R

Readers, examples of, 55
Reading habit, characteristics of, 55
Reading power, defined, 55
Reading power drill
   alarm timer, 57-58

two facts, 56
Reading, secondary learning skill, 8
Reading speed,
  college student, 55
  high school student, 55
  maintaining your, 67
  measure, 61-63
Reading test records, purpose of, 169
Readrite system, steps in, 28
Recall, influenced by context, 215
Reciting, important, 51
Recording behavior, problems of, 174
Recording information, importance of, 84-85
Record keeping, advantages of, 169-171
Records
  of reading rate, 61
  reinforcement, 176-177
Records questionnaire, 173
Regression, in eye movement, 64
Rehearsal, for exam, 116-117
Reinforcement
  continuous 227
  defined, 42, 52, 221
  delayed, 226-227
  dynamite, 219-220
  effect on behavior, 221-222
  feedback, 35-36
  from co-teaching, 53
  immediate, 226-227
  increases behavior, 221-222
  student to teacher, 127
  the teacher, 126
  when needed, 59-60
Remember, what you use, 205
Remembering, cues for, 42
Repetition
  defined, 42, 52
  law of, 229

Repetitive work, time scraps, 149
Re-study procedure, when to use, 15
Retrieval cue, tagging of, 40
Reward
  defined, 222-223
  discovering results, 35
  is not reinforcement, 222-223
Routine work, time scraps, 149

S

Schedule, mini-max, 148
Schedule, preparation of, 24
Scholarship students, need study power, 9
Scientific apparatus, Skinner box, 212
Seat choice, habit, 74-76
Seat, in class, 20-21
Self taught learners, students as, 8
Self testing
  immediate, 29
  when, 18-19
Sentence style, of notes, 92
Shaping, building behavior, 228-229
Short term memory
  brief, 202
  explanation of, 200-203
  forgetting, 207-208
  like electricity in wires, 205
  small, 202-203
Shy People, co-teaching, 48
Skinner box, scientific apparatus, 212
Specific practice, defined, 216
Speed improvements, shown, 55
Stimulus control
  defined, 42, 212
  experiment, 212
  redefined, 216
Stimulus, defined, 220
Stimulus Deprivation

INDEX

experiments, 182-183
hallucinations, 182
Stimulus generalization
   defined, 214-215
   people, 215
   pigeons, 214-215
Stimulus intensity dynamism,
   defined, 75
Student
   anonymous, 128-129
   loneliness, 51
   professionalism, 121
Student records, purpose of, 172
Student's illusion, explanation of, 203
Student-teacher relations, 20
Student-teacher relations, establishing, 122
Study place
   and people, 136
   bedroom as, 133
   importance of, 131-132
   needed, 14-15
   radio, 136
   regular time habits, 138
   requirements for, 19
   respect for, 136
   the physical side, 135-136
   the social side, 136
   unique work space, 131-132
   where, 131-132
Study power, defined, 6, 7
Study power records, introduction, 165
Study problems form, instructions, 15
Study problems list, purpose of, 168-169
Study time, importance of, 137-138
Subconscious memory
   purpose of, 106
   steps to tap, 106-108

Success
   reinforcing, 225-226
   results of, 35-36
Successive approximations, technique of, 228-229

T

Teacher's axiom, defined, 44
Teacher's help, changes over years, 127-128
Teacher
   help student, 127-128
   rotten, 129
   style of exam, 116-117
Teaching machine, new invention 220
Teaching, preparation for, 44
Tests
   chapter, instructions, 15
   purpose of, 41
Test yourself
   at the end of class, 80-81
   how to, 29
   important, 41
Textbooks, not for readrite technique, 15-16
Tip-of-the-tongue
   experiment, 104
   generic memory, 105
Time budget, three steps, 144, 147
Time
   budget, 147
   five planning rules, 147-148
   like money, 143-144
   mini-max, 148
   scraps of, 149
   the great multiplier, 77
   where it goes, 144
Time scraps
   repetitive work, 149
   routine work, 149
Time sheet, how to use, 23-24, 146-147

Time spent, poor memory for, 145
Tool, learning skill, 8
Tutoring, co-teaching, 47

U

Underlining, 36
Underlining words, purpose, 31
Useful memory, transferred, 204
Use it or lose it
    an explanation, 204
    knowledge, 33
Underline, key points, 36
Underlining, adult finger reading, 37

V

Variety, beats boredom, 184

W

Warm-up, importance of, 78
Weekly schedule, purpose of, 169
Words, number on page, 61
Words per minute, defined, 62
Working day, the students', 150
Work plan, how evolved, 12
Work, quality of, 7
Writing, secondary learning skill, 8